65.

Making Sense of Agile Project Management

Making Sense of Agile Project Management: Balancing Control and Agility

Charles G. Cobb, PMP

JOHN WILEY & SONS, INC.

This book is printed on acid-free paper. ♾

Published by John Wiley & Sons, Inc., Hoboken, New Jersey

Published simultaneously in Canada

Library of Congress Cataloging-in-Publication Data:
Cobb, Charles G., 1945-
Making sense of agile project management : balancing control and agility / Charles G. Cobb.
p. cm.
Includes index.
ISBN 978-0-470-94336-6 (pbk.); ISBN 978-1-118-01568-1 (ebk); ISBN 978-1-118-01569-8 (ebk); ISBN 978-1-118-01570-4 (ebk)
1. Software engineering. 2. Computer software–Development–Management. 3. Agile software development. I. Title.
QA76.758.C57 2011
005.1–dc22

Printed in the United States of America
10 9 8 7 6 5 4 3 2 1

Contents

Preface

WHO SHOULD READ THIS BOOK?

The goal of this book is to help companies see both agile and non-agile methodologies in a whole new light and understand how they can use these approaches effectively in an overall strategy to gain the right balance of both control and agility. The book is intended for a fairly broad audience—some of the examples in the book are from a software development perspective; however, most of the book is applicable to improving any product development process for software, hardware, and services.

Audience	Primary Benefits
All Readers	• Unravel and demystify a lot of confusing and competing approaches for agile and traditional product development • Avoid the "program du jour" mentality that all traditional development methodologies and practices are obsolete and that newer agile methodologies and practices replace them all • Better understand how these approaches are complementary to each other rather than competitive and how they might be used more effectively in an overall strategy
Business Leaders, CIOs and IT Managers, Product Development Managers	• Learn how to develop a balance of agility and control to maximize business results without unnecessarily sacrificing other management goals such as risk management and control of project costs and schedules • Develop an understanding of the alternative approaches, benefits, and tradeoffs associated with implementing a more agile product development approach • Develop a strategy, an action plan, and an approach for improving your company's product development processes that is well aligned with your business objectives
PMO Leaders, Project Managers and Business Analysts	• Develop a deeper understanding of the principles behind agile and non-agile methodologies in order to design and tailor a project methodology that is well aligned with the business environment it supports and the risks and complexities of individual projects • Understand the impact of agile methodologies on the future of project management and business systems analysis and develop a very proactive approach to meet these new challenges

BRIEF OVERVIEW OF THE BOOK

Many businesses have cumbersome and bureaucratic product development processes that can seriously hamper their competitive ability. Typically, these processes have been developed to satisfy a need to provide control and predictability for costs and schedules; however, an overemphasis on control can lead to rigid and inflexible processes that may not be well designed to adapt to business needs. In many businesses today, flexibility and responsiveness to change are as important as control of costs and schedules:

- A project that successfully meets its cost and schedule goals but misses an important market window because the schedule wasn't aggressive enough might not be considered very successful overall.
- A project that fails to achieve the desired business outcome because the development process didn't provide a sufficient level of flexibility to rapidly adapt to new and changing business requirements might also not be considered very successful even if it met its cost and schedule goals.

If we accept a broader definition of how to determine the success or failure of projects, it forces us to take a close look at the level of emphasis that has traditionally been put on establishing a level of control designed to meet cost and schedule goals. Achieving a more balanced approach might mean rethinking the way projects are managed, but if it is done correctly, it is not necessary to completely sacrifice control over costs and schedules in order to achieve agility. It does require some skill to achieve the right balance of control and agility, and the right approach may be somewhat different from one business to the next.

Implementing a balanced approach successfully in a business environment poses some significant new challenges for project managers:

- There's a much greater range of methodologies, principles, and practices (both agile and traditional) that a project manager needs to consider.
- There's a need to fit the methodology (or combination of methodologies—either agile or non-agile) to the business environment as well as the risks and complexities of typical projects rather than trying to force-fit projects to any standard methodology (agile or non-agile).

That requires a broad-based understanding of different methodologies and practices as well as a deeper understanding of the principles behind them to tailor and customize an approach to fit with the business environment and the risks and complexities of individual projects.

In the past, some project managers may have acted as "cooks"—they knew how to prepare a limited number of recipes (methodologies) and sometimes did so "by the book". In the future, being a good "cook" may not be good enough, and more project managers may need to become "chefs"—they will need to know how to prepare a much broader range of dishes and go beyond preparing standard recipes by the book to create highly customized and innovative "recipes" tailored to fit a particular business and project environment. The agile movement forces project managers to consider a much broader range of "recipes" and "ingredients" to "cook" with and requires a much more customized and tailored approach.

This book has two major objectives:

1. For all readers (and, in particular, business leaders); this book is intended to provide an understanding of how to fit agile methodologies into an overall business strategy that provides the right balance of control and agility for their business. Doing that effectively requires analysis and planning. In many cases, agile methodologies have been implemented from a development perspective—they need to be understood from a much broader business strategy, project management, and project governance perspective in addition to a development perspective.
2. For project managers, this book is intended to provide a much deeper understanding of agile principles, methodologies, and practices to enable project managers to develop a more agile project management approach and understand how to blend and tailor both agile and traditional principles, methodologies, and practices to create an appropriate balance of control and agility to fit a business environment, as well as the risks and complexities of any individual project. Key topics include:
   - How the project management role is changed in agile projects and what new skills and career directions may be needed to grow into agile project management roles.
   - How to develop a project management approach that can be adapted to agile as well as non-agile project environments.
   - How to integrate existing project management knowledge such as the *A Guide to the Project Management Body of Knowledge* (*PMBOK® Guide*)—Fourth Edition with new and rapidly evolving agile principles, practices, and methodologies
   - How to design and tailor the right combination of principles, practices, and methodologies (agile as well as non-agile) to provide a balance of control and agility to fit the needs of a business and the risks and complexity of projects rather than attempting to use a standard "off-the-shelf" methodology (either agile or non-agile) for projects.

This book has intentionally been designed to avoid an in-depth discussion of the mechanics of implementing any particular methodology (either agile or non-agile) for two primary reasons:

- There are already numerous other books on the market that are readily available to provide that kind of information.
- Digressing too far into the details of the mechanics of how any particular methodology is implemented would distract the reader from the high-level view that this book is intended to focus on.

WHY I WROTE THIS BOOK

I recently attended a local agile group meeting to hear the presentation "Essential Deprogramming for Traditional Project Managers." The person who gave the presentation had over 15 years of project management experience, and the tone of her presentation was that she has now "seen the light," forsaken all the things she used to do as a project manager, and transformed herself into an agile coach.

She made a number of very negative comments about project management that were based on a lot of popular stereotypes, myths, misconceptions, and clichés about what project management is, and she made a particular statement that "'Agile Project Management' is an oxymoron." I don't agree with that point of view at all, but it indicates how large a "chasm" there is between the traditional project management perspectives and newer, more agile approaches to project management. One of the major obstacles to crossing this "chasm" is that there are people on both sides of the "chasm" who are somewhat opinionated and narrow-minded:

- There are some project managers who are deeply entrenched in thinking that traditional, plan-driven, control-oriented approaches are the only way to do project management.
- There are many agilists who are equally entrenched in their perspective that the only way to be "agile" is the pure agile way and that there is no need for project management at all—they see project management as a role rather than a set of skills that can be adapted to a broad range of different environments, just as the agile principles can also be applied to a broad range of different environments.

I've been doing project management in product development and other project environments for a long time. That has given me a very broad view of what works and what doesn't work in different situations, and I've learned that there is no single methodology (agile or non-agile) that works for all projects. One of the risks in project management is that if you are schooled in one particular methodology (either agile or non-agile), it's easy to get lost in the mechanics associated with implementing that methodology and not step back and consider that an entirely different methodology or approach might make much more sense for a given project.

A major goal of this book is to help build a bridge across this "chasm" between traditional and agile project management approaches and help people see these methodologies in a very different light. This "chasm" really isn't as large as people think it is, and the "chasm" is as much perceived as it is real. This is an extremely strategic and important topic for the project management profession. For many project managers who have been schooled in traditional project management approaches, agile methodologies will require developing a new perspective:

- Project managers need to expand the tools in their toolkit to embrace newer, more agile forms of project management in addition to traditional project management approaches.
- In the past, project managers may have attempted to force-fit a project to a given methodology (either agile or non-agile) because that's what they're most familiar with. Agile methodologies will require tailoring the methodology (or combination of methodologies) to fit the business environment and the risks and complexity of the project.

These factors will require project managers to develop a broad-based understanding of agile and non-agile methodologies at a deeper level to apply them successfully in the right combinations for a given project. CIOs, CTOs, development managers, and business leaders also need to understand the potential role that agile methodologies can play in improving the effectiveness of their organization in meeting increasing demands for timely and flexible software solutions that satisfy very demanding business requirements.

I've had some unique experiences in my career that ultimately led me to write this book:

1. In the mid-1990s I was the director of corporate quality for a company that developed hardware and software products for telecommunications applications. It was quite a challenge:
   - The quality of the products was weak, and the company had ongoing customer service issues to try to keep up with problems generated by software quality issues.
   - The software development organization had a number of very bright developers who didn't want anything to do with any defined methodology or process.
   - The company had grown by acquisition and had acquired other companies in four different worldwide locations (Manchester, UK; Canton, Massachusetts; Dallas, Texas; and Wichita, Kansas) and each of those organizations had its own way of doing things.
   - My primary job at the time was to get the entire company to agree on a single development methodology, and get everyone to adopt and consistently implement that methodology and then pass an external audit on the process implementation. I had moved into the quality management arena from a project management background, so my natural orientation was toward the control and predictability provided by the Waterfall model; however, I was working with a number of software developers and managers who knew a lot more about software development than I did at the time, and I learned a lot from that.
   - To make a long story short, I came to realize that forcing people to adopt one methodology like the Waterfall wasn't going to work—it was overkill, it had way too much overhead for many of the company's

projects, and the software developers would never follow it if we implemented it as a standard methodology for the whole company. On the other hand, there were some projects for which it did make sense. The end result was that we wound up with several different life-cycle models and the project manager could pick one of those models that he/she felt was most appropriate for the project, and he/she could also tailor it as needed to fit that particular project.

- Another lesson I learned is that no methodology (agile or non-agile) should ever be taken as absolute dogma. Project managers must have some ability to apply it intelligently and make changes as needed to fit the scope, risks, and complexity of the project.
- That implies that those project managers have a sufficient level of training and understand the concept and principles behind the methodology to make those decisions intelligently.
- The impact of those decisions is understood, reviewed, and approved if necessary by the project's stakeholders.

2. Since that time, I've worked with many companies in many different application environments, using numerous project management methodologies (both agile and not-so-agile) to help them improve their product development processes. I also have a very strong background doing hands-on development work, so I understand first-hand what it takes to develop good software.

3. In 2003, I published a book called *From Quality to Business Excellence—A Systems Approach to Management*. A key objective of that book was to try to demystify and unravel a lot of confusing and competing approaches to process improvement and quality management that were in use at that time (Six Sigma, TQM, BPR, etc.). At that time, Six Sigma was very hot, as agile is today, and people were just jumping into it, treating it as a "panacea" for solving almost any kind of problem, and doing it superficially without fully understanding what it took to do it successfully. I hope that this book will play a similar role in understanding the potential business impact of agile product development methodologies.

HOW TO USE THIS BOOK

The following is a summary of how the book is organized to meet these objectives.

Part I

Part I of the book is designed to satisfy the first objective of the book:

> Understanding how to fit agile methodologies into an overall business strategy that provides the right balance of control and agility for a business.

This part of the book is appropriate for all readers. It consists of the following chapters:

Chapter #	Chapter Title	Description/Comments
1	Introduction	This chapter sets the stage for the rest of the book. It introduces the main points and provides an executive summary of the book.
2	Agile Values, Principles, and Practices	This chapter is intended to provide an overview of the principles behind agile and clear up some of the confusion that exists about agile and traditional methodologies by separating some of the perceptions from the reality. Users who are familiar with agile may want to skim through some of this material; however, this is an important chapter for all readers to clear up any misconceptions that exist before proceeding on into the rest of the book. The chapter also provides an understanding of the principles behind Lean Software Development, which is the foundation of most agile methodologies and can be used to streamline traditional plan-driven methodologies.
3	Becoming More Agile	This chapter is designed to provide a management-level perspective for anyone faced with making business decisions related to developing a more agile development strategy for their business. It provides an understanding of the benefits of agile approaches as well as the obstacles that must be overcome and the commitments needed to implement an agile strategy. It also discusses alternatives that can help provide a balance of control and agility for those businesses that are unable to completely implement a pure agile strategy.
4	Case Studies	This chapter discusses some case studies of companies that have crafted successful methodologies that blend a combination of methodologies, practices, and principles to fit the needs of their business.
5	Part I Summary and Action Plan	This chapter provides a summary of some of the key points to consider when developing a strategy and plan for your business and discusses some recommended next steps for companies to put the information learned in this book into operational use to improve your business.

Part II

Part II of the book is designed to satisfy the second objective of the book:

> Understanding how to develop a more agile project management approach, including how to customize and select and tailor methodologies, practices, and principles to provide a balance of control and agility.

This part of the book is primarily designed for project managers to enable them to more effectively help their companies implement an agile strategy. It is also appropriate for business leaders who want to get a deeper understanding of agile methodologies and how to apply them in an overall business strategy in more detail. Part II consists of the following chapters:

Chapter #	Chapter Title	Description/Comments
6	Agile Project Management	This chapter discusses: How the project management role is changed in agile projects and what new skills and career directions may be needed to grow into agile project management roles. How to develop a project management approach that can be adapted to agile as well as non-agile project environments, including how to integrate existing project management knowledge such as the *A Guide to Project Management Body of Knowledge* (*PMBOK® Guide*) with new and rapidly evolving agile principles, practices, and methodologies
7	Fundamental Principles Behind SDLC Models	This chapter is designed to provide a deeper level of understanding of the fundamental factors that should be considered in the selection and tailoring of life-cycle models to provide the right balance of control and agility to align with the company's business strategy and the scope and complexity of typical projects. It is designed to enable the user to go beyond the constraint of simply implementing standard off-the-shelf life-cycle models (either agile or non-agile) and more effectively use life-cycle models as a tool for meeting business requirements.
8	Software Development Life Cycles	This chapter provides a high-level overview of some major types of software development life cycles to help understand how these different software development life cycles might be used in an overall development strategy.
9	Part II Summary and Action Plan	This chapter summarizes the contents of Part II of the book and what it means to project managers.

Part III

Appendix #	Appendix Title	Description/Comments
Appendix A (Optional)	Overview of Agile Development Practices	These two appendices are intended as background reading for anyone who is not familiar with agile development practices and project delivery frameworks. It is a high-level overview only and does not go into great deal of detail on any of these development practices or project delivery frameworks.
Appendix B (Optional)	Overview of Agile Project Delivery Frameworks	

Acknowledgments

Writing this book has been a lot like writing software in many respects—the methodology I used for the writing of this book has had a number of attributes of an agile project in itself:

- It started out with a few core ideas that were the seed of this book, and it developed iteratively and incrementally from there. Originally, it was just going to be a paper or a magazine article, and it grew from there into a book. I didn't have a completely firm idea of where it was going when I started—it just evolved.
- It was a team approach—a number of very experienced project managers collaborated with me and made helpful comments and suggestions on the direction of the book as it evolved.
- I also kept users well connected into this effort by publishing draft copies of the book for review on several web sites for feedback and comments from potential readers as it was being written.
- Another agile idea that I've used is the principle of keeping this book as simple as possible, yet getting across the key ideas that I believe are important. There is an enormous amount of information from a number of different sources on agile product development, and it would have been very easy to stray too far into going into a lot of detail in a number of different areas. Loading the book down with all that information would have been similar to what software products go through when they get loaded down with features no one uses that only make them more complicated and difficult to use.

If I had used a traditional approach to try to write this book, and if I hadn't received a lot of help from a very good team of people who made numerous contributions and suggestions throughout the development process, this book probably would have never even gotten off the ground. There are two people, in particular, who made very significant contributions to this book:

- Martin Burns, PMP®, project manager at IBM Global Business Services—Martin has some very deep insight into the this area, spent a lot of time reviewing a number of early drafts of this book, and provided numerous comments and suggestions that were very helpful.

- Erik Gottesman of Sapient has provided an enormous amount of thought leadership in this area and has very generously shared a lot of information about the Sapient|Approach development process that has been used in this book. Erik has been a very energetic supporter of the effort to publish this book and has provided many very insightful comments and suggestions on its development.

I would also like to thank the following individuals who took the time to review an early draft of this book and provided helpful comments and suggestions:

Dr. David F. Rico	Adjunct Instructor at George Washington University
Gina Abudi	Partner and VP, Peak Performance Group, Inc.
David Peterson, PMP®	Technical Project Manager/Lead Business Analyst
John Balog, PMP®	Sr. Project Manager, Software, Hardware
Cornelis (Kees) Vonk, PMP®	Consultant/Instructor Project Management
Glenn Deles, PMP®	IT Project Manager
Michael Hoffman, PMP®	Senior Development Analyst at Time Warner Cable

PART I
OVERVIEW

The primary objective of Part I of the book is to help companies understand how to fit agile methodologies into an overall business strategy that provides the right balance of control and agility for their business. Doing that effectively requires analysis and planning. In many cases, agile methodologies have been implemented from a development perspective; they need to be understood from a much broader business strategy, project management, and project governance perspective in addition to a development perspective.

In order to accomplish that, it is essential to overcome some popular misconceptions associated with "agile" such as:

- "Agile" is an undisciplined process of simply writing code with no planning, no documentation, and no disciplined methodology for how it is done.
- The only way to be "agile" is to implement pure agile methodologies such as Scrum.
- At one end of the spectrum is the most extreme forms of traditional plan-driven, control-oriented methodologies like the Waterfall process; at the other end are pure agile approaches like Scrum, with nothing in between.

The truth is that:

- Implementing an "agile" process requires just as much or more discipline as traditional approaches such as the Waterfall model, but it's a different kind of discipline. Rather than relying on rigidly defined and prescriptive methodologies, agile approaches rely much more heavily on the training and skill of collaborative, cross-functional teams to adapt the methodology to the problem that they are attempting to solve.
- Pure forms of agile like Scrum have many advantages, but they can be very difficult to implement and aren't necessarily appropriate for all business environments and projects. Many businesses require a balance of control and agility, which may be more suited to a hybrid approach.
- There are many ways companies can become "more agile" without necessarily going to the extreme of a pure agile approach, but it may take a more sophisticated approach to blend together the right combination of agile and non-agile methodologies and practices to craft a customized

approach. The best approach is always to fit the methodology and practices to the business environment and problem you're trying to solve rather than force-fitting a project to a particular methodology, but doing that requires a much higher level of skill and it requires developing an understanding of the methodologies and practices at a deeper level.

There are many companies that are locked into very cumbersome and bureaucratic traditional methodologies that don't see how to improve that situation, because it can be so difficult to move to a pure agile approach and there is also a fear of losing control in the process. Part I of the book is designed to help companies understand some of principles behind agile approaches in order to see how to develop an appropriate strategy for how to integrate more agile practices into the way they do business.

CHAPTER 1

INTRODUCTION

"Agile" is definitely the latest and coolest buzzword in the software development world—everyone wants to be "agile," but there are many misconceptions of what "agile" means, and many people don't fully understand the implications of what it takes to develop an effective agile development process.

MEANING OF THE WORD "AGILE"

First, it is essential to define what we mean by the word "agile". In the software development arena, the word "agile" has become synonymous with specific forms of agile such as Scrum and Extreme Programming (XP):

> Scrum is an agile software development model based on multiple small teams working in an intensive and interdependent manner. The term is named for the scrum (or scrummage) formation in rugby, which is used to restart the game after an event that causes play to stop, such as an infringement.
>
> Scrum employs real-time decision-making processes based on actual events and information. This requires well-trained and specialized teams capable of self-management, communication and decision making. The teams in the organization work together while constantly focusing on their common interests.[1] (See Appendix B for more detail.)

> Extreme Programming is a discipline of software development based on values of simplicity, communication, feedback, and courage. It works by bringing the whole team together in the presence of simple practices, with enough feedback to enable the team to see where they are and to tune the practices to their unique situation.
>
> In Extreme Programming, every contributor to the project is an integral part of the "Whole Team." The team forms around a business representative called "the Customer," who sits with the team and works with them daily.

[1] What is Scrum?, http://searchsoftwarequality.techtarget.com/sDefinition/0,,sid92_gci1230820,00.html

> Extreme Programming teams use a simple form of planning and tracking to decide what should be done next and to predict when the project will be done. Focused on business value, the team produces the software in a series of small fully integrated releases that pass all the tests the Customer has defined.[2] (See Appendix A for more detail.)

This connotation of the word "agile" has become widely accepted in common usage in software development and creates the impression that the only way to be "agile" is to practice those specific methodologies. In other words, if you're not doing Scrum and/or Extreme Programming, you're not agile at all.

The meaning of the word "agile" has become confusing because of these widely-used specific connotations that have become associated with it. These connotations are also in the context of a development perspective and a much broader context is needed. A more general connotation of the word "agility" is defined by Dr. David Rico[3] as follows:

> - "The ability to create and respond to change in order to profit in a turbulent global business environment
> - The ability to quickly reprioritize use of resources when requirements, technology, and knowledge shift
> - A very fast response to sudden market changes and emerging threats, by intensive customer interaction
> - Use of evolutionary, incremental, and iterative delivery to converge on an optimal customer solution
> - Maximizing the business value with right-sized, just enough, and just-in-time processes and documentation"[4]

The word "agility" as defined above has a much broader meaning than the meaning that has typically been associated with the word "agile"—it implies that there are many different levels of "agility" and not just a limited number of specific ways to being "agile". A key idea that this book will develop is that there is a spectrum of different approaches to "agility":

- At one end of the spectrum, there are approaches such as the traditional Waterfall methodology that heavily emphasize upfront planning and control and have a very limited amount of agility. These approaches might be classified as "plan-driven" or "predictive" because they use upfront

---

[2] What is Extreme Programming?, http://xprogramming.com/book/whatisxp

[3] Rico, David F., Lean and Agile Systems Engineering, http://davidfrico.com

[4] Rico, David F., "Lean and Agile Systems Engineering, http://davidfrico.com

planning heavily to attempt to predict the cost and schedule for a project. They also typically place an emphasis on controlling changes once the project is in progress to manage the scope of the effort to ensure that the original predictions of costs and schedules remain valid.

- At the other extreme, there are approaches such as Scrum and Extreme Programming (XP) that have a much higher level of agility and would be considered much more "adaptive" because they place a much higher level of emphasis on being flexible to user needs and requirements as the project progresses and they have a much lower level of emphasis on upfront planning and control of costs and schedules.

In the middle of these two extremes, there are many ways to blend together different levels of agility and control to fit a given business environment.

This definition of the word "agility" also acknowledges that "agility" includes a higher-level business perspective as well as a development practice perspective and that the two must be integrated. Scrum and Extreme Programming (XP) are excellent methodologies that can have an enormous impact on improving a company's software development process, but too often, a migration to agile is led from a development strategy perspective driven primarily by implementing a new development methodology such as Scrum and XP, and there are much broader implications that need to be considered such as:

- What role does the product development process play in the company's business? What are the advantages to be gained by becoming more agile?
- What is the most appropriate balance of agility and control for the company's business environment and competitive strategy?
- What are the benefits and tradeoffs associated with different levels of agility that might be used to provide that balance?

In this book, to avoid confusion about terminology, the phrase "pure agile" or "extreme agile" will be used to refer to the most adaptive forms of agile methodology such as Scrum and Extreme Programming (XP).

MEANING OF THE WORD "WATERFALL"

The agile movement started out as a revolution against traditional development practices, such as the Waterfall, process that have been perceived as heavily laden with documentation and were perceived as cumbersome, ineffective, and extremely bureaucratic. Figure 1.1 shows a typical Waterfall model.

The Waterfall process is called that because it is a series of sequential phases that have to happen in sequence, and each phase cascades into the next. For example, one of the early phases is a requirements definition phase, where the user requirements are defined and documented and then handed off to the

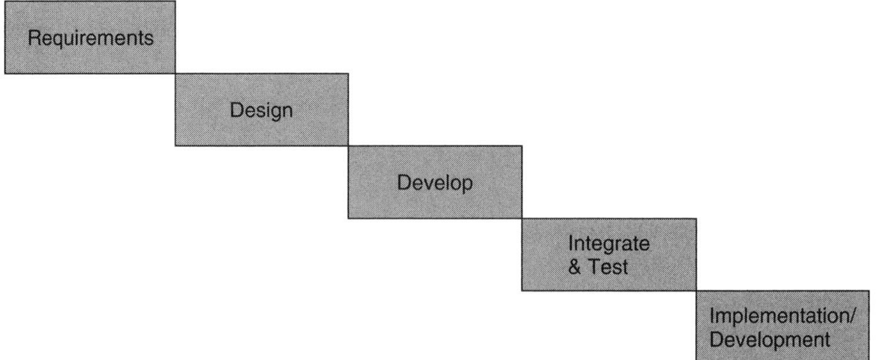

Figure 1.1 Typical Waterfall model

development team in the next phase to develop a solution. There are several significant problems that are inherent in that kind of process—it assumes that:

- The users are capable of defining explicitly detailed requirements for everything that they need without seeing it at all.
- The business environment is also very stable and the requirements aren't going to change much throughout the rest of the project.
- The requirements can be accurately documented in a way that developers are going to easily understand what needs to be done to satisfy those needs and nothing will be lost in translation.

Those may not be very realistic assumptions in many situations today, but the Waterfall approach has appealed to companies who have seen it as a way to get control and predictability over project costs and schedules. The truth is that control over costs and schedules is an illusion if the requirements are uncertain and are likely to change significantly. It may appear that there is a well-defined plan with accurate and predictable estimates of costs and schedules, but one of two things is likely to happen:

1. The rigidity of the requirements and the change control process make it difficult to adapt to user needs as the project progresses. The project may meet its cost and schedule goals but miss the mark in satisfying the business need if changes in user needs are overly controlled.
2. On the other hand, if users are allowed to make changes freely, attempting to impose a rigorous change control process in an environment with very uncertain user requirements can create enormous amounts of unnecessary bureaucracy processing change requests on top of change requests and can make the earlier estimates of costs and schedules meaningless.

Attempting to apply a Waterfall model in that kind of environment is unrealistic, yet many project managers attempt to do it anyway because it provides an "illusion" of control. It's much better to just accept the fact that the user requirements are uncertain and choose a model that is designed to be more flexible and adaptive to uncertain user requirements. The cost and schedule estimates may not be as exact and precise as you might like, but it's unrealistic to believe that the cost and schedule estimates can be any more exact and precise than the requirements are.

POLARIZATION OF AGILE AND TRADITIONAL WATERFALL APPROACHES

There has been a considerable amount of polarization associated with traditional Waterfall and agile approaches:

- The agile movement was essentially a revolution against bureaucratic, Waterfall-style processes, and people in the agile community wanted to distance themselves as far as possible from those practices. For that reason, when the agile movement started out, it moved the pendulum to an extreme point in the other direction away from the traditional Waterfall approach (little or no documentation, process, or methodology, etc.).
- At the other extreme, some companies and practitioners of the traditional Waterfall approach have developed a strong and deeply rooted control orientation with an emphasis on accurately estimating and managing costs and schedules that can be difficult to change. If your goal is to accurately manage costs and schedules, any good project manager knows that it is essential to control and manage changes in requirements and scope. For that reason, it's very understandable why agile methodologies that emphasize unrestricted flexibility to adapt to change would feel very uncomfortable to those people.

In 2003, Barry Boehm and Richard Turner observed:

> "Unfortunately, rather than find ways to support each other, these two approaches to software development have considered each other opposites in a zero-sum game. The agilists rail against the traditionalists and lament the dehumanization of software development by 'Taylorian' reductionists who worship process. The establishment has responded with accusations of hacking, poor quality, and having way too much fun in a serious business. True believers on both sides have emerged to proclaim their convictions with near messianic stridency, raising the perplexity level of software developers and managers trying to evolve their success strategies."[5]

[5] Boehm, Barry and Turner, Richard, *Balancing Agility and Discipline—A Guide for the Perplexed*, New York: Addison-Wesley, 2003, p. 4

Since that time, the reality is that both sides of this conflict have evolved considerably, yet there is still a perception in some cases that they are far apart:

- The agile movement has matured rapidly and considerably. Methodologies like Scrum have evolved that are more than just a development process and have a strong base of knowledge and experience behind them, yet many people still retain an image of the agile movement as just an undisciplined development process from its early anarchist, revolutionary days.
- Many people have found innovative ways to make traditional development approaches more agile by making the documentation and process requirements much more sensible and adopting more iterative development approaches that balance control with agility, yet many people still have an image of traditional development approaches as highly dogmatic and bureaucratic.

It's time to find the middle ground and start to build a bridge across this chasm—much of these differences are more rooted in perceptions and misconceptions rather than in reality and, in many cases, the judgment and skills associated with how the methodology is applied has as big an impact as the methodology itself.

There is much to be learned from both of these areas and a broad base of knowledge and a continuum of different methodologies, practices, and principles from both the agile and traditional project management approaches need to be considered in many cases to develop an effective overall strategy. The selection of a project methodology (or methodologies) is a very important strategic decision for all organizations that depend on effective project management. The approach needs to be well aligned with the company's business strategy, culture, and business environment, as well as the risks and complexity of individual projects. For example:

- In very high-risk industries and application areas, depending on the nature of the risk, a considerable amount of upfront planning may be needed to ensure that the risks have been defined and mitigated.
- In highly regulated environments, project requirements, test plans, and test results may have to be well documented to satisfy regulatory requirements.

In these situations and many others, a balance of control and agility is needed to satisfy these requirements, and there are many ways to provide some level of agility without completely sacrificing control. Selecting an overall approach that provides the right balance of control and agility should be done jointly by the business and development sides of the organization based on an objective understanding of the alternatives and all the issues and tradeoffs involved. Attempting to use any standard methodology (either agile or non-agile) by the book that doesn't fit the risks and complexity of the business and project environment is not likely to be very successful. And, in many cases, the optimum solution may not be a single, standard methodology at all, but a combination of methodologies that can be customized and tailored to the requirements of each project.

THE PROGRAM DU JOUR EFFECT

Any new methodology, when it is really the hot thing to do, has a tendency to become the "program du jour." (Or program of the day) Agile methodologies have the potential to have an enormous impact; however, like many other new and hot methodologies:

- Consultants tend to swarm all over them and sell them as a cure for almost anything that ails you.
- Many companies and managers want to jump on this bandwagon, and that further builds the hysteria in the market.

The result of this can be:

- Jumping into agile looking for a "quick fix" without fully realizing that it takes a significant commitment to make it successful, resulting in superficial implementations that are likely to fail
- Attempting to implement agile methodologies in a business environment or organizational culture that is inconsistent with an agile approach
- Attempting to use agile methodologies for projects that they are inappropriate for or failing to blend a sufficient level of agility with the level of control that is needed

I've seen this phenomenon before. When I did the research for my book on business excellence,[6] I looked at a number of companies that were implementing Six Sigma, which was a very hot methodology at that time:

- There were some companies where the implementation followed the program du jour pattern—there was a lot of hoopla about the implementation, there were green belts and black belts and many of the other rituals that go along with Six Sigma, but if you looked under the surface, you quickly discovered that it didn't go very deep.
- On the other hand, there were other companies where it wasn't even obvious that they were doing Six Sigma because it was so well engrained into their business, and they took the time to understand the principles behind Six Sigma at a deeper level. They didn't even necessarily call it Six Sigma. These companies had their own process improvement methodology that was really fully integrated into how their business operated, and the methodology behind Six Sigma was only one tool in their toolbox.

---

[6] Cobb, Charles G., *From Quality to Business Excellence*, ASQ Quality Press, Milwaukee, WI, 2003

Another phenomenon I've seen before is the tendency to "throw the baby out with the bath water" whenever a hot new methodology comes along. In many of these situations, there is a lot to be learned from the previous methodology, but the previous methodology is considered obsolete and passé, and lessons learned from the past are forgotten when people move on to a hot new methodology like Six Sigma or agile. There is a tendency to think that traditional development methodologies and everything we've learned from them are now completely obsolete and have been replaced by agile, and that's not the case at all. There's a huge body of knowledge that has been developed over many years that should not be lost or ignored. Many of those principles, such as those in *A Guide to the Project Management Body of Knowledge* (PMBOK® Guide)—Fourth Edition are still valid; they just need to be applied intelligently in a different context.

A key objective of this book is to try to avoid the "program du jour" effect and present an objective and unbiased view of agile—where pure agile methodologies work and where a more traditional or hybrid approach may be a better solution, how agile methodologies fit with other methodologies, and what it takes to understand all of these methodologies at a deeper level and apply them successfully.

IMPACT ON PROJECT MANAGEMENT

The Standish Group recently released a report called "CHAOS Summary 2009" that has some disturbing statistics that show a very low percentage of projects met their desired objectives:

> "This year's results show a marked decrease in project success rates, with 32% of all projects succeeding which are delivered on time, on budget, with required features and functions" says Jim Johnson, chairman of The Standish Group, "44% were challenged which are late, over budget, and/or with less than the required features and functions and 24% failed which are cancelled prior to completion or delivered and never used."[7]

Jamie Capella of the Corporate Executive Board[8] presented data that showed a similar result. They did a study that indicated that a large number of projects (greater than 50 percent) that had successfully met their cost and schedule goals failed to deliver the business value that was intended. Both of these reports indicate a need to take a hard look at how project management is being done to determine what could be wrong.

The fundamental problem, in many cases, is one of two things:

- An overemphasis on control of costs and schedules can cause losing focus on the successful achievement of business results.

---

[7] Standish Group, http://standishgroup.com/newsroom/chaos_2009.php

[8] Capella, Jamie, Presentation to PMI MassBay Chapter, March 18, 2010

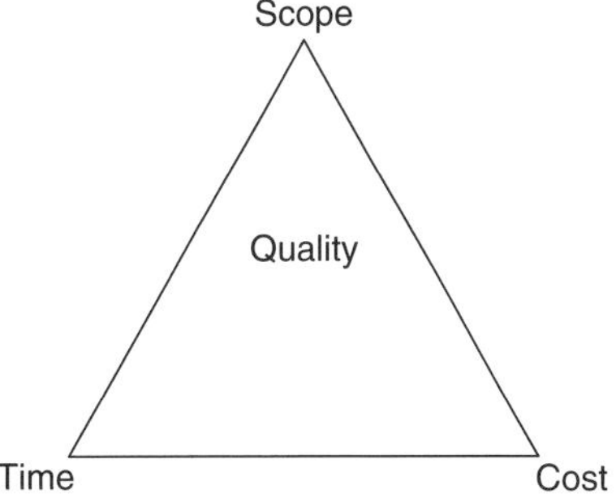

Figure 1.2 Traditional Project Management Triangle

- In a situation where the requirements are very uncertain and difficult to define upfront, attempting to force-fit that kind of project to a rigidly controlled, traditional Waterfall model is probably not the best model.

The traditional Project Management triangle in Figure 1.2 shows a project management approach that has been used for years.

If the project was managed within the constraints of time, cost, and resource availability, and it delivered the items that were within the scope of the project with an acceptable level of quality, it was considered a success. That's the predominant way that projects have been managed for a long time. There is nothing explicit in that triangle about providing business value unless you make the assumption that delivering what is in the scope is going to provide that value, and that's a *very big* assumption.

> "Too often project managers (and those above them) focus on the usual constraints of time and cost. There are times when value doesn't seem to matter at all—its schedule, schedule, schedule, as if value will take care of itself. Then there are those that focus on scope and detailed requirements but not the end goal of value . . . The assumption gets made that delivering on scope, schedule, and cost means delivering value."[9]

In the same PMI® Meeting[10] where Jamie Capella spoke, there was a panel discussion with seven Boston-area CIOs that followed. The message they gave was very loud and clear—in today's world, successful project managers need to go well beyond managing costs and schedules and focus on achieving successful business outcomes. This will require rethinking and rebalancing priorities in some cases. For example, the emphasis on management of project costs and schedules can have a negative impact:

---

[9] Highsmith, Jim, *Agile Project Management: Creating Innovative Products*, New York: Addison-Wesley, 2010, p. 18

[10] PMI MassBay Chapter Meeting, March 18, 2010

- In order to control costs and schedules, users are expected to sign off on requirements at the start of a project, and any changes from that point on are well controlled and minimized.
- The level of user involvement in the development effort after the project has entered the design stage may be very limited in order to control changes.

When projects fail to provide the business value that they were intended to provide, there's a usual list of suspects to blame such as:

- The users didn't adequately specify the requirements or the requirements weren't sufficiently defined.
- The project team didn't understand the requirements or the business need changed.

The root cause of the problem may be in the way that projects have been typically managed. Attempting to use an inappropriate methodology on a project may not satisfy *either* the objectives of managing costs and schedules or providing the desired business value:

- Too much emphasis on managing costs and schedules can lead to a somewhat rigid management of project scope that makes it difficult for the users to provide sufficient input and to react to change.
- In an unclear, uncertain, or rapidly changing environment, a very different kind of approach may be needed that has much more emphasis on satisfying business needs as a primary goal and has a lot more flexibility to adapt to change. Attempting to use a methodology that is optimized around managing costs and schedules in that environment is not likely to be successful.

A very different approach is needed to provide the right balance of flexibility and responsiveness to adapt to user needs in an uncertain environment:

> "Traditional Project Managers tend to focus on requirements as the definition of scope, and then concentrate on delivering those requirements. Agile Project Leaders focus on delivering value and are constantly asking questions about whether different renditions of scope are worth the value they deliver."[11]

Naturally, in this environment, the estimates of costs and schedules cannot be much more accurate than the user requirements are, but that doesn't prevent establishing a ballpark estimate for the project based on high-level requirements that are defined upfront and are further elaborated as the project progresses.

---

[11] Highsmith, Jim, *Agile Project Management-Creating Innovative Products*, New York: Addison-Wesley, 2010, p. 27

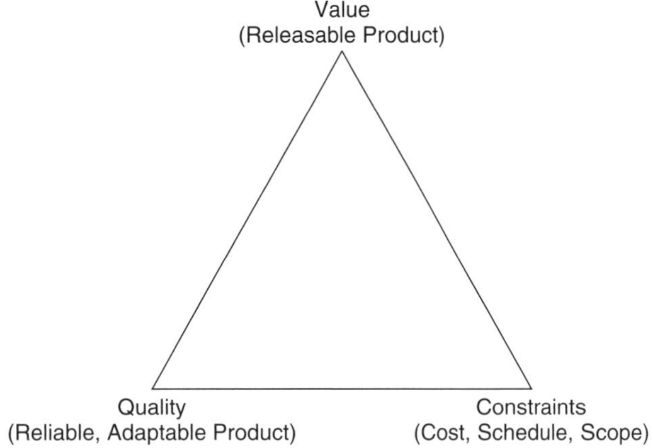

Figure 1.3 Agile Project Management Triangle

Jim Highsmith in his book *Agile Project Management*[12] proposes an agile triangle shown in Figure 1.3.

In an agile project, there is a much stronger focus on producing value for the customer. The customer is directly involved in the development effort, and it is understood and *expected* that the customer is going to introduce changes throughout the project to try to optimize the business value the project produces. In today's world:

- It may be unrealistic to expect that users can totally predict all the business requirements for a project far in advance of when the project will be delivered.
- In many cases, business results and software application solutions are so intimately intertwined, that achieving successful business outcomes requires a much more collaborative and integrated approach.

The trend towards more agile project management raises some important questions for project managers and any organization that depends on effective project management discipline for successful implementation of product development projects. For example:

- How does "agile" impact existing project methodologies? Is there still a need for traditional plan-driven development approaches?
- How do I reconcile all the traditional project management practices, such as those in the Project Management Institute's *A Guide to the Project Management Body of Knowledge*—Fourth Edition (PMI® *PMBOK® Guide*—Fourth Edition), which has been the foundation of project

[12] Highsmith, Jim, *Agile Project Management-Creating Innovative Products*, New York: Addison-Wesley, 2010, p. 21

management for so long, with many of the new ideas and principles that are the foundation of the agile movement?

- What is the impact of the agile movement on the future of project management? How does it change the project management role? What skills are needed for a project manager to be effective in an agile environment?

The answers to these questions are not immediately obvious, and these are very important and strategic questions for businesses, as well as the project management profession.

COMMON AGILE MISCONCEPTIONS

Our understanding of agile methodologies is rapidly evolving; however, there are a number of misconceptions that seem to persist about agile development. It is essential to clear up some of these misconceptions in order to objectively understand the benefits, limitations, and requirements of implementing an agile strategy.

The Pizza Box Methodology

There are people who think that being agile is nothing more than some businesspeople sitting down with some developers over a box of pizza and starting to write code with no structure, process, tools, or methodology for how it is done. The truth is that being agile does require a planned approach and a very disciplined process for doing the work, and in a very fast-paced development environment, having appropriate tools to manage the effort can become imperative.

> "Agility without discipline is the unencumbered enthusiasm of a startup company before it has to turn a profit. Great companies have both (discipline and agility) in measures appropriate to their goals and environment."[13]

An effective implementation of an agile approach can require a *much higher* level of skill and self-discipline from everyone on the project team:

> "Although it may seem counter intuitive [sic], agile is an extremely disciplined approach to working. Agile does not equal sloppiness. Most people will have a difficult time adjusting to this."[14]

---

[13] Boehm, Barry and Turner, Richard, *Balancing Agility and Discipline—A Guide for the Perplexed*, New York: Addison-Wesley, 2003, p. 2

[14] "'Gotchas': Common Pitfalls when Moving to Agile," Sapient Corporate White Paper, www.sapient.com

All-or-Nothing Thinking

There are people in the agile community who are very zealous and aggressive about promoting the benefits of Scrum and Extreme Programming (XP) to the extent that it seems to be a black-and-white proposition—either you fully adopt those specific agile approaches or you're not agile at all. The truth is that:

- The principles behind agile methodologies, including Scrum, can be customized and tailored to fit different kinds of projects and can be used in combination with other project management approaches as necessary to provide a balance of control and agility.
- There are many alternative approaches between pure forms of agile at one end of the spectrum and traditional Waterfall development approaches at the other end, and there are many ways an organization can become *more agile* through incrementally adopting new development practices and approaches without necessarily going to pure forms of agile, as shown in Figure 1.4.

Traditional Development Approaches Are Dead

There is also a misconception that traditional methods of doing development and all the practices and tools that have been commonly associated with them are either obsolete or irrelevant and are completely replaced by agile methodologies, practices, and tools. The truth is that:

- There are many good reasons why traditional plan-driven development approaches still can make sense for a given project, depending on the risk and complexity of the project and other factors.
- There are a number of ways to apply agile principles to traditional methodologies in order to make them more agile.

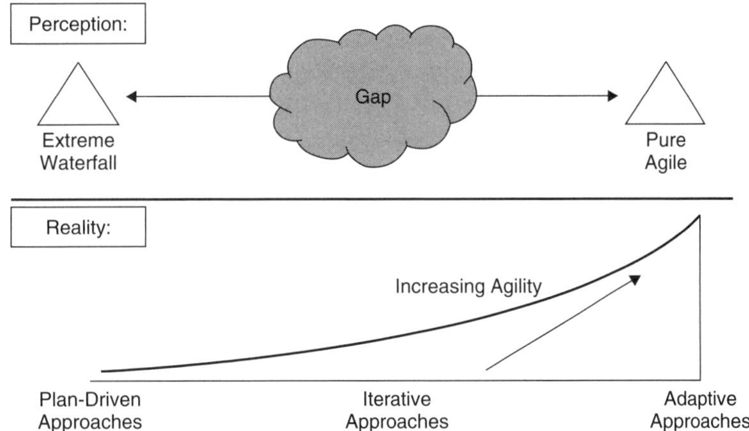

Figure 1.4 All-or-nothing thinking

- There are lots of ways to apply more traditional practices and tools to agile projects to achieve higher levels of control and predictability if necessary.

Just Do It Faster

Software development projects are notorious for becoming "death march" projects. Edward Yourdon defines a "death march" project as:

> "Quite simply, a 'death march' project is one whose "project parameters" exceed the norm by at least 50 percent. In most projects, this means one or more of the following constraints have been imposed upon the project:
>
> - The schedule has been compressed to less than half the amount estimated by a rational estimating process; thus, the project that would normally be expected to take 12 calendar months is now required to deliver its results in six months or less...
> - The staff has been reduced to less than half the number that would normally be assigned to a project of this size and scope...
> - The budget and associated resources have been cut in half...
> - The functionality, features, performance requirements, or other technical aspects of the project are twice what they would be under normal circumstances..."[15]

Basically a "death march" project amounts to pressuring project teams to just do the same work faster without necessarily changing anything about the process and methodology of how the work is done. It's a brute force approach to compress the project schedule, which is fraught with many potential problems.

John Wooden is a famous American basketball coach at the University of California at Los Angeles (UCLA). "In Coach Wooden's last twelve years as coach, UCLA won ten National Collegiate Athletic Association (NCAA) championships. In the 27 years he led the Bruins, they never had a losing season. Their record of 88 consecutive winning games will probably never be surpassed."[16] He is noted for saying "Be quick, but don't hurry".[17] Being quick requires discipline and training, hurrying can be just a brute force way to try to get it done faster and is likely to have a much lower success rate.

Becoming Agile Only Impacts the Development Organization

Many people think that becoming agile only impacts the product development organization. This is a quite common misconception on the business side—if we

[15] Yourdon, Ed, "What is a Death March Project and Why Do They Happen?", www.informit.com /articles/article.aspx?p=169512

[16] John Wooden, Academy of Achievement, www.achievement.org/autodoc/page/woo0pro-1

[17] "The Wizard's Wisdom: Woodenisms," http://sports.espn.go.com/ncb/news/story?id=5249709

can just get our development organization to be more agile and speed up the way they do things, it will solve all our problems. The truth is that becoming more agile impacts much more than just the development side of the organization—it requires a broad-based commitment from the business side of the organization to work in a close, collaborative partnership with the development side of the organization, and it may also require some major shifts in organizational culture and thinking to make that work.

Migration toward an agile approach without substantial sponsorship and long-term commitment from the business is probably doomed to failure. In many cases, the business side of the organization should take a major leadership role in driving the change that is needed.

> "The business stakeholders involved must learn the process as it is very different for them... if this group is not brought into the fold, there will be major disconnects (in terminology, approaches to situations, etc.) Once educated, they will be able to see the benefits of being able to direct the development as it progresses. The business also needs to clearly understand the expectation that it will also be frustrating for them to see the "dirty laundry" being aired each iteration: unfinished work, team mistakes, and other issues that are often hidden in a methodology with long breaks between business reviews."[18]

Agile Is Just a Development Methodology

A similar misconception is that agile is just a development methodology and not a project management methodology or framework. That perception is probably a carryover from the early days when agile was primarily a development methodology with little or no structure or process. Since that time; however, "agile" has matured significantly and Scrum is a relatively well-defined methodology and process with a significant knowledge base associated with it.

However, there are probably several key reasons why that perception still persists:

1. In an agile project, the line between what is a development methodology and what is a project management methodology is often blurred:
   - The development process may not be a discrete function separate from requirements and other project management aspects of the project—they are typically very well integrated.
   - The project management methodology may not be as formally defined as a separate process from the development process, and in many cases, agile methodologies don't use the term "project manager" at all.

---

[18] "'Gotchas': Common Pitfalls when Moving to Agile" Sapient Corporate White Paper, www.sapient.com

2. Agile methodologies are meant to be building blocks and combined and extended as necessary to create a complete project methodology. Agile does not specifically define all of the higher-level planning and project management that might be necessary for larger, more complex projects, but it would be inaccurate to characterize it as just a development methodology.

WHAT AGILE DOESN'T TELL YOU

There are a couple of key reasons why there are misconceptions about agile:

1. Agile methodologies, by design, are not prescriptive—they don't tell you exactly what needs to be done to implement the methodology or how to do it in many cases. In general, agile methodologies define some principles that intentionally require interpretation for a given situation. For example, the Agile Manifesto defines four values and twelve principles. The four values are as follows:

> "We are uncovering better ways of developing software by doing it and helping others do it. Through this work we have come to value:
>
> - Individuals and interactions over processes and tools
> - Working software over comprehensive documentation
> - Customer collaboration over contract negotiation
> - Responding to change over following a plan
>
> That is, while there is value in the items on the right, we value the items on the left more."[19]

It's up to the person implementing agile to interpret what those values mean in a given situation and determine how to apply them in the context of his/her business and project environment. In some cases, they've been misinterpreted. For example, some have taken an extreme view to interpret them to mean that:

- There is no documentation, and no processes and tools.
- Agile is not consistent with environments based on customer contracts.
- Change control is not consistent with agile.

It certainly wasn't the intent of the people writing the Agile Manifesto that the contents would be interpreted as absolutes[20]— they were intended to be relative statements. The key point is that you have to interpret those principles in the context of your business and project environment and

---

[19] Agile Manifesto, http://agilemanifesto.org

[20] Highsmith, Jim, *Agile Project Management-Creating Innovative Products*, Addison-Wesley, New York, NY 2010, p. 16

apply them intelligently. Unfortunately, that has not always been the case and agile methodologies have been misapplied or poorly implemented in some situations.

2. Agile methodologies are still maturing, and there's a lot to be learned about what works and what doesn't work. In fact, agile is heavily based on continuous improvement, the whole methodology is meant to evolve, and there is an evolution taking place as the body of knowledge associated with agile grows. Jim Highsmith[21] breaks down the most important agile tools and techniques fall into the following levels:
   - Technical Practices
   - Iteration Management
   - Project Management
   - Portfolio Governance

   Agile has its roots in technical practices and that area is the most mature and most established in terms of having a widely accepted body of knowledge associated with it, but as you move up the ladder, the levels of knowledge associated with the other areas are progressively less defined. For example, a few books have touched on the portfolio governance area, but there is much to be learned in that area.

   Traditional Project Management Office (PMO) organizations need to change radically in some cases to adapt to agile. In many cases, instead of being only an enforcer of rigidly defined corporate processes and policies about how to manage projects, PMO organizations need to shift their focus to a value-added consulting orientation to help their companies learn to successfully implement more flexible and adaptive processes.

The important thing about agile is that implementing it mechanically "by the book" is not the right approach, you really need to understand the principles underneath it at a deeper level to know how to apply it in the context of your business and project environment. That's why you won't find a prescriptive approach defined for how to implement every aspect of agile.

Understanding any methodology at a deeper level (understanding the principles behind it) is essential for selecting a methodology (agile or non-agile) that is consistent with your business environment and tailoring it as necessary to fit specific projects. That is the approach behind this book.

---

[21] Highsmith, Jim, *Agile Project Management-Creating Innovative Products*, Addison-Wesley, New York, NY 2010, p. 78

CHAPTER 2

AGILE VALUES, PRINCIPLES, AND PRACTICES

It is outside the scope of this book to provide in-depth background on agile methodologies; however, it is important to at least provide a general understanding of agile values, principles, and practices and how they have evolved. That is the purpose of this chapter: it is intended to provide background reading for anyone who does not already have a background in these areas. I highly recommend the books listed in the Additional Reading section at the end of this book as resources for additional in-depth reading in this area.

LEAN SOFTWARE DEVELOPMENT PRINCIPLES

Before getting into agile, it's worthwhile to understand the principles behind Lean Software Development for several reasons:

1. Lean Principles Are the Foundation for Agile:
   First and foremost, agile has adopted the fundamental value system of lean: delivering and maximizing net customer value. Understanding the lean principles provides a deeper understanding of why agile makes sense from a broader business and operational management perspective rather than just a development perspective.
2. Operational Management Perspective:
   The principles behind lean manufacturing have been well-proven and widely used to provide significantly improved business results in many industries and application areas. An understanding of Lean Software Development principles will provide a deeper understanding of why agile methodologies have the potential to significantly improve product development processes and business results from an operational management perspective.

   In many cases, agile methodologies have been sold primarily on the basis of improving software development processes from a development perspective; however, successfully developing a more agile product development approach can have much broader implications that impact many portions of the business and might require a significant organizational transformation to be successful. The Lean Software Development principles provide a way to better understand the impact from an operational management perspective so that it can be well-aligned with an overall business strategy.

3. Improving Traditional Development Processes:
In many situations, the best solution for companies will not be to completely discard traditional development processes and replace them with agile development processes. There are a lot of reasons why traditional development processes may still make sense in many business and project environments. In those environments, the right solution may be to improve and streamline those traditional development processes rather than replace them The principles behind Lean Software Development can be applied to improve almost any development process (either agile or non-agile).

Lean Principles

The roots of the agile methodology are in "lean" thinking, which originated in lean manufacturing concepts. Lean manufacturing or lean production, which is often simply known as "Lean" is defined as:

> "A systematic approach to identifying and eliminating waste through continuous improvement by flowing the product at the demand of the customer."[1]

"Lean" considers the expenditure of resources for any goal other than the creation of value for the end customer to be wasteful and a target for elimination. "Value" is defined as any action or process that a customer would be willing to pay for.

Agile is based on taking that same thinking from lean manufacturing and applying it to a software development process. It involves looking at a software development process and making some critical decisions about whether each activity in the process adds value. There are three kinds of work in any process:

- **Value-Added**—Process steps that produce value the customer is willing to pay for or are essential to directly meeting customer requirements
- **Non-Value-Added**—Process steps that are not directly required to produce customer value but are required for other reasons such as meeting regulatory requirements, company mandates, legal requirements, and so forth
- **Waste**—Process steps that consume resources but produce no value in the eyes of the customer

Applying these concepts to a software development life cycle model requires evaluating the various steps in the process and making a judgment as to whether

[1] Lean Manufacturing Guide, www.leanmanufacturingguide.com/

they really produce value in the eyes of the customer or not. Dr. David Rico provides a definition of "Lean Systems Engineering" as follows:

> "Lean (lēn): Thin, slim, slender, narrow, adequate, or just-enough; Without waste
>
> - A customer-driven systems engineering process that delivers the maximum amount of business value
> - An economical systems engineering way of planning and managing the development of complex systems
> - A systems engineering process that is free of excess waste, capacity, and non–value adding activities
> - Just-enough, just-in-time, and right-sized systems engineering processes, documentation, and tools
> - A systems engineering approach that is adaptable to change in customer needs and market conditions"[2]

INCOSE[3] has developed a list of systems engineering enablers to support the six key principles of lean:

Lean Principle	Enablers
Value	**Focus on delivering customer value:** • Use a defined process for capturing requirements focused on customer value. • Establish the value of the end product or system to the customer (what are the business objectives?). • Frequently involve the customer.
Map the Value Stream	**Use a well-defined methodology for executing projects:** • Poor planning is the most notorious reason for wasteful projects. • Plan to develop only what needs developing. • Plan leading indicators and metrics to manage the project.
Pull	**Tailor the process to the risks and complexity of the project to achieve maximum efficiency:** • The Pull Principle promotes the culture of tailoring tasks and pulling them and their outputs based only on legitimate need and rejecting others as waste. • Pull tasks and outputs based on need, and reject others as waste.

[2] Rico, David F., Lean and Agile Systems Engineering, http://davidfrico.com

[3] International Council on Systems Engineering—Lean Systems Engineering Working Group, http://cse.lmu.edu/about/graduateeducation/systemsengineering/INCOSE.htm

Lean Principle	Enablers
Flow	**Eliminate bottlenecks that are likely to obstruct or delay progress:** • In complex programs, opportunities for the progress to stop are overwhelming, and it takes careful preparation, planning, and coordination effort to overcome them. • Clarify, derive, and prioritize requirements early and often during execution. • Front-load the architectural design and implementation. • Make progress visible to all. • Use the most effective communications and coordination practices and effective tools.
Respect for People	**Build an organization based on respect for people:** • Nurture a learning environment. • Treat people as most valued assets.
Perfection	**Strive for excellence and continuous improvement in the software development processes:** • Use lessons learned from past projects for future projects. • Develop perfect communication, coordination and collaboration policy across people and processes. • Use effective leadership to lead the development effort from start to finish. • Drive out waste through design standardization, process standardization, and skill-set standardization. • Use continuous improvement methods to draw best energy and creativity from project teams.

Each of these topics is discussed in more detail in the following sections.

Customer Value

Many businesses focus on financial results rather than customer value as a primary goal—one problem is that without understanding the cause-and-effect relationships that drive those financial results, you're always in reactive mode. When the financial results for the current quarter go down, there's a lot of scrambling around to figure out what went wrong and what caused that to happen and to try to fix the problem.

A more proactive approach is to develop an understanding of the factors that drive financial results for your business and focus on those factors—if you focus on customer value and you do that successfully, the financial results should follow and it provides a much more reliable and consistent approach for managing a business successfully. Figure 2.1 is a model I used several times in my *Business Excellence* book.[4]

[4] Cobb, Charles G., *From Quality to Business Excellence*, ASQ Quality Press, 2003

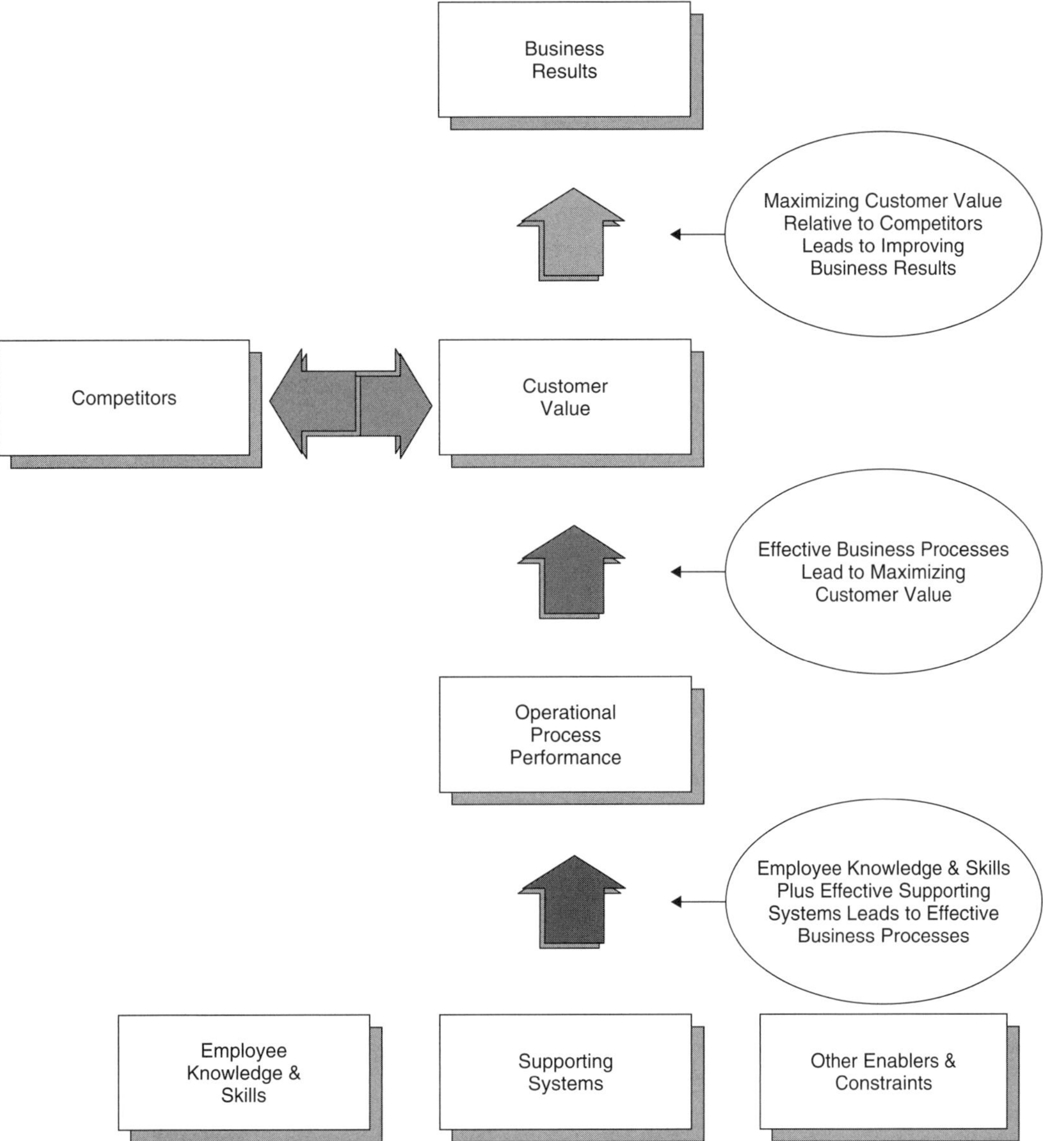

Figure 2.1 Business Excellence model

This is a relatively simple model, but it's useful to understand some of the general cause-and-effect relationships that drive business results in a typical business. Here's a summary of some key points in this model:

1. Customer value is the primary focus of this model—if you improve customer value relative to your competition, it should have a direct impact on driving business results.

2. Customer value is a function of effective business processes that are designed to maximize value to the customer—if you continuously improve those processes to consistently deliver high levels of customer value, it should have a direct impact on driving both customer value and business results.
3. Operational process performance is a function of a number of things including:
   - Employee knowledge and skills
   - Supporting systems
   - Other enablers and constraints, which include:
     - Cultural and behavioral factors
     - Organizational structure
     - Technology

The idea of this model is that businesses need to have an integrated, cross-functional view of how their business works to develop a proactive, systems approach to management that is focused on customer value. It's fairly obvious that a focus on customer value should be a strong driving force in any business, but "customer value" can mean different things:

- In a company that produces products or applications for sale to external customers, customer value is what the buyer of the product is willing to pay for and what makes the product unique relative to the competition.
- In a company where the products are primarily for internal use, (for example, an IT organization that produces applications for internal use), it may be more difficult to define customer value because:
  - The relationship to the value that the application provides to the ultimate external customer may be indirect.
  - The internal customer may not have a very clear or well-defined idea of what he/she would value in the application.
  - If it is a unique application, there may not be something to compare it to as a reference.

Naturally, the more uncertain the customer requirements and value are, the more of an iterative and adaptive discovery approach may be needed to define a product or application to satisfy those values.

Map the Value Stream

Lean Software Development is a software development approach developed by Mary Poppendiek based on the lean principles. A more detailed description of Lean Software Development can be found in Appendix B. An important principle of both lean manufacturing and Lean Software Development is to "map the value stream." This process basically involves starting from the point that the product or service is delivered to the customer (either an internal customer or external customer) and working backward from that point to map all the process steps that lead to fulfilling that customer value. The next step is to identify and differentiate steps in that process that produce value to the customer from steps in the process that produce no value to the customer and may constitute waste.

An important factor is to identify "waste." Mary Poppendiek has translated the seven wastes found in a manufacturing process to the equivalent seven wastes found in Software development:[5]

The Seven Wastes of Manufacturing	The Seven Wastes of Software Development
Inventory	Partially Done Work
Extra Processing	Extra Processes
Overproduction	Extra Features
Transportation	Task Switching
Waiting	Waiting
Motion	Motion
Defects	Defects

Pull

One of the key differences associated with lean is the difference between a "push" approach and a "pull" approach—this difference is also found in most agile approaches. In a traditional manufacturing process approach, production output is forecast, inventory is stocked at various points, and raw materials are then "pushed" through the process to fulfill that forecast. This type of process has been predominantly used in manufacturing for many years to maximize the efficiency of the production equipment used in the process. By stockpiling all the raw material required, the process is designed to maximize the efficiency of the equipment used in the process; however, it has some serious potential deficiencies such as:

- The forecasting process requires attempting to make an intelligent guess at what the customer demand is well in advance of when it is actually expected to be delivered from production, which is very difficult to do accurately and is fraught with lots of potential problems.
- The process is very difficult to adjust to changes in customer demand—if there is a change in customer demand, it can take a considerable amount of time and effort to replan the entire process to adjust to that change, and there also may be a considerable lag associated with restocking material

[5] Poppendiek, Tom and Mary, *Lean Software Development—An Agile Toolkit*, New York: Addison-Wesley, 2003, p. 4

to support the revised plan. If the forecast is wrong, there are significant potential risks including:

- Winding up with a significant amount of unusable inventory that might have to be scrapped (In a software project "unusable inventory" translates to extra features that no one needs or is likely to use that complicate the product and cause unnecessary maintenance if they are not removed).
- Not having sufficient inventory to fill customer demand if the forecast is wrong, (In a software project this translates to not having the right features to satisfy customer needs).
- Having to stockpile or store inventory beyond the originally planned duration (In a software project this translates into undesirable product management overhead.) "I've often seen this administrative burden lumped onto the project manager who must now wade through bloated scope matrices, backlogs of change requests, and unwieldy specifications."[6]

Most traditional product development processes, such as the Waterfall process, are based on a similar "push" process. All the requirements are gathered upfront and are "pushed" through the rest of the development process in a sequential fashion just like a manufacturing assembly line. In a traditional product development process, the "push" approach may have the advantage of optimizing the utilization of the resources in a development process if the requirements are relatively certain and known in advance, but that is often not the case. It can result in serious potential problems and inefficiencies if there is uncertainty in the requirements. Those potential problems and inefficiencies are similar to those associated with a "push" manufacturing process:

- The product requirements for a new product development effort are essentially a "forecast" of the requirements for a product or application that a customer will need in the future that may be very uncertain and not very well defined. Attempting to forecast (or guess at) product requirements well in advance of when the product will actually be deployed and used has even more risk than forecasting production output in a manufacturing process. In addition to the normal risks of forecasting customer demand, the customer may not really know what he/she wants without seeing the product and seeing first-hand how it works. For that reason, the requirements might easily change over that time.
- The process also can be difficult to adjust to changes in customer requirements. Typically, many assumptions are made about what the customer requirements are, and elaborate plans, resource assignments and documentation will be created to support those assumptions.

---

[6] Gottesman, Erik, E-mail comments on book review

- There is also a significant risk that the assumptions in the requirements are wrong, don't really reflect the real needs of the customer, and that may not be discovered until the final product is ready for final acceptance testing.

The result of inaccurate or changing customer requirements may require a significant amount of lost time and effort to replan around a different set of requirements and assumptions and might also require substantial amount of rework. If a typical change control system is used, the process for doing that may also be very cumbersome and difficult. Lean and agile approaches avoid these problems by:

- Deferring the resolution of uncertain requirements until a decision is required (when that particular requirement is "pulled" into development for further processing). Avoiding guessing at the requirements upfront and waiting till more information is known will typically result in better decisions and avoid many of the problems associated with inaccurate and changing requirements.
- Lean and agile systems openly acknowledge and are built around the assumption that requirements are uncertain and are likely to change as the project progresses. Many traditional processes do not recognize or acknowledge the uncertainty in the requirements and attempt to superimpose a rigid control model on top of a very uncertain environment.

A "pull" system works by only producing the required amount to meet demand at each stage. In a manufacturing system, this would be characterized by a just-in-time production scheduling system. Many of the ideas for lean manufacturing came from the Toyota Production System and *kanban*. If the word *kanban* is translated literally; "*kan*" means visual and "*ban*" means card or board. The idea is based on inventory demand cards that are sometimes used in a manufacturing system:

> "Picture yourself on a Toyota production line. You put doors on Priuses. You have a stack of 10 or so doors. As you keep bolting them on, your stack of doors gets shorter. When you get down to 5 doors, sitting on top of the 5th door in the stack is a card—a Kanban card—that says "build 10 doors." Well it may not say exactly that—but it is a request to build exactly 10 more Prius doors."
>
> You pick the Kanban card up, and run it over to the guy who builds doors. He's been waiting for you. He's been doing other things to keep busy while waiting. The important thing here is that he's NOT been building Prius doors. He takes your Kanban card and begins to build doors.
>
> You go back to your workstation, and just a bit before your stack of doors is gone, the door guy comes back with a stack of 10 doors. You

> know that Kanban card is slid in between doors 5 & 6. You got the doors just in time."[7]

The process flow works in a similar way for the rest of the plant—when the guy who makes the doors for the Prius runs out of parts that he needs to build the doors, he has a similar Kanban card to request more parts from the process that provides those parts to him. The whole process flow is "pulled" by *actual* customer demand rather being pushed by a forecast of someone guessing at what they *think* the customer demand is. Of course, in many situations, this process is computerized and actual cards are not physically used to signal demand.

In a software development process, there is a direct analogy between Kanban cards and "User Story Cards" that are used in an agile process. "User stories" are a high-level description of a capability that the system needs to provide—the following is an example of a user story:

> "As a banking customer, I need to be able to withdraw funds from my account through an ATM machine"

User stories are typically defined early in the project to identify the capabilities the system must provide to a sufficient level of detail to do a rough estimate of the level of effort associated with each and the details of how the user story will be implemented will be deferred until it is time to do the design:

- Instead of attempting to define all of the requirements in detail, only the high-level requirements are defined upfront without a lot of detail typically to the level of user stories.
- Instead of treating all requirements equally, the requirements are prioritized based on their value to the customer. After they are prioritized and broken up into releases and/or iterations, the most important requirements that are at the top of the list and ready for development get developed first.
- Once the developer has picked up a "User Story" to begin working on, he/she will then work directly with the user to "pull" more detail as needed to fill that requirement.

A "story card" is equivalent to a "Kanban" card in a manufacturing system and describes one particular feature that a user needs. As in the manufacturing system, physical cards may or may not be used—there are computerized tools that will automate this task and eliminate the use of physical story cards if desired. However, in many cases, physical cards may actually be used and put on a board and each developer picks up a card to start working on it similar to the way a Kanban card works in a factory.

---

[7] "Kanban Development Oversimplified," www.agileproductdesign.com/blog/2009/kanban_over_simplified.html

Flow

"Flow" is an important principle to understand to maximize the efficiency of any process.

Importance of Small Batch Sizes: In a manufacturing process, it is well known that small batch sizes are much better for optimizing the "flow" of the process than large batch sizes. If large batch sizes are used, bottlenecks develop at various points in the process and material winds up waiting at those bottleneck points to be processed creating waste. There are at least a couple of types of "waste" associated with that:

1. Excess material inventory is used in the process, which creates unnecessary inventory cost, space for storage, and additional handling costs. Mary Poppendiek uses an example of the construction of the Empire State Building in New York. The entire Empire State Building, which was the tallest building in the world at that time, was built in a total of 20 months, including demolition of existing buildings and planning and design of the new building.[8]

   One of the most serious constraints that needed to be dealt with in that project is that there was only a limited amount of vacant real estate in the area where the building was built to store the materials needed for the building and the flow of the project had to be carefully planned. The building was built in iterations of a few floors at a time, and the arrival of material had to be scheduled meticulously to have just the right materials available at the right time to maximize the flow.
2. If the material is perishable, it can go stale and become unusable. By "perishable," I'm not necessarily referring to fruits and vegetables. Dell Computer is a good example—Dell builds systems for customers out of a variety of different components (disk drives, graphic cards, etc.), and those components become obsolete quickly and are constantly being replaced by newer versions. Using small batch sizes and building systems on demand as customers need them reduces the risk of winding up with too much obsolete inventory of components in the pipeline.[9]

The other major advantages of using small batch sizes are[10]:

- It reduces the end-to-end cycle time (via Little's Law of Queuing[11])
- It makes waste very hard to ignore, as any waste in a small batch size system will cause much larger problems than when you've got inventory at hand to smooth it over. You then have to confront and fix the waste.

---

[8] Poppendiek, Tom and Mary, Leading Lean Software Development—Results Are Not the Answer, New York: Addison-Wesley, 2010, p. 102

[9] Poppendiek, Tom and Mary, Implementing *Lean Software Development—From Concept to Cash*, New York: Addison-Wesley, 2007, p. 12

[10] Burns, Martin, E-mail comments on book review

[11] "Principle: Little's Law," htwww.factoryphysics.com/Principle/LittlesLaw.htm

> The visual metaphor often employed is that a stream running low uncovers the rocks on its bed.

Attempting to define all the requirements for a product or application upfront in a traditional development process like the Waterfall process is equivalent to attempting to process large batch sizes in a manufacturing process. It's impossible to work on all the requirements at once, so bottlenecks develop at various points in the process and requirements wind up waiting to be processed. The impact of that is similar to a manufacturing process—having an excess of requirements sitting around waiting to be processed is similar to having excess inventory in a manufacturing process:

- There are "handling costs" associated with managing those requirements waiting to be processed—they have to be well documented and tracked or they may be forgotten and left out of the design.
- The requirements are also "perishable"—if they wait for a long time to be processed, they could easily become obsolete and if that is the case, either someone winds up designing and building a product or application on obsolete requirements or unnecessary labor is consumed in redefining and rewriting the requirements.

An iterative development process is analogous to small production batch sizes in a manufacturing operation—by breaking up the requirements into iterations, the overall development process is likely to flow much more smoothly and avoid the bottlenecks associated with traditional development processes.

Of course, in actual practice, there are limits to how far it is practical to break down the requirements to optimize flow. For example:

1. **Requirements Management Considerations**—From a requirements management perspective, it may be necessary to group requirements into related feature sets that are interrelated to each other and those feature sets might be bigger than the effort that can be realized in a single iteration. That requires some compromises between:
   - An idealized approach where individual sets of requirements are completely processed immediately in each iteration, and
   - A more realistic hybrid approach where there some of the requirements might be "pipelined" for processing and spread across more than one iteration

   The idea of buffering some of the requirements that cannot be fulfilled immediately is called "story pipelining."

   > "Story pipelining is often seen by purist agile practitioners as "strictly un-agile" as it violates the oft-held view that working software is the only thing that represents value and anything less is a cop out. In practice, however, pipelining is often the best way to balance

> agility with the realities of real-world delivery constraints. You gain a measure of project progress that's still closer to real doneness in the eyes of the customer, you retain a lifecycle that encourages regular and frequent feedback, but you also recognize that complex software systems have a gestation period."[12]

2. **Testing/Release and Configuration Management Considerations**— There are also some testing and release management considerations that might require compromises from the ideal flow model:
   - Testing may want a functionality set to test (particularly regression test) against that's a relatively complete subset of functionality and is stable for the duration of the test cycle.
   - Release and configuration management might have similar needs.

Both of these issues can be overcome but may require a major rethinking of how the process works and very strong coordination of test planning, as well as release and configuration management with the rest of the development effort.

Concurrent Processing (or Engineering): Concurrent processing is another well-known way to improve "flow" in any process. In a manufacturing process, it is much more likely for bottlenecks to develop if there is only one path through the system and everything is sequential than if there are parallel paths available and some work can be done concurrently.

In a product development process, there are typically large opportunities for concurrent engineering to improve the flow through the process. Here are a few examples:

- Requirements development can be overlapped with design instead of being sequential and quality testing can also overlap with design instead of being sequential. This requires a much more collaborative, cross-functional approach to development, which can be difficult to achieve, but the potential payoff is significant.
- Within a given iteration some of the testing and development tasks can be overlapped. For example, a tester can begin testing one user story in an iteration while the developers are working on the next user story rather than the tester waiting for all user stories to be complete.
- Design teams can work on multiple iterations concurrently. This requires breaking up the design effort into iterations and requires some coordination among design teams.

[12] Gottesman, Erik, E-mail comments on book review

Respect for People

In the early days of manufacturing, processes were designed so that the people performing those processes did not require a high level of skill. An individual working on an assembly line could be assigned a small repetitive task such as putting a tire on a car which required only a minimum amount of skill and training. The primary requirement for higher levels of skill and training could be limited to a relatively few people who were responsible for designing and managing the overall process and training the workers to perform each task. There are several problems with that approach:

- No one really takes overall responsibility for the overall quality of the complete vehicle.
- It might rely heavily on quality control inspectors at the end of the line to try to find defects and send the vehicles back for rework if necessary.
- It can be a dehumanizing experience for anyone to perform that kind of limited, repetitive task.
- It doesn't take advantage of the complete range of skills and judgment of the people performing the tasks.

For a long time, those designing manufacturing processes have recognized the need to respect and empower the people performing the processes as much as possible. In a manufacturing process, having people take pride in workmanship is extremely important to achieving high levels of quality and productivity. The need for fully utilizing the capabilities of people and motivating them is even more critical in a product development process, where the overall effectiveness of the process is so critically dependent on the performance of the people performing the process. Both lean and agile methodologies seek to eliminate those problems by empowering individuals and the team as a whole to take responsibility for the overall quality of their work.

Many traditional development processes have been modeled on the early manufacturing processes, where the process defines in detail the work to be done and how it should be done, and the process requires a lower level of skill to perform those tasks that are relatively well defined. Agile methodologies are generally much less well defined and rely heavily on the skill and training of the people performing the process to tailor it to a particular project, task, and business environment. That is a very key reason why respect for people is so important in an agile environment.

Perfection

In the early days of manufacturing, there was a high level of reliance on quality control and inspectors to find defects at the end of the assembly line. The problems with that approach are apparent:

- It takes a lot of resources to do inspection that wouldn't be necessary if the defects were eliminated at the source.

- This method for finding defects is not totally reliable because it typically relies on sampling, and since it's impossible or impractical to do a 100 percent sample, at least some small percentage of defects is not going to be detected before they get to the customer.
- A lot of rework and scrap can result from defective products that are found at the end of the assembly line.

Total Quality Management (TQM), which came about in the early 1990s taught us to go upstream in the process and build quality into the process so that the process itself is inherently reliable. This approach is based on finding the sources of defects in the process, putting controls in place at the source to prevent those defects from happening at all rather than relying on inspection at the end of the process to find the defects just before the product is shipped to the customer, and using continuous improvement to continually improve the reliability of the process on an ongoing basis.

Continuous improvement is built into most lean and agile methodologies. For example, Scrum has a "Retrospective" at the end of each iteration to look back at the work that was done and assess how the process worked. Since the iterations are very short, learning what works and what doesn't work happens quickly, and the processes are also very flexible and adaptable, which makes it relatively easy to improve the process. Lean Software Development puts an even stronger emphasis on having defined processes and a very aggressive focus on continuous improvement of the process. Scrum and agile methodologies have continuous improvement within a given project (for example, retrospectives are used within a project to learn and redefine the process as necessary as the as the project progresses), but they may have no defined mechanism to capture those lessons learned and incorporate them into a more global process that spans multiple projects.

Many times, traditional development methodologies attempt to force-fit a project to a particular methodology and don't allow sufficient flexibility to the people implementing that process to tailor it to fit a particular project or to easily make improvements to the process based on lessons learned on previous projects.

There is also a direct relationship with the principle of respect for people—in many cases, the people performing the process are the first ones to see opportunities for improvements in the process to prevent defects and/or to do the process more efficiently, but many times they are not empowered to suggest or make those changes. Lean and agile methodologies recognize that and are not rigidly defined or prescriptive—they provide some fundamental principles and practices that are common to most projects and are expected to be tailored to a given situation. Naturally, it requires more skill to make good judgments about how to tailor a process to fit a business and project environment.

Interrelationship of Lean and Agile

The interrelationship of lean and agile is shown in Figure 2.2.

The following is a summary of how the lean and agile disciplines are related to each other:

1. Process Orientation
   Lean Software Development has a bit stronger process orientation than most agile methodologies.
   - Lean Software Development has its origins in lean manufacturing; Mary and Tom Poppendiek have done a lot of work to translate the principles of lean manufacturing to a software development environment. Lean manufacturing has a strong process orientation—Lean Software Development still has a process orientation, but it is primarily a set of principles that can be applied to almost any other development process (agile, iterative, or traditional). It does not explicitly define processes, but it does recognize the iterative and adaptive nature of processes that are needed in a software development environment.
   - The original Agile Manifesto and Principles were somewhat of a revolution against rigidly defined processes, such as the Waterfall approach, that were perceived to be very mechanistic rather than humanistic. One of the statements in the Agile Manifesto is "We value individuals and interactions over processes and tools" to reflect a bias for a more humanistic orientation and less of a mechanistic, process orientation. Current agile methodologies, such as Scrum, have recognized the need for process discipline, but it's a different kind of process discipline that relies much more on highly trained people with skill and judgment rather than rigidly defined, mechanistic processes.
2. Developer-Centric versus Operational Management Orientation

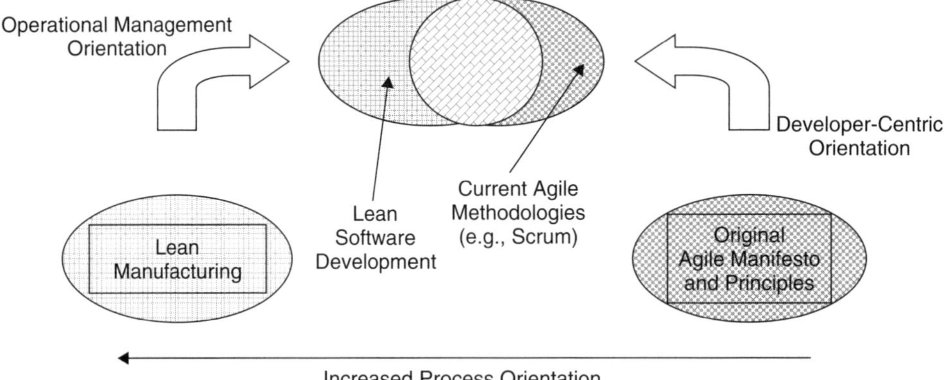

Figure 2.2 Interrelationship of Lean and agile

Many agile methodologies have a very strong developer-centric orientation while Lean Software Development has a little more of an operational management orientation; however, they have begun to merge:

- Scrum has gone beyond a developer-centric orientation and provides somewhat of a framework for project management and has a disciplined process designed to eliminate waste similar to Lean.
- The work of Mary and Tom Poppendiek has adapted the original lean manufacturing principles to a software development environment that is very congruent with the original agile principles.

The principles in Lean Software Development provide a way to go beyond a developer-centric orientation and view agile methodologies in a broader operational management perspective.

3. Common Principles

Current agile methodologies and Lean Software Development have many principles in common such as:

- Focus on Customer Value
- Respect for People and Empowerment
- Emphasis on Learning and Continuous Improvement
- Iterative Development Approach
- Designing Quality and Integrity into the Product
- Deciding as Late as Possible
- Eliminating Waste

4. Differences

The differences between current agile methodologies and Lean Software Development are more in the implementation than in the principles behind them. Both are not prescriptive and allow a lot of flexibility in how they're implemented, so there may be significant differences in implementation, but there is very little difference in the underlying principles. The following are a few examples of how they might differ:

- An agile methodology like Scrum might do continuous improvement within a project through retrospectives, but might not have a strong enough process orientation to transfer those lessons learned into a broad-based process definition that is carried forward to other projects. Lean Software Development would tend to put more emphasis on having a defined process (or set of processes) that is used across projects and constantly improved.
- A Lean Software Development approach could be applied to iterative and even traditional methodologies that might not be considered to be "agile." In some situations, there might be a need for a more controlled, process-driven approach, and the principles behind Lean Software Development can be used to streamline that approach.

Martin Burns and Erik Gottesman have also pointed out some additional differences that can arise between lean and agile methodologies:

- Lean practitioners will tend towards automated methods because they enable the standardization that is the enabler for a lean approach, while some agilists tend to minimize the use of tools and not attempt to standardize processes across projects[13]
- An agile approach typically has a stronger emphasis on human factors—for example, most agile practices are based on a "sustainable pace". The idea of a "sustainable pace" is "... predicated on the concept that software developers should not work more than 40-hour weeks, and if there is overtime one week, then the next week should not include more overtime. This also carries with it the implied suggestion that people perform best and most creatively if they are rested. I do not believe that a Lean adherent would take exception to this suggestion or argue that overworked developers are *more* productive, but Lean does not incorporate an implicit or explicit prohibition on overtime"[14]
- Lean approaches tend to put a stronger emphasis on "just barely good enough" thinking:

> "In many areas of life, there are strengths that—if overplayed—can become weaknesses. In agile development, it's craftsmanship: the urge to create something ever more worthy and beautiful. Where Agile and Lean often part company is the point at which doing so no longer creates value, relative to the cost incurred: it becomes waste_*even if the result is truly of higher quality*. If there were a path to enlightenment for developers, then the 6th step would require recognizing the point of "Just Barely Good Enough" and knowing to stop there."[15]

Again, the preceding differences are not really differences in principle—the principles are probably much more consistent than the typical implementation. Both Lean and agile allow considerable latitude in how they are implemented, and there may be significant differences in practice, while the principles behind the methodology are not that different at all.

AGILE HISTORY AND OVERVIEW

Agile methodologies are not new—people have been doing various kinds of agile projects for a long time; however, in today's world, the movement to adopt

---

[13] Burns, Martin, E-mail comments on book review
[14] Gottesman, Erik, E-mail comments on book review
[15] Burns, Martin, E-mail comments on book review

more agile methodologies seems to be gaining a lot more momentum for several reasons:

- Some of the methodologies and tools for implementing agile projects such as Scrum, are becoming much more widely understood and accepted.
- Many companies have demonstrated success in implementing agile projects in actual practice and have added to the knowledge base of what works and what doesn't work in different projects and environments.
- The tradeoffs associated with balancing a need for sufficient project control and achieving greater agility are also better understood, and there are many ways to achieve a balance of those objectives with the appropriate blend of agile and traditional methodologies.

The origins of much of today's agile movement can be traced to the Agile Manifesto, which was originally developed in February 2001, at The Lodge at Snowbird ski resort in the Wasatch mountains of Utah[16] The Agile Manifesto itself is fairly simple and consists of four value statements:

> "We are uncovering better ways of developing software by doing it and helping others do it. Through this work we have come to value:
>
> - Individuals and interactions over processes and tools
> - Working software over comprehensive documentation
> - Customer collaboration over contract negotiation
> - Responding to change over following a plan
>
> That is, while there is value in the items on the right, we value the items on the left more."[17]

It's important not to misinterpret the intent of these statements—the intent behind them was a *shift* in emphasis. That doesn't mean that the items on the right are unimportant:

> "Over the years, the manifesto statements have been misinterpreted, primarily in confusing less important with unimportant: This should not be construed as indicating that tools, process, documents, contracts, or plans are unimportant. Tools are critical to speeding development and reducing costs. Contracts are vital to initiating developer-customer relationships. Documentation aids communication. However, the items on the left are the most critical. Without skilled individuals, working products, close interaction with customers, and responsiveness to change, product delivery will be nearly impossible."[18]

---

[16] "History: The Agile Manifesto," http://agilemanifesto.org/history.html

[17] Agile Manifesto, http://agilemanifesto.org/

[18] Highsmith, Jim, *Agile, Project Management—Creating Innovative Products,* New York: Addison-Wesley, 2009, p. 16

The Agile Manifesto Principles elaborate on this overall value statement. The following is a summary of the Agile Manifesto Principles[19] and their relationship to traditional project management practices.

Agile Manifesto Principle	Relationship to Traditional Project Management Practice
Our highest priority is to satisfy the customer through early and continuous delivery of valuable software.	There is no real contradiction in principle; however, traditional practice in many cases has emphasized control, predictability, and thoroughness of testing over early delivery because the tradeoffs required to deliver early in many cases have been perceived to be severe. However, with the right approach and methodology, those tradeoffs may not be that severe and may be very manageable. Of course, the priority given to early delivery of software needs to be weighed against other factors in any project or business environment. For example, the process needs to be matched to the customer's ability to actively engage in the project and provide feedback and inputs. It is difficult to make a statement that early and continuous delivery of software is *always* the highest priority in all projects.
Welcome changing requirements, even late in development. Agile processes harness change for the customer's competitive advantage.	Change control has always been viewed as a very essential element of stabilizing a project, but a change control process does not necessarily have to be extremely rigid. If it is done properly, it does not equate to stifling or *preventing* change—it means ensuring that unnecessary change (as defined by the sponsor, ultimately) is rejected, but that necessary change is brought into the project with the full awareness of all concerned and that necessary adjustments to designs, plans, timescales, tests, contracts (etc.) are made, and with the minimum of wider disruption. Change control also can be valuable for configuration management and validating that any new changes are not inconsistent with other previously developed requirements and assumptions. For that reason, developing a more relaxed approach toward managing changes might not be acceptable in all projects. (See the discussion that follows.)
Deliver working software frequently, from a couple of weeks to a couple of months, with a preference to the shorter timescale.	Achieving these times with most traditional development methodologies may be difficult, and this is the area that agile really pays off; of course, the gains in this area need to be weighed against potential impact in other areas. It is certainly possible with traditional development approaches to break the project up into individual releases or iterations in order to deliver functionality early and that can be a very realistic approach in many cases; however, there is also typically some overhead involved in developing truly releasable software that should be considered.
Business people and developers must work together daily throughout the project.	This is a significantly increased role for the business people to play in the project that goes well beyond the typical requirements definition and testing phases of most traditional development methodologies. It also implies a very close and collaborative working relationship between the business and development staff and a strong commitment of the business side to fully participate in the project throughout the development process.

[19] "Principles behind the Agile Manifesto," http://agilemanifesto.org/principles.html

Agile Manifesto Principle	Relationship to Traditional Project Management Practice
	Many business people are not prepared to make the kind of commitment that is needed and, in some cases, that level of participation may not be necessary. As a result, the project methodology needs to be tailored to the need for participation and the availability of business people to provide that participation.
Build projects around motivated individuals. Give them the environment and support they need, and trust them to get the job done.	There is no question that building a project around motivated individuals is a good thing for any project methodology; however, this particular principle might imply a higher level of delegation and trust than might normally be found in many traditional development projects. A higher level of delegation might involve some loss of control, but that could be a very acceptable tradeoff in the right environment with the right people on the project team. It does, of course, also imply that the people are well trained and capable of taking an increased level of responsibility. Some people have used this statement to justify having complete anarchy and chaos without any leadership at all and that clearly wasn't the intent behind it. Trust in motivated individuals is always a balance—you can move a long way back from micro-management without entirely sacrificing an appropriate level of leadership and management. Knowing what's on track, what's not on track, and deliberately deciding whether, when, and where to undertake corrective action (and what that should be) is essential to any project. Without that, you're "managing by hope" which is never a wise approach.
The most efficient and effective method of conveying information to and within a development team is face-to-face conversation.	There is no question that maximizing the use of face-to-face communications is a good thing in any project. However, the ability to do that is dependent to some extent on the ability to co-locate members of the team to allow face-to-face communications and also might be limited by the size of the team. In many situations, tools such as desktop sharing (with or without video) and collaboration portals can alleviate some of the need for direct face-to-face communications for distributed teams especially when used with web-based development tools. This principle has often been interpreted to imply relaxing the emphasis on project documentation in favor of direct face-to-face communications. That can also be an acceptable tradeoff under the right circumstances based on project size, complexity, and other factors; however, some level of documentation may still be valuable and isn't inconsistent with an emphasis on face-to-face communications. Oral communication is great, and very quick, but places an overreliance on memory for information that may have a shelf life of no longer than a few days. Careful reading of the agile principle helps: it's about *conveying* information, not originating it, or keeping it available for future use. Not everyone who comes into contact with the product (or its components) is a member of the current development team. Think of the member of the support team in 5 years' time or other occasions when more formal and/or documented communication may be necessary to convey or preserve information outside of the development team or for future use after the development effort is finished.

Agile Manifesto Principle	Relationship to Traditional Project Management Practice
Working software is the primary measure of progress.	There is no real contradiction with traditional development processes in this as long as the entire team (business and development) agrees on what "working software" means, what it consists of (including whatever documentation may be needed to support it), and what "done" means. What artifacts are deemed valuable by the customer apart from software? What makes up a working solution? Many traditional development processes fall short because the software is tested against documented requirements, and the requirements are either incomplete or inaccurate in reflecting the real needs of the users. What is implied here is "working software" in the eyes of the user, since the user is more directly involved throughout the development process. Working software is only the primary measure of progress when that's the project's only deliverable, which is probably true for a software coding team but not at all so for many projects. The primary measure of progress should be whatever the sponsor defines as value. Think about user training for example or process change, for example.
Agile processes promote sustainable development. The sponsors, developers, and users should be able to maintain a constant pace indefinitely.	There is no real contradiction with traditional development processes, but this does imply that *all* the members of the team (both business and development) keep pace with each other throughout the whole duration of the project. • In many traditional projects, the participants come in and out of the project as needed at different phases and, in some cases, that may be the best way to manage resources. • In many projects, the business users may not have a sufficient capability to provide dedicated resources to participate in the project team on an ongoing basis and if the requirements are more certain and can be defined upfront, that level of participation may not be necessary. A key factor here is the motivation of the team—the theory behind this is that by empowering the team, they will be more highly motivated and energized and capable of more sustained development work. The need for leadership and skill to develop that kind of motivation is not limited to agile. It can also be done in a traditional environment if the development team understands the business need for additional control and is involved in the decision making behind the project.
Continuous attention to technical excellence and good design enhances agility.	There is no real contradiction with traditional development processes; however, it should be well understood that technical excellence and good design are not the only factors to determine a successful project development approach. This statement can be interpreted to be very developer-centric and needs to be understood in the context of the overall project goals.
Simplicity—the art of maximizing the amount of work not done—is essential.	There is no real contradiction with traditional development processes. This is basically the "keep it simple" principle. Projects should not be overburdened with overly complex features that may be unnecessary. The main advantages of simplification are speed and reduced complexity and reduced complexity can lead to better maintainability.

Agile Manifesto Principle	Relationship to Traditional Project Management Practice
The best architectures, requirements, and designs emerge from self-organizing teams.	This is certainly a very arguable principle behind agile that will not always be true. For example, it is hard to make a categorical statement that the best architectures *always* emerge from self-organizing teams. The approach for determining the best architecture probably depends on the scope and complexity of the project. A similar argument could be made about requirements—this principle makes an implication that using self-organizing teams is the strongest factor in determining the quality of the requirements. It is certainly a factor, but not necessarily the only factor. Developing well-defined requirements that are testable and traceable to the design is a skill that is extremely important especially on large, complex projects.
At regular intervals, the team reflects on how to become more effective, then tunes and adjusts its behavior accordingly.	There is no real contradiction with traditional development processes. This is probably a very strong point in favor of agile methodologies. Most methodologies emphasize the idea of a postmortem to stop and reflect on what went right and what went wrong and to use that learning as a basis for ongoing continuous improvement of the process. A big advantage of the agile approach is that the sprints are much shorter so that learning and correction can take place much more frequently as the project progresses.

Adopting many of these agile principles might involve some tradeoffs with accepted project management practices that have traditionally received so much attention such as:

- Control and predictability
- Management of project risk
- Delivering an acceptable level of software quality

In many cases, that has been perceived as an all-or-nothing proposition, and the choice has been between:

- Very rigid and tightly controlled methodologies like the waterfall approach with lots of documentation, and
- Using no methodology and documentation at all

I've seen organizations where that pendulum has swung back and forth between total overcontrol to almost no control. The key lessons I've learned over the years are:

- It takes a well-planned and sophisticated approach to achieve the right balance of agility and control—if it is done right, it doesn't require completely sacrificing control to achieve agility, but it takes skill to achieve *both* agility and control without sacrificing one to achieve the other.
- Making the right decisions about what is the right balance of agility and control is something that should be done jointly by the business side of the organization and the development side of the organization based on a mutual understanding of the tradeoffs and their potential impact. It

takes a certain amount of organizational maturity to make those decisions effectively.

Many organizations are not at the level of maturity that it takes to create the collaborative, cross-functional environment to make this successful, and that can be a very difficult thing to achieve. I've seen many situations where either:

- There is an adversarial relationship between the business and the development organization, and the business organization might feel that the development organization does not understand their needs or is not sufficiently responsive to their needs.
- The business organization doesn't want to understand or be actively involved in the product development process and has chosen to abdicate the responsibility for developing solutions to the development organization.

That happens particularly often in business organizations whose primary focus is not on product development—for example, where an internal IT organization develops applications only intended for internal business use. In many of those situations, the company doesn't recognize the strategic impact of these internal applications on the business and developing a much more collaborative partnership approach that is well aligned with achieving the company's business goals may require very strong senior management leadership.

AGILE PERCEPTIONS AND REALITY

There is somewhat of a perception that agile and traditional plan-driven methodologies are at odds with each other. Certainly, the agile movement started out as a rebellion against what it perceived as rigid bureaucratic management styles with excessive documentation and overhead and a heavily mechanistic process-driven style as opposed to a much more fluid, humanistic, and dynamic orientation. In describing their original meeting in February 2001, Jim Highsmith characterizes the creators of the Agile Manifesto by saying "a bigger gathering of organizational anarchists would be hard to find"[20]. It was, in a sense, an uprising of the developer community to "define a developer community freed from the baggage of Dilbertesque corporations... In order to succeed in the new economy, to move aggressively into the era of e-business, e-commerce, and the web, companies have to rid themselves of their Dilbert manifestations of make-work and arcane policies."[21] He goes on to say:

> "The agile movement is not anti-methodology; in fact, many of us want to restore credibility to the word methodology. We want to restore a balance.

[20] "History: The Agile Manifesto," Jim Highsmith, http://agilemanifesto.org/history.html
[21] "History: The Agile Manifesto," Jim Highsmith, http://agilemanifesto.org/history.html

> We embrace modeling, but not in order to file some diagram in a dusty corporate repository. We embrace documentation, but not hundreds of pages of never-maintained and rarely-used tomes. We plan, but recognize the limits of planning in a turbulent environment."[22]

There are a number of commonly held perceptions about agile and traditional plan-driven software methodologies—some of these perceptions do have some basis in reality; however, in many cases, the perceived difference is much greater than the real difference.

Perception	Reality
• Agile is based on highly empowered teams. • Teams associated with traditional plan-driven methodologies are not empowered.	There is nothing that prevents using an appropriate level of empowerment with traditional plan-driven methodologies. Of course, the degree of team empowerment should be appropriate to the level of control desired. "Although self-organizing is a good term, it has unfortunately become confused with anarchy."[23] It is also not understood across all cultures.[24]
• Agile teams are highly motivated. • Traditional plan-driven teams are not.	• With the right management and leadership style it is certainly possible to have highly motivated teams using traditional plan-driven methodologies as well as agile methodologies. • The key thing is the perception that traditional plan-driven methodologies are always based on out-of-date management philosophies, and that is not necessarily the case.
• Agile projects value working software over documentation. • Traditional plan-driven projects focus too heavily on creating documentation.	No project (either agile or non-agile) should focus on creating documentation for the sake of documentation. Any document should serve a useful purpose in the project. The perceived gap in this area is probably much greater than the reality: • Agile methodologies have embraced the need for documentation where it serves a useful purpose, and • Traditional plan-driven methodologies provide the capability to limit and tailor the level of documentation to the project.
• Agile emphasizes customer collaboration over contract negotiation. • Traditional plan-driven methodologies are based on formal contracts with customers without a significant amount of collaboration.	In some cases, it may be essential to use a contracting approach with only a limited amount of collaboration—an example is a contracting firm performing fixed-price software development work. However, in most traditional plan-driven development approaches, there is nothing that prevents the project from becoming more collaborative. It is simply a matter of encouraging rather than limiting customer inputs throughout the design and development process, recognizing the importance of customer collaboration in the development process, and dedicating and training the resources to provide that collaborative input.

[22] "History: The Agile Manifesto," Jim Highsmith, http://agilemanifesto.org/history.html

[23] Highsmith, Jim, *Agile Project Management—Creating Innovative Products*, New York: Addison-Wesley, 2010, p. 60

[24] Gottesman, Erik, Comments on book review

Perception	Reality
• Agile is focused on responding to change rather than following a plan. • Traditional plan-driven methodologies are heavily focused on following a plan.	Both agile and traditional plan-driven methodologies incorporate some level of planning; the primary difference is in how much planning is done upfront versus planning that happens as the project progresses. • Agile projects typically use a "rolling wave" approach, which is based on a developing a high-level plan upfront and further refining the plan as the project progresses. This approach avoids wasted effort that might be needed to replan efforts that were based on too much "speculative" planning. • In the pure Waterfall model, a completely detailed plan is typically developed upfront; however, many variations on that are possible. As an example, in an iterative development approach, the high-level requirements are defined upfront and the detailed requirements for each iteration are developed prior to each iteration.
• Agile projects rely heavily on face-to-face communications. • Traditional plan-driven projects rely heavily on documentation as a means of communication.	In most cases, there is nothing to prevent a traditional plan-driven project from incorporating a significant amount of face-to-face communication.

It seems that a number of the differences between agile approaches and traditional plan-driven methodologies are at least as much perception as they are reality. There is no reason why this perceived gap can't be easily narrowed—a number of practices that have been associated with agile can also be applied to traditional plan-driven methodologies to increase the emphasis on people and output rather than the traditional emphasis on project control. An example is respect for people—there is no reason why traditional plan-driven methodologies can't incorporate respect for people as a value and it is probably just largely perception that they don't. Another example is customer collaboration—there is nothing to prevent an increased level of customer collaboration in conjunction with a traditional plan-driven methodology.

Closing this gap has proven elusive because it takes a higher level of sophistication to mix and match these attributes of agile approaches with traditional approaches as opposed to simply adopting some kind of canned, predefined, off-the-shelf methodology, but it is mostly a matter of changing our mindset about how we think of agile and traditional plan-driven methodologies:

- Instead of thinking in black-and-white terms that there is agile at one extreme and Waterfall at the other extreme and nothing in between, we need to see these methodologies as more of a continuum with lots of shades of gray in between that can provide an appropriate balance of agility and control for a given situation.
- Instead of thinking of rigidly defined methodologies with fixed characteristics, we need to recognize that any methodology can and should be

customized and tailored to fit the situation at hand, and there are numerous characteristics of any methodology (agile or non-agile) that can be adjusted.

GENERAL AGILE PRACTICES

Most project managers are used to seeing methodologies that are very well defined, complete, and well-integrated with the tools and practices that are needed to support them. That isn't necessarily the case with agile—it is more like a restaurant menu where there may not be a full-course entrée, and you order individual menu items a-la-carte to make up a full meal. That is a result of several factors:

1. Many agile methodologies are not highly prescriptive and expect the person implementing the methodology to use his/her judgment to adapt the methodology to a specific situation. Agile methodologies are also meant to be much more fluid and dynamic than traditional methodologies. That may be unsettling for some people, but that is probably the way of the future—instead of force-fitting projects to fit any predefined methodology (either agile or non-agile), we should be adapting the methodology (or combination of methodologies) to fit the project.

   With traditional, plan-driven methodologies, there were fewer variables to worry about—in theory, you could freeze the requirements early on in the project and optimize the project methodology around controlling costs and schedules. In that environment, relatively well-defined and repeatable project methodologies might work, but if you accept the notion that the model must now be optimized around a much more uncertain environment, where it may be impossible to define all requirements upfront, it is an entirely different ballgame.
2. Agile methodologies are based on using continuous improvement to further optimize the methodology to best fit the project as the project progresses. It would be difficult to achieve that goal with a very rigidly predefined methodology.
3. Many agile methodologies are still in an early stage of evolution, and there are gaps and inconsistencies in some of the tools and practices for that reason.

If you go into agile methodologies expecting to be handed a canned and well-defined approach that works in all situations right out of the box, you may be disappointed, because that's not likely to happen. It requires a considerable amount of skill and sophistication to successfully apply the right combination of these tools and practices in a given situation.

Jim Highsmith[25] breaks down the most important agile tools and techniques into the following levels:

1. Technical Practices
2. Iteration Management
3. Project Management
4. Portfolio Governance

The order in which they are listed is also the order from most to least mature and well defined. Technical practices are naturally where the roots of agile have evolved from and are most well-defined and mature. Portfolio governance and the other higher-level practices are least defined at this point in time.

The following sections provide a brief overview of some of these areas of practice. Appendix A provides more detail on agile technical practices and the Additional Reading list at the back of this book provides a much more detailed and complete coverage of these areas.

Organizational Practices

The following are some of the organizational practices that are critical to most agile projects.

Teamwork

I can't imagine a company that doesn't practice "teamwork" to some extent, but there are different levels of "teamwork." In many companies, good teamwork means that people from various functional organizations can go to meetings, collaboratively discuss issues, and come up with a solution that is for the common good of the whole organization. Agile projects go well beyond that level of teamwork—in an agile project, people from functional organizations are assigned to the project and from that point on, the agile project team works as a highly integrated individual entity to take collective ownership for the success of the project from both an engineering design and a business results perspective.

Respect for People, Self-Organization, and Empowerment

All agile methodologies are based on a high level of respect for people, as well as self-organization of teams and empowerment. Instead of people on a team being told individually and explicitly what to do, the team, as a whole, establishes the direction and divides up the tasks to be done among the members of the team. Each member on the team is fully empowered to do the tasks that he or she is assigned, and the team as a whole feels joint responsibility for the results—if one member on the team fails to deliver his or her expected results, the team as a whole has failed.

[25] Highsmith, Jim, *Agile Project Management—Creating Innovative Products*, New York: Addison-Wesley, 2010, p. 78

Transparency and Trust

Most agile methodologies are based on a close and collaborative relationship between the business user and the development team. In a traditional project environment, there may have been a tendency to not air the "dirty laundry" with the business user. In an agile environment, problems, risks, and issues are normally shared openly and transparently with the business user, and the business user normally plays an active role in helping to set the direction to resolve those issues. It is more of a true partnership than an arm's-length, vendor-style contractual relationship, and it requires a level of maturity and sophistication that isn't present in many organizations to evolve to that level of partnership and trust. For example, in some organizations:

- Business users, who are used to getting some kind of firm upfront commitment from a development organization on the costs and schedules for a project against detailed requirements will need to understand and trust a very different kind of commitment process, where the business users and the development organization will jointly own responsibility for delivering the functionality that is needed over a period of time in increments. In these circumstances, it may not be possible to completely and accurately estimate the costs and schedule of the overall project upfront. That involves some level of trust that the project team will be able to deliver the expected results with a reasonable cost and schedule.
- Internal organizations such as QA will need to also develop more of a partnership relationship with the development team based on transparency and trust. For example, if the QA organization is testing unreleased software they need to trust the development team that the software has reached a sufficient level of stability and completeness to not waste their time doing unnecessary testing. They also have to trust that the continuous integration process is going to detect and resolve any regression problems that might be introduced by changing software to fix defects.

Planning Practices

The following are some of the key principles involved in planning an agile project.

Just-in-Time Planning

Many people think of an agile project as completely unplanned—people just start writing code with little or no planning. The planning in an agile project may be just as deep as a traditional plan-driven project—it's just done very differently, which may be a more effective way of doing planning in some cases. Most agile methodologies are based on the idea of "just-in-time" planning. Rather than attempting to plan the entire project upfront, the upfront planning is limited to only the amount of planning that is needed to get the project started, and other planning is generally deferred until further into the project when it becomes essential. That approach:

- Allows the project to get started quickly and
- Also avoids unnecessary effort that might be needed with traditional approaches if things further out in time are planned upfront but only need to be replanned later as the project progresses and more information about them becomes known.

Of course, the tradeoff associated with this is that, without doing a complete detailed plan upfront, it is more difficult to accurately predict the overall costs and schedules of the entire project.

Levels of Agile Planning

Agile project methodologies such as Scrum typically include five levels of planning:

1. Vision

   The purpose of the vision planning effort is to define the business goals and objectives that the project is intended to accomplish. A suggested format for an agile vision statement follows (this is commonly called an "elevator statement" in agile terminology:

   > - For (target customer)
   > - Who (statement of the need or opportunity)
   > - The (product name) is a (product category)
   > - That (key benefit, compelling reason to buy)
   > - Unlike (primary competitive alternative)
   > - Our product (statement of primary differentiation)[26]

   An example is:

   > "For a mid-sized company's marketing and sales departments who need basic CRM functionality, the CRM-Innovator is a Web-based service that provides sales tracking, lead generation, and sales representative support features that improve customer relationships at critical touch points. Unlike other services or package software products, our product provides very capable services at a moderate cost."[27]

---

[26] Moore, Geoffrey A., *Crossing the Chasm: Marketing and Selling High-Tech Products to Mainstream Customers*, New York: Harper Business Books, 1999

[27] Moore, Geoffrey A., *Crossing the Chasm: Marketing and Selling High-Tech Products to Mainstream Customers*, Harper Business Books, 1999

2. Roadmap
   The purpose of the roadmap planning portion of the effort is to break the vision down into releases to describe how the overall functionality required by the vision will be delivered over a period of time. Each release is a working subset of the overall functionality that will be incrementally delivered to the user. The roadmap plan describes which features of the overall functionality will be included in each release and approximately when each release is likely to be delivered.
3. Release
   The purpose of the release planning portion of the effort is to break each release down into iterations to describe how the functionality required for each release will be incrementally developed. The results of each iteration should be working software, which may not be releasable. The plan for each release would normally require breaking the features required in the product backlog into user stories, estimating the time required for each user story, and grouping the user stories into iterations to satisfy the overall plan for delivering the functionality required for that release.
4. Iteration
   The purpose of the iteration planning portion of the effort is to define the tasks to be performed during that iteration to develop the user stories required for that iteration. The tasks are also assigned to members of the team for completion.
5. Daily
   The daily planning sessions are primarily to review progress against the planned effort for that iteration and to identify and resolve any obstacles that might be inhibiting progress.

Each of the preceding levels of planning represents different levels of precision, with the highest level of precision and detail being at the daily level and the lowest level of precision and detail being at the vision level.

Requirements Definition Practices

The process for defining requirements is one of the most critical parts of any development process. The following are some commonly used agile practices for requirements definition. These practices are not necessarily the only way to define requirements for agile projects.

User Stories

User stories provide an easy-to-understand and simplified way of stating requirements that is commonly used with many agile methodologies such as Scrum and Extreme Programming. A user story is a very high-level definition of a requirement, containing just enough information so that the developers can produce a reasonable estimate of the effort to implement it without a lot of detail. It is generally of the following form:

"As a <type of user>, I want to <goal>, so that <reason>."

The user story should describe the user need from the perspective of the user. An example is something like the following:

> "As a banking customer, I want to be able to easily make an online deposit of a check into my bank account through my iPhone® so that I can save the time required to send a check for deposit through the mail and I can have the money immediately credited to my checking account as soon as the deposit is completed electronically."

In many agile methodologies, a user story is a sufficient level of definition of a requirement to estimate the level of effort needed to implement it at the beginning of an iteration. The details of a user story are normally further elaborated as necessary as the iteration progresses. The use of user stories does not necessarily preclude or replace other forms of requirements, such as use cases, that might be useful in an agile project. It also doesn't necessarily mean that the requirements definition effort is limited to user stories:

- Many user stories will have business rules associated with them and may also have more detailed functional requirements.
- Most of those details can be elaborated as the iteration progresses. The creation of further detailed documentation to capture this information should be done based on the needs of the project.

Acceptance criteria for user stories are normally defined prior to the beginning of an iteration so that they can be tested as "done" at the end of the iteration.

Story Points

"Story points" are a method of estimating the relative size of a user story. The typical form of story points is a Fibonacci series, such as 1, 2, 3, 5, 8, 13, with 1 being a minimal level of effort and 13 being a maximum level of effort for a user story in an iteration. A user story with story points greater than 13 indicates that it is too big to be accomplished in one iteration and probably needs to be broken down.

The team is asked to vote on the number of story points to assign to each user story as a way of estimating the magnitude of effort required. Sometimes a method called "Planning Poker"[28], which uses playing cards, is used to reach consensus on an estimate of story points to assign to each user story. An experienced agile team has a known velocity of how many story points it is able to produce in each iteration, and that becomes a metric for sizing the work that can be done in future iterations.

---

[28] "Planning Poker," www.planningpoker.com

Epics: An "epic" is just a large user story that needs to be broken down into smaller user stories prior to the start of an iteration. The previous example of depositing a check through an iPhone® might be considered an "epic" that needs to be broken down into smaller user stories such as:

- As an Electronic Banking Customer, I want to be able to scan an image of the front and back of a check into the iPhone® so that it can be deposited electronically.
- As an Electronic Banking Customer, I want to be able to enter the deposit information associated with an electronic deposit so that the correct amount will be deposited into the correct bank account when the electronic deposit is processed.
- As an Electronic Banking Customer, I want to be able to electronically submit a scanned check and deposit information to the bank for deposit so that I can save the time associated with sending deposits by mail.
- As an Electronic Banking Customer, I want to be able to receive confirmation of a completed electronic deposit so that I will know that the deposit was successfully processed

User Persona: A "User Persona" is a description of a specific type of user that impacts the requirements. For example, a "Banking Customer" is an example of a User Persona. User Personas are useful ways of characterizing the users of the system and keeping the development effort focused on satisfying their needs. A "User Persona" can be as detailed as necessary to differentiate and capture the characteristics of individual users who might have a different impact on the system. For example, there could be different User Personas to differentiate an Online Banking Customer from a Non-Online-Banking Customer.

Product Backlog: The product backlog is a high-level document list of all required features, wish-list items, and the like, prioritized by business value. It is the "what" that will be built. It is owned by the product owner and continuously prioritized and reprioritized as the project progresses, work is completed, and detailed requirements are better understood.

Spikes: Iterations in an agile methodology typically result in delivering working software to implement user stories and the detailed requirements associated with that user story are normally defined during the iteration. In some cases; however:

- Significant uncertainties may be associated with a particular user story or a broader area of functionality, or
- An investigation of alternative design approaches may be needed to better define the architecture and design approach before an iteration can take place.

In those situations, a special kind of iteration called a "spike" may be appropriate. "A spike is an experiment that allows developers to learn just enough about the unknown elements in a user story, e.g. a new technology, to be able to estimate that user story. Often, a spike is a quick and dirty implementation or a prototype which will be thrown away. When a user story on the product backlog contains unknown elements that seriously hamper a usable estimation, the item should be split into a spike to investigate these elements plus a user story to develop the functionality."[29]

Requirements Prioritization: All agile methodologies rely on the user to prioritize requirements. The exact approach for prioritizing requirements might vary, but it is generally done on the basis of importance. Other factors that might be considered include risk and difficulty. Breaking up the requirements into individual requirements (typically user stories), prioritizing them, and incrementally developing them using an iterative approach provides a way of delivering the most important functionality to the user as quickly as possible.

A commonly used prioritization technique in agile projects is called "MoSCoW." It consists of breaking up requirements into four categories:[30]

- **Must have**—Requirements labeled as *MUST* have to be included in the current delivery timebox in order for it to be a success. If even one *MUST* requirement is not included, the project delivery should be considered a failure.
- **Should have**—*SHOULD* requirements are also critical to the success of the project but are not necessary for delivery in the current delivery timebox.
- **Could have**—Requirements labeled as *COULD* are less critical and often seen as *nice to have*.
- **Won't have**—*WON'T* requirements are either the least critical, lowest-payback items, or not appropriate at that time.

SUMMARY OF AGILE TECHNIQUES AND PRACTICES

As previously mentioned, it may be necessary to pick the right combination of techniques and practices in an à la carte manner and customize them as needed to build a complete enterprise-level development process rather than attempting to force-fit a project to any particular standard, predefined methodology. The best approach for a particular business may not be a pure agile approach at all—there is still a need for traditional plan-driven approaches in many situations, and there may be a need for a hybrid approach that offers a balance of control and agility.

---

[29] Phillipus, Erik, "Architecture Spikes," www.agile-architecting.com/Architecture%20Spikes.pdf

[30] "MoSCoW Method," http://en.wikipedia.org/wiki/MoSCoW_Method

The table that follows is a comparison of some of the characteristics of pure agile and hybrid methodologies.

> **Note**
> If you are new to agile and need to understand agile technical practices in more detail, each of these practices is defined and discussed in more detail in Appendix A and Appendix B of this book.

	Agile		Hybrid		
Characteristic	XP	Scrum	FDD	AUP	DSDM
Core Agile Characteristics:					
• Direct Customer Engagement	√	√	√	√	√
• Frequent Incremental Releases	√	√	√	√	√
• Adaptability to Change	√	√	√	√	√
• Self-Organization/ Empowerment	√	√	√	√	√
• Emphasis on Simplicity	√	√	√	√	√
• Continuous Improvement	√	√	√	√	√
General Lean Systems Engineering Principles					
• Focus on Customer Value (Eliminate Waste)	√	√	Limited	Limited	√
• Map the Value Stream (Eliminate Waste)	Very Limited	Limited	Optional	Optional	Optional
• Use the "Pull" Principle	√	√	Optional	Optional	Optional
• Optimize the Flow to Eliminate Bottlenecks	√	√	Limited	Limited	Limited
• Respect for People (Empower the Team)	√	√	Not Defined	Not Defined	√
• Perfection (Continuous Improvement Emphasis)	√	√	Optional	Optional	√
Lean Software Development Principles					
• Amplify Learning	√	√	Optional	Limited	√
• Decide as Late as Possible	√	√	Optional	Limited	Limited
• Deliver as Fast as Possible	√	√	Optional	Limited	Limited

	Agile		Hybrid		
Characteristic	XP	Scrum	FDD	AUP	DSDM
• Build Integrity In	√	√	Limited	Limited	√
• See the Whole	Limited	Limited	√	√	√
Technical Practices:					
• Continuous Integration	√	√	Optional	Optional	Optional
• Timeboxing	√	√	Optional	Optional	Optional
• Architectural Design Approach	Not Specified	Not Specified	UML	UML	UML
• Test-Driven Development	√	Optional	Optional	Optional	Optional
• Code Refactoring	√	Optional	Optional	Optional	Optional
• Pair Programming	√	Optional	Optional	Optional	Optional
Project Management:					
• Planning & Estimation Approach	Rolling Wave with Very Limited Upfront Planning	Product Backlog Release Plans	More Emphasis on Upfront Planning	More Emphasis on Upfront Planning (Inception Phase)	High-level Scope & Requirements Base-lined Upfront
• Requirements Management	User Stories	User Stories	Hierarchical Product Features & Use Cases	Agile Model-Driven Development	Prioritized Requirements List
• Risk Management	Not Specified	Not Specified	Not Specified	Not Specified	Upfront Feasibility & Business Analysis Ongoing Risk Mgt.
• Extensibility to Distributed Teams (Multiple Sites, Time Zones)	Difficult	Very Limited	√	√	√
• Configurable to Accommodate a Wide Range of Project Types	Very Limited	Limited	√	√	√
Project Governance:					
• Methodology Change Mgt & Organizational Consistency	Difficult	Difficult	Not Defined	Not Defined	√

CHAPTER 3

BECOMING MORE AGILE

AGILE BENEFITS AND TRADEOFFS

There are a number of very significant benefits of successfully implementing a more agile approach. Jim Highsmith cites the following business objectives that potentially result from a successful agile methodology implementation:

> **1.** Continuous Innovation—to deliver on current customer requirements
> **2.** Product Adaptability—to deliver on future customer requirements
> **3.** Improved Time-to-market—to meet market windows and improve return on investment (ROI)
> **4.** People and Process Adaptability—to respond rapidly to product and business change
> **5.** Reliable Results—to support business growth and profitability[1]

In many cases, if it is done correctly, an agile transformation can change the culture and chemistry of the whole company to dramatically improve its competitive advantage. However, there is no "free lunch"—there is a lot of work that needs to be done to achieve these objectives, and there are some significant tradeoffs associated with achieving these benefits, which are discussed in the sections that follow.

Focus on Successful Business Outcomes

One of the biggest impacts of implementing a more agile approach is likely to be more successfully achieving business outcomes. Agile projects are probably more likely to accomplish the business outcomes that they were intended to achieve if the business users actively participate in the development effort and a more flexible and adaptive development approach is used. The impact of this is

[1] Highsmith, Jim, Agile Project Management—Creating Innovative Products, pg 10, Addison-Wesley, New York, 2009

likely to be most significant in companies that have a very uncertain environment that requires high levels of flexibility and adaptability. That's a very significant benefit; however, there are tradeoffs associated with it:

- Adopting a more flexible development approach will probably reduce the ability to accurately predict upfront development costs and schedules for the overall project. It requires some trust between the business organization and the development organization to create a working relationship where the uncertainty in the product requirements, as well as the costs and schedule, is understood and acknowledged, and both sides partner in a collaborative approach. This is very different from a "contractual relationship, where both sides agree to work together based on some well-defined upfront requirements and a well-defined cost and schedule estimate for fulfilling those requirements.
- In some cases, a more agile approach may also increase the total cost and schedule for the project because it may require more trial-and-error attempts to find an optimal solution. The cost and schedule increase will be determined primarily by the amount of experimentation that is needed to find an optimal solution.
- A much more significant commitment of resources from the business side is required. Business resources need to take a much more active role throughout the entire development process and should feel some primary ownership for making it successful.

Jim Highsmith summarizes the advantage agile methodologies provide for developing better products:

> "...When we reduce the cost of experimentation enough, the entire economies of how we develop products changes—it switches from a process based on anticipation (define, design, and build) to one based on adaptation (envision, explore, and refine). When the cost of generating alternatives plunges and the cost of integrating them into a product is low, then great products aren't built, they evolve—just like biological evolution, only much faster than in nature. Biological evolution begins with experimentation (mutation and recombination), exploration (survival of the fittest), and refinement (producing more of the survivors). Increasingly, product development processes are being built using this biological metaphor."[2]

With traditional plan-driven methodologies, you typically have one shot at getting it right—you attempt to define and document the requirements as best

---

[2] Highsmith, Jim, *Agile Project Management—Creating Innovative Products*, New York: Addison-Wesley, 2009, p. 7

you can at the start of the development effort and *hope* that those requirements are going to produce the business outcome that they were intended to produce. Typically, companies focus very heavily on the risks of not meeting cost and schedule goals, and that tends to favor more traditional plan-driven approaches; however, there's a much bigger risk in that the project won't successfully achieve the business outcome it was intended to achieve. Management of this kind of risk may call for a very different approach to product development:

> "The key point is that opportunity, uncertainty, and risk reside in the proposed product—not in the approach to project management. Our approach to project management needs to fit with the characteristics of the product to improve our chances of capitalizing on the opportunity by systematically reducing the uncertainty and mitigating the risks over the life of the product....
>
> Linear thinking, prescriptive processes, and standardized, unvarying practices are no match for today's volatile product development environment. So as product development processes swing from anticipatory to adaptive, project management must change also. It must be geared to mobility, experimentation, and speed. But first of all, it must be geared to business objectives."[3]

Both of these types of risks need to be considered to develop a balanced approach that blends the right level of control to provide a reasonable level of predictability over costs and schedules with sufficient agility to ensure that the product successfully achieves the business outcome it was intended to achieve. The level of volatility and uncertainty in each business will be different, and each business needs to find the balance that is most appropriate for its business environment:

- In some businesses that have a highly volatile and uncertain product development environment, it probably makes sense to adopt a pure agile approach.
- In other businesses that do not have that level of volatility or that operate in a high-risk and/or regulated environment, a pure agile approach may need to be tailored to the business environment or a more plan-driven approach or hybrid approach may me more appropriate.

The key point is to open up our thinking to new ways of doing things and not restrict the selection of approaches to standard, off-the-shelf methodologies (either agile or non-agile) that may not be optimum for the business environment.

---

[3] Highsmith, Jim, *Agile Project Management—Creating Innovative Products*, New York: Addison-Wesley, 2009, pp. 8–9

Customer Satisfaction and Competitive Advantage

A transformation to a more agile product development approach should not be considered simply from a development perspective—it has the potential to have a much broader impact on customer satisfaction and competitive advantage if it is done properly. However, achieving those advantages may require a significant, broad-based initiative that is not limited to development—it could be an expensive and time-consuming effort that requires a significant organizational commitment.

For companies that depend heavily on the effectiveness of their product and application development processes to gain competitive advantage, that effort could have huge potential to leverage a major change to make the whole company more competitive in its marketplace. It could result in faster times to market for new products and mission-critical applications and products that are also much more successful because they better fit user needs.

Organizational Effectiveness, Cross-Functional Synergy, and Employee Morale

In addition to the benefits of improved customer satisfaction and competitive advantage, an agile initiative could be the catalyst that is used to bring about higher levels of cross-functional synergy by breaking down barriers between various functional organizations that are typically engaged in the product development effort, and that is likely to result in higher levels of organizational effectiveness. Higher levels of engagement and empowerment of employees who participate in the process is also likely to result in improved levels of employee morale.

Higher Productivity and Lower Costs

A number of books have published data showing productivity gains as well as reductions in development cost from implementing agile methodologies; however, it is somewhat difficult to make a very universal and meaningful quantitative comparison. It's difficult to make an apples-to-apples comparison between two identical projects and the productivity gain depends on a number of factors that might not be the same for each project such as:

- What was the starting-point methodology and what was the ending-point methodology that the comparison was based on (for example, extreme Waterfall to pure agile or something in between?)
- How unaligned was the previous methodology with the company's business environment and projects and how well aligned is the new methodology?
- What were the characteristics of each project really similar (e.g., uncertainty of requirements)?

From a business perspective, as previously discussed, the payback of going to a more agile methodology is likely to be much greater for companies that have an uncertain business environment that requires flexibility and adaptability to succeed in spite of those conditions. For companies that do not have a business environment with a high level of uncertainty and don't require the level of flexibility and adaptability that a pure agile methodology provides, the gains are likely to be much less and a less agile approach may still be more efficient overall.

One of the things that make it difficult to really quantify the productivity gains is that, in many cases, each potential gain has an offsetting potential loss and the net gain that might be realized depends a lot of on how skillfully the methodology is implemented. The following is a summary of some of the potential gains and losses that can result from moving to a more agile approach:

Potential Productivity Gain	Offsetting Potential Productivity Loss
• Simplified and prioritized requirements combined with a more iterative development process reduces unnecessary functionality and delivers high-priority functionality more quickly.	• More business user involvement is needed throughout the development process.
• More direct engagement of the users in the development process is likely to better satisfy business needs and could significantly reduce rework that might be needed when problems associated with meeting user needs are not discovered until late in the project with a traditional development process.	• More business user involvement is needed throughout the development process. • More direct involvement of the business user in the development process might introduce delays if timely participation isn't available and might introduce unnecessary churning of requirements if the business users are not skilled in performing that role.
• Reduced number of defects and higher-quality products are more likely because quality and testing are a much more integral part of the development process.	• Implementing this successfully requires a much more rigorous and continuous integration and testing approach that might require the purchase of test tools to automate the process.
• Higher employee morale and levels of participation can result in significant productivity gains.	• It may take a considerable amount of training, coaching, and mentoring to get employees to a level to effectively perform this role.
• Timeboxing of development efforts is likely to improve productivity and development schedules.	• Effective use of timeboxing requires some skill and might require training, coaching, and mentoring to get a team to the point where they can use that technique effectively.
• Emphasis on continuous improvement is likely to result in ongoing improvement of the process, which will further improve productivity over a more statically defined traditional process.	• The teams may need to be trained and skilled in how to do process improvement in order to do it effectively.
• Deferring decisions using rolling wave planning is likely to result in better decisions, based on facts rather than speculation.	• A higher level of skill and training is probably needed to perform this role effectively as opposed to traditional upfront planning methods. • The organizational culture must also support this approach.

Potential for Higher Quality

If it is done successfully, an agile approach has the potential to significantly improve the quality of products because:

1. It creates an environment that is much more heavily focused on producing a high-quality product as seen directly from the perspective of the primary user.
2. The focus on making testing an integral part of the development process, doing testing as the development progresses, using pair programming, and emphasizing collective ownership of responsibility for the quality of the product by the team are all practices that can have a big impact on improving the level of quality of the final products and applications.

OBSTACLES TO BECOMING AGILE

Developing a pure agile approach is not for everyone, and the obstacles that must be overcome to successfully implement a full implementation of agile are significant. Mike Cohn's book *Succeeding with Agile: Software Development Using Scrum* is an excellent resource to better understand some of the obstacles that must be overcome in the typical organization to become more agile. He has defined a number of attributes of Scrum that make it a difficult transition:[4]

1. **Successful change is not entirely top down or bottom up.** An effective agile implementation requires real buy-in from everyone involved. A superficial implementation may have limited success and a significant change management initiative may be needed to change the culture and operating style of the organization to be consistent with Scrum. This type of change cannot be dictated from the top down nor can it be done entirely from the bottom up without a sufficient level of top-down support.
2. **The end state is unpredictable.** Since Scrum and other agile methodologies are heavily based on continuous improvement, it is difficult to say when the transition is really complete. There are some assessments that can be used to assess the level of agility, but it is a very subjective measurement. There is no such thing as saying something like "we're an "agile level 2 organization" or an "agile level 3 organization."
3. **Scrum is pervasive.** Scrum impacts many areas of the organization—the impact is not limited to simply the development side of the organization. A successful Scrum initiative will require a broad-based commitment of many areas of the organization to be successful. For example:
   - Business owners who have been used to providing a basic level of overall direction at the front end of a project will now find that a much

[4] Cohn, Mike *Succeeding with Agile: Software Development Using Scrum*, New York: Addison-Wesley, 2009

higher level of commitment is required for the entire duration of the project.

- Organizations that have built a focus on project governance, such as Project Management Offices (PMOs), will have to change, and metrics for measuring and tracking project progress may also have to change.

4. **Scrum is dramatically different.** Scrum will cause many people in the organization to do things differently, for example:
   - Developers who are used to coming in to the office, going to their cube, and immediately putting on their headphones and writing code will now have to work much more as part of a team, where they will have to interact and collaborate with others much more than ever before.
   - Testers who are used to being given a completed application to test against a defined requirements document or specification will have to learn entirely new ways of testing code that may only be partially developed collaboratively with the development team as the design progresses.
   - Users who are used to only a limited involvement in the development process will be required to have a much higher level of direct participation in the process, they will have to share ownership of the success of the project, and they will be much more directly exposed to risks and partially complete products as the project progresses.

   The impact in these changes in the way people work is significant and should not be underestimated. Because it is such a big change, a significant amount of training, mentoring, and coaching may be needed; some people are likely to resist this transition, and some changes in personnel may also be necessary.
5. **Change is coming more quickly than ever before.** If it is successful, a transition to Scrum is likely to bring about a significant amount of change to the organization very rapidly. It may be a challenge for many organizations to absorb that kind of change so quickly.

The following sections discuss some of the most important obstacles to overcome.

Corporate Culture

Corporate culture can be one of the biggest obstacles to overcome in developing a more agile product development approach.

1. Management and Leadership Style
   Many companies have a management and leadership style that is not well aligned with adopting agile methodologies and shifting to a more flexible

and distributed form of management might be a significant cultural change for some companies:

> "For decades now, corporations have been changing from a hierarchical approach to being more collaborative as knowledge work has grown in importance. A September 2005 article in the *Project Management Journal* expresses similar sentiments for the management of projects as the authors question the 'veracity of tight centralized management,' 'rationalist' discourse, and a 'command and control' approach to project management. Instead, the authors recommend allowing for flexibility of local response in order to be able to constantly adjust to emerging problems in the project system. This need to distribute responsibility and initiative in support of adaptation to change is familiar territory to 'agile'approaches to projects."[5]

Some companies have built a significant culture and infrastructure around a "command-and-control" approach to managing projects. They may have a very well-established methodology for how projects are managed, which is in some cases enforced by a PMO. The emphasis in many of these organizations is on well-controlled, plan-driven projects that provide high levels of cost and schedule predictability. Shifting to a different orientation that balances control of costs and schedules with a sufficient level of flexibility to adapt to customer needs in an uncertain environment can be a challenge:

- Very different methodologies may be needed with higher levels of flexibility and adaptability.
- Significant amounts of training might be needed to develop project managers and project teams to take on more responsibility to implement a more distributed style of leadership and management.
- The role of the PMO organization might shift significantly from the role of a "process enforcer" to a value-added process consultant to support project teams.
- It may be necessary to break down traditional organizational barriers to create a more collaborative, cross-functional approach
- Business models and measurement systems might also need to be changed to be more consistent with this new environment.

2. Cross-Functional Collaborative Approach
Adopting a pure agile methodology like Scrum requires a collaborative approach at a number of different levels, and this may also require a major shift in organizational culture in some companies:

---

[5] Fernandez, Daniel J. and Fenandez, John D., "Agile Project Management—Agilism versus Traditional Approaches," *Journal of Computer Information Systems*, Winter 2008–2009

a. Business sponsors and development teams need to work collaboratively to choose an appropriate methodology for a project, customize it as needed to fit the risks and complexity of the project, and work jointly to implement the process, including taking joint ownership for the success of the process and quickly making decisions to resolve any issues that may arise during the course of the project. In some organizations, the product development process is seen as totally the responsibility of development to just "make it happen" and to do it faster, better, and cheaper without a significant amount of direct intervention from the business side in the development process. Many organizations are not at a level of maturity to develop the kind of collaborative, cross-functional approach that's needed, and it may take strong senior management leadership to bring about that kind of change.

b. Within the development organization, all the functions (development, QA/test, etc.) need to work closely and collaboratively to become more agile. By design, many development organizations have some natural barriers that make it difficult to achieve full collaboration. In some cases, there may be good reason for maintaining some level of separation. For example, many organizations preserve some separation between the development function and the QA/test function as a way of providing objectivity in the testing effort and maintaining checks and balances in the development process. There may be situations where that kind of separation is justified, but in many situations, it is also a sign of limited organizational maturity.

Breaking down these barriers and achieving effective cross-functional collaboration both between the business and development organizations and within the development organization requires creating an environment based on trust, and that may require a strong level of leadership to achieve:

- The business organization has to learn to trust that, if they work collaboratively with the development organization, they're going to get what they want and even get a better-quality product than they would have gotten with a well-defined contractual commitment based on firmly defined requirements.
- The internal organizations within development, such as QA, need to learn to trust that they can still achieve the same or higher levels of quality by relaxing some of the boundaries and controls that may have been developed between organizations.

3. Learning Environment

Agile heavily emphasizes continuous improvement, and that requires a culture that is consistent with that approach. Some companies do not learn from their mistakes and, in some cases, they don't even acknowledge them. A culture of covering up mistakes and not being transparent about them is not consistent with an agile approach. Agile is based on the philosophy "fail early and fail often"—in the right culture, mistakes are synonymous with learning.

If the culture of the organization is not consistent with openly and transparently finding and acknowledging defects in products and processes and aggressively learning from those mistakes to implement more effective processes to prevent those problems from happening again, a successful agile transformation will be difficult to achieve.

Organizational Commitment

Adopting a pure agile methodology such as Scrum also requires a broad-based organizational commitment from both the business and development sides of the organization. If the software development organization tries to implement a more agile development process and there isn't a sufficient level of commitment from the business side to fully participate in the process; chances are that it will have very limited success. In many companies, it is very difficult to expect a customer or sponsor to stay attached on a regular basis to the development team throughout the entire project.

Agile methodologies also require a high level of skill and training of the project teams. Implementing an agile approach might require a significant amount of retraining of personnel and, in some cases; it might even require replacement of personnel who are unable to make the transition to an agile approach.

Risk and Regulatory Environment

Many companies operate in a high-risk industry and/or a regulated environment, which requires a high level of control over the software development process. There are certainly situations where more of a traditional plan-driven development approach may be more appropriate based on the risks and complexity of the project. In these organizations, it may not be a simple matter of implementing an agile methodology out of the box; a significant effort might be required to design a customized process that blends an appropriate level of control with more agility.

For example:

- In a high-risk environment, depending on the nature of the risks; more upfront planning might be needed to analyze and plan for the risks prior to implementing the project—that doesn't preclude using an agile methodology for the majority of the development effort, but it might require wrapping an additional layer of planning and management around it.
- In a highly regulated environment, more rigorous documentation might be needed for such things as specifications and test results. That also

doesn't preclude the use of an agile methodology for some portion of the development effort, but it might also require wrapping more documentation and management around it.

In both of these situations, some kind of a hybrid approach may be appropriate, which might be either:

- Starting with a pure agile approach like Scrum and adding additional layers onto it to satisfy the risk and regulatory requirements, or
- Starting with a plan-driven approach and making it more agile

The best alternative of those two would probably depend on the magnitude of the effort that is needed to satisfy the risk and regulatory requirements.

DEVELOPING A MORE AGILE APPROACH

In some organizations, a pure agile approach may not be appropriate or the obstacles associated with adopting a pure agile approach can be formidable to overcome, and it may require a significant change management effort to make a complete jump to agile. In these situations, there are many ways for an organization to become *more agile* without going all the way to the most pure forms of agile such as Scrum or Extreme Programming. There are many ways to integrate a sufficient level of control with some of the principles of agile development in a customized development process. It requires a more sophisticated project management approach to:

- Design an effective development process that blends a level of control and agility that is appropriate for the business environment that the company operates in.
- Tailor the overall development process as needed to fit each project.

Of course, a good process is one that people really use, is well aligned with the business environment and projects it is used for, and adds value without unnecessary overhead. There is a level of organizational maturity implied in developing a process (or processes) that really works and is used to add value to the business. That is a key strategic decision for any business—a project manager might recommend these decisions, but they should be reviewed and approved by an appropriate level of management who can assess the impact of these decisions from an overall business management perspective.

Developing an Agile or Lean Mindset

To some extent, agile is a way of thinking. Many of the statements in the Agile Manifesto are values that can be practiced to some extent with many different methodologies. (See the "Agile Perceptions and Reality" section) For example, the following statement is an excellent goal that can be applied to any methodology:

> "Our highest priority is to satisfy the customer through early and continuous delivery of valuable software"[6]

Of course, it requires some good judgment to figure out how this goal can actually be achieved with different life-cycle models other than a pure agile (e.g., Scrum) approach—applying this value to a traditional plan-driven development model requires some creative thinking (See "Software Development Life Cycles").

> "An overemphasis on linearity leads to stagnation, just as an overemphasis on evolution leads to endless and eventually mindless change. With either model, development team members, product team members, and executives need to exercise judgment in its application."[7]

What's required is to understand the principles behind Lean and agile and apply those principles to the way the organization thinks and its culture. An organization that has built these principles into the way the organization works and has developed a mindset among all its people that supports this way of thinking has gone a long way toward creating the right framework to support a more agile development approach.

The important thing is to focus on the principles rather than getting lost in the mechanics of any methodology (either agile or non-agile). Rather than attempting to force-fit your business and projects to fit into the mechanics of any given methodology, the right approach is to focus on the business objectives you want to achieve, including customer satisfaction goals; create a business environment and culture for achieving those goals; and then select or design supporting development processes that are consistent with that environment.

Hybrid Approaches

In many cases, it may not make sense for a company to go all the way to a pure agile approach like Scrum or Extreme Programming right away for a variety of different reasons, such as:

- The organizational culture and other factors may not support it and too much of a change management effort may be needed for success.

---

[6] "Principles Behind the Agile Manifesto," http://agilemanifesto.org/principles.html

[7] Highsmith, Jim, Agile Project Management-Creating Innovative Products, pg 87, Addison-Wesley, New York, NY 2010

- The risk and regulatory environment the company operates in may require a balance of control and agility.
- A more gradual and incremental migration to agile may be appropriate because of the level of change and training needed to go to a full agile approach.
- The level of uncertainty in the company's business environment or in individual projects may not justify a pure agile approach.

In these situations, a hybrid approach that provides a compromise between a traditional plan-driven environment and a pure agile environment may be a good solution. Steve Pieczko has written a nice article indicating that "The journey to full agile development often begins with a hybrid approach"[8]

> "So why do so many organizations aspire to become Agile yet are still only implementing a few aspects of it? Most likely, they're not given enough time to plan the process of becoming Agile. Or, it may be because Agile is usually introduced by the development community in a bottom-up style that isn't understood or appreciated from the top-down [sic]. Regardless, many teams end up implementing a hybrid methodology."

The following are some possible alternatives for developing a hybrid approach:

1. Use an iterative approach to break up large projects into smaller chunks, develop the high-level requirements and plan upfront, and continue to refine the requirements and plan with each iteration.
2. Prioritize requirements to ensure that the most essential requirements are done first to accelerate the delivery of the most important capabilities.
3. Develop a higher level of engagement of business users in the oversight of the development effort, and develop a more flexible and adaptive approach to requirements definition if necessary.
4. Integrate QA testing into the development effort using a Test-Driven Development approach and adopt the agile principle that software is not "done" until it is tested and provides the business value it is intended to provide.
5. Streamline the documents and artifacts required for traditional development process by eliminating documents and artifacts that do not provide value.
6. Use agile technical practices such as pair programming, continuous integration, code refactoring, and timeboxing to improve development productivity.

[8] Pieczko, Steve, "Agile?, Waterfall? How about WetAgile?" www.agilejournal.com/articles/columns/column-articles/3080--agile-waterfall-how-about-wetagile

7. Begin to create an organizational culture that is more agile including:
   - Train people in the organization in adopting agile thinking and practices.
   - Implement a facilitative management and leadership approach with empowered teams.
   - Develop a spirit of partnership between the business users and developers to jointly own the success of development efforts.
   - Within the development organization, create a spirit of joint ownership of project results among the members of the development team.
   - Build closer, cross-functional teamwork among the development team by co-locating members of the team and developing a sense of shared ownership of work. Use daily standups to build and reinforce a shared commitment to goals
   - Develop and implement a more sophisticated project management approach, where project managers are trained and skilled in selecting from a broader range of methodologies, principles, and practices and tailor them to fit projects rather than force-fitting a project to a well-defined methodology.

CHAPTER 4

CASE STUDIES

When I published my first book, *From Quality to Business Excellence* in 2003.[1] I saw an interesting pattern. I was looking at how companies used a variety of process improvement techniques that were in use at the time and, in particular, Six Sigma was very hot at that time. I researched a lot of companies for my book, and I found that there were many companies I looked at that just did Six Sigma like the "program du jour" because it was the latest and coolest thing to do at that time. Other companies that I looked at, had implemented Six Sigma; but, in many cases, it was just one of several tools that they used for process improvement.

The difference in these two kinds of companies was striking:

- In the first type of company, Six Sigma was highly visible with all the hoopla associated with it (black belts, green belts, and so on), but many of these implementations turned out to be superficial and not very effective. In many cases, they were also not very long-lasting—as soon as Six Sigma went out of vogue, the companies moved on to something else.
- In the second kind of company, there was an entirely different pattern; the companies really took the time to understand Six Sigma at a much deeper level and really integrate it into the way they did business. In many cases, it wasn't even obvious that they were dong Six Sigma because it was so well integrated into the way they did business and tailored, if necessary, to fit with their business and other complementary tools.

I've seen a similar pattern with the adoption of agile methodologies. Many companies want to jump on the agile bandwagon and attempt to implement standard agile methodologies out of the box without necessarily taking the time to fully understand them and/or customize and tailor them to fit their business. That may work in some situations, but it's not surprising that it has mixed results in others. The companies that really impressed me are the ones that took the time to understand agile methodologies at a deeper level and really put a lot of effort into making them a part of the way they do business. In many cases, that has meant picking and choosing the right combination of agile practices and methodologies

[1] Cobb, Charles G., *From Quality to Business Excellence*, Milwaukee, WI, ASQ Quality Press, 2003

and, if necessary, crafting unique methodologies that are customized to fit their business.

Here are a few common characteristics I saw in many of these companies:

- They were "learning organizations" and demonstrated "thought leadership." They were driven by ongoing process improvement and learning and openly shared their knowledge with others.
- They had a broad, cross-functional view of how their business worked as a complete system (not just from a product development perspective) and aligned their product development strategy into that broader perspective.
- They were innovators—they didn't just accept the status quo of implementing standard agile methodologies; they developed innovative approaches that went beyond just doing things by the book and adapted the methodologies to fit their business rather than force-fitting their business to fit any specific methodology.

The following is a summary of general characteristics I would associate with "learning organizations":

Characteristic	"Traditional" Organization	"Learning" Organization
Control vs. Empowerment Orientation	• Emphasis on control. • Processes are more rigidly defined and do not allow for significant deviation.	• Emphasis on individual empowerment. • Processes are typically not as rigidly defined and rely much more heavily on the skill and judgment of the people performing the process.
Process Standardization	• Standardized, "textbook" processes (agile or non-agile) out of the box.	• Processes are highly tailored and customized to fit the business.
Key Differences	• The process manages the organization. • The organization attempts to force-fit their business environment and projects to a predefined methodology (agile or non-agile) • Processes are implemented somewhat mechanically.	• The organization manages the process. • The organization selects the principles, methodologies, and practices from a variety of sources (agile or non-agile) that are best suited to their business environment and customizes them as needed to fit individual projects. • The people in the organization understand the principles behind the process and are able to implement them much more intelligently.

Characteristic	"Traditional" Organization	"Learning" Organization
Emphasis on Continuous Improvement	• Processes are relatively static and don't change often. • The organization does not actively seek out new ideas and practices to improve process effectiveness.	• Processes are regularly updated to reflect lessons learned and opportunities for improvement. • The organization takes a leadership role in exploring and developing process improvements and best practices.
Change	• May be resistant to change.	• Change is welcomed and embraced.
Approach to Failures	• Failures are seen as things that should be punished or covered up if they happen and are too be avoided at all costs.	• Failures are expected to occur as a natural outcome of trying new ideas and are seen as opportunities for learning and continuous improvement.
Management and Employee Engagement	• Management may be more focused on driving results (process outputs) than on understanding the process factors that contribute to achieving the results. • Employees might follow the process mechanically without a significant level of commitment or may not follow the process at all.	• Management is focused on making the processes more effective to drive results and leads and champions ongoing process improvement. • Employees are fully engaged in the process and fully believe in what they're doing.

SAPIENT

Sapient is headquartered in Massachusetts and operates in other international locations throughout the world. The company helps clients achieve extraordinary results from their customer relationships, business operations, and technology. Leveraging a unique approach, breakthrough thinking, and disciplined execution, Sapient leads its industry in delivering the right business results on time and on budget.[2]

Unique Challenges

Sapient has developed a unique and innovative agile methodology called Sapient|Approach (S|A), they have fully integrated agile into their own business, and they have also helped many clients become more agile. Some of the unique challenges that Sapient faced were:

1. A large portion of Sapient's business is focused on providing services to clients. In many cases, these services have been provided on a fixed-price

[2] Sapient Company Profile, www.fullinterview.com/phpkb/article/sapient-company-profile-5135.html

basis because their clients value the ability to budget and control costs accurately. Adopting an agile business model required some rethinking of the fixed-price business model and also required developing partnerships with their clients to achieve a balance of cost control and the flexibility that was needed to be adaptive to very dynamic client needs that evolved as the project progressed.

2. Sapient focuses on helping their clients achieve business outcomes as a primary goal, and their services are holistic in their nature and typically include all of the following:
   - Working with the client to define top-level strategies and objectives
   - Designing and implementing business processes to support those strategies and objectives
   - Implementing IT systems and applications that are well-integrated with those business processes
   - Providing change management to help clients achieve the organizational transformation that might be needed to successfully implement a more agile approach

   These factors have required a highly integrated approach that puts the agile practices and principles into the context of how it enables their clients to achieve those business outcomes.
3. Many of Sapient's customers are in a government environment, which adds another layer of challenges and complexity including:
   - Overcoming bureaucracy within and among government agencies to help them become more agile and to help them develop collaborative, cross-functional relationships within the government environment
   - Developing close collaborative partnerships with their government customers to develop more agile working relationships in spite of typical government contractual requirements

Process Methodology Selection and Design

Sapient had to craft a unique methodology to fit their business called Sapient| Appproach because existing "out-of-the-box" agile and non-agile methodologies were not adequate to provide an effective, overall business solution for their business:

> "When we began to consider the role that agile methods would play in our delivery methodology, we were met with a daunting proliferation of choices: Crystal, Extreme Programming (XP), Scrum, and Dynamic Systems Development Method (DSDM), just to name a few. Each of these, while rightfully attesting to being agile, approaches agility in a unique and nuanced fashion.

> For instance, XP takes a heavily developer-centric view, focusing on engineering practices such as continuous integration and test-driven development (TDD) and collaboration techniques like the planning game and pairing. It does not; however, provide the robustness of project management processes offered by Scrum. Similarly, DSDM provides risk management practices which are more conspicuously missing from Scrum. Furthermore, Agile Unified Process (AUP) and Agile Modeling offer tools and techniques for requirements development not found in any of the other aforementioned methodologies.
>
> Thus, many of the discrete methodologies beneath the agile umbrella, when taken in isolation, leave something to be desired from an enterprise delivery perspective. Luckily; however, most of the "offenders" are complementary to one another and can be creatively combined to provide the breadth of process necessary to deliver complex projects. You simply need to be selective and understand how elements of each method satisfy specific needs within your organization."[3]

Developing the Sapient|Approach methodology required mixing and matching a number of methodologies and practices as well as customizing and scaling them to fit their business environment and large, complex projects:

> "For us, being selective meant considering our needs across a number of process areas. In the end, we based the core of our development process on XP and Lean Development, but found a great deal of augmentation was required from an analysis and design perspective in order to deal with the complexity of the systems we often encounter. So, we dropped XP's 'system metaphor' concept in favor of some of the more robust modeling techniques provided by Agile Modeling. To this, we added Scrum-based project management techniques, but deviated from both Scrum's guidance on sprint length as well as XP's approach. We have opted to allow teams to select an iteration length ranging from one to four weeks in duration. The iteration length is chosen based on a decision-making framework that respects such influencing factors as team size and structure, degree of geographic collocation or distribution, the number of integration partners and the nature of their delivery methods, and the customer's level of experience and comfort with working with a highly iterative model."[4]

---

[3] Gottesman, Erik, "Growing Agility in a Large and Distributed Enterprise," Agile Project Leadership Network, Agile Business Conference, London, UK, 2006, p. 2

[4] Gottesman, Erik, "Growing Agility in a Large and Distributed Enterprise," Agile Project Leadership Network, Agile Business Conference, London, UK, 2006, p. 3

Sapient recognized that many times, off-the-shelf implementations of standard agile methodologies don't work, but standard agile methodologies provide "building blocks" for building a complete methodology:

> "The myriad agile methods existing today offer the basic mechanics required to deliver valuable software solutions early and continuously with a high standard of quality. However, what happens when you seek to institutionalize these methods in organizations consisting of hundreds of teams (large and small) working across multiple industries and using sometimes markedly dissimilar technologies? Simply put, today's agile methods fall short of providing what is needed to cope with such complexity and variation in a consciously reasoned fashion which promotes organizational knowledge."[5]

Sapient also recognized the value of traditional standards and principles such as CMMI that might not normally be considered a part of an agile implementation and blended and integrated those into their approach:

> "More often than not, agile teams shun such models as Capability Maturity Model Integrated (CMMI), ISO, ITIL, and Six Sigma as being bureaucratic and representative of the 'old guard'—i.e., favoring processes and tools over individuals and interactions. We, on the other hand, felt this to be a short-sighted view. Is it not possible to combine the best of agile with the best these models have to offer? For example, ITIL service delivery practices provided us a means to more seamlessly integrate agile methods into an application support context.
>
> Similarly, we drew practices from CMMI for configuration management, product distribution, defining and provisioning training, and identifying and deploying process improvements. CMMI also prompted us to invoke one very specific change in how we do development. As mentioned earlier, the core of the S|A development process is based on practices established in XP. However, we did away with XP's insistence on pairing. As a services firm we must often work side-by-side with many partners. Effectively integrating such a team often means bringing together many different working styles and organizational cultures. Thus pairing is not always preferable or possible. In cases where pairing is not practiced, other techniques must be employed to ensure the quality of work products. To this end, CMMI provides a wealth of guidance on verification."[6]

---

[5] Gottesman, Erik, "Growing Agility in a Large and Distributed Enterprise," Agile Project Leadership Network, Agile Business Conference, London, UK, 2006, p. 3

[6] Gottesman, Erik, "Growing Agility in a Large and Distributed Enterprise," Agile Project Leadership Network, Agile Business Conference, London, UK, 2006, p. 4

Mixing and matching these various agile and non-agile methodologies, principles, and practices requires a very high level of skill. On the surface, they may not appear to be congruent with each other at all; however, understanding the principles behind them at a deeper level has enabled Sapient to leverage a very broad range of knowledge from a variety of sources such as:

- Lean and Theory of Constraints
- Function Points
- User-Centered Design

Sapient also recognized that they didn't need to throw away a lot of their existing traditional processes in order to move to agile.

> "Lastly, when transitioning to agile methods, one should not believe that every practice in place before the transition is unnecessary or wrong. Your organization must have been doing some things right to begin with; otherwise you wouldn't be in business, would you? We point this out because we have seen a disturbing tendency among organizations to think that in order to be agile; you must unlearn and divorce yourself from all of your old behaviors. This simply isn't true. You must let go of some things. For us, this included evolving our attitude toward fixed pricing. We also had to get very disciplined about managing WIP and deferring decisions until the last responsible moment in order to avoid speculation and waste.
>
> Conversely, over the course of Sapient's history, we had developed some highly effective processes of our own design for such things as aligning stakeholders around a common vision, eliciting customer requirements, and running Project Management Offices (PMOs). All of this was good and required neither disposal nor significant overhaul in order to integrate with the new techniques introduced."[7]

Methodology Summary

The following is a high-level summary of the major elements of the Sapient| Approach methodology:

Factor	Description
Unique Features:	• Highly customized and well-integrated methodology • High-level focus on business outcomes in addition to development process • Excellent blend of control and adaptability • Innovative use of "non-agile" practices integrated with agile approach

[7] Gottesman, Erik, "Growing Agility in a Large and Distributed Enterprise," Agile ProjectLeadership Network, Agile Business Conference, London, UK, 2006, p. 5

Factor	Description
Scalability Approach:	Modified Scrum-of-Scrums approach plus some PMO processes
Overall Life-Cycle Model Approach:	Agile Unified Process
Iteration Management Approach:	Scrum with modifications: • Modified role definitions • Variable iteration lengths within a project
Development Approach:	Extreme Programming (XP) with modifications: • Dropped XP's 'system metaphor' in favor of Agile Modeling • Eliminated pair programming
Agile Practices Included:	• Scrum (modified) • Extreme Programming (modified) • Product Backlog • Timeboxing • User Stories • Daily Standup Meetings • Heavy emphasis on customer engagement and continuous improvement • Transparency and Visibility
Tools Used:	Sapient uses its own tool called ResultSpace® but not to the exclusion of other tools

Other Methodologies Used:	• CMMI
	• Lean and Theory of Constraints[8]
	• Function Points from COCOMO II for software estimation
	• User-centered Design (UCD) for user interfaces
	• Process Auditing
	• Agile Modeling and Model-Driven Development
	• Existing Sapient processes for:
	  • Aligning stakeholders around a common vision
	  • Eliciting Customer Requirements
	  • Running Project Management Offices (PMOs)

Methodology Description

Sapient has recognized that the overall methodology needed to be easily tailored to fit a variety of projects and a layered approach is used to provide that level of flexibility as shown in Figure 4.1.

[8] Goldratt, Eliyahu, *Theory of Constraints*, Great Barrington, MA, North River Press, 1999

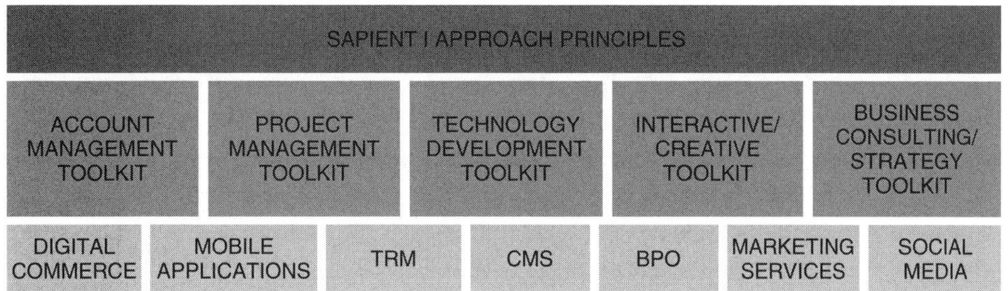

Figure 4.1 Sapient|Approach layered approach

The layered approach consists of:

1. Universal principles that apply to *any* type of work at Sapient
2. Domain-specific "Toolkits" describe general processes typical in most Sapient engagements.
3. Engagement or offering "Playbooks," including detailed, more prescriptive guidance and custom assets for executing specific engagement types or projects

The core principles which are common to all Sapient projects are:

- Partner with Clients
- Communicate and Collaborate
- Provide Value Early
- Define and Manage Scope
- Front Load Risk
- Timebox Work
- Measure Success

Sapient|Approach is a very complete methodology that embraces the areas shown in Figure 4.2.

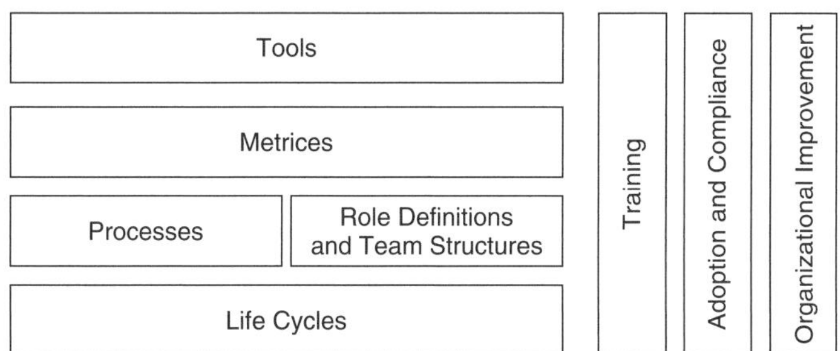

Figure 4.2 Sapient overall methodology (Source: Gottesman, Erik, "Growing Agility in a Large and Distributed Enterprise," Agile Project Leadership Network, Agile Business Conference, London, UK, 2006, p. 6)

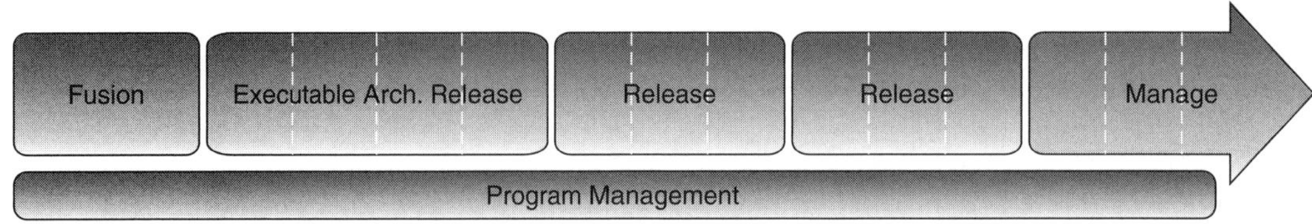

Figure 4.3 Sapient|Approach life-cycle model (Source: "The Right IT Results Faster with Sapient|Approach," Sapient Corporation White Paper, 2005, p.13)

Figure 4.3 is a high-level view of the Sapient|Approach life-cycle model. The following is a description of each of the phases in the life-cycle model:

- "In **Fusion**^{SM}, key members of the development team and core client stakeholders chart the vision; high-level features; and technological context, constraints and requirements—producing a plan for solution delivery. Fusion^{SM} uses facilitative workshop techniques that can be used at any time during the project.
- In the **Executable Architecture Release**, which is typically made up of two or more iterations, the development team delivers the core 10–20 percent of the completed application, fully implemented and tested, on the target technical architecture
- **Subsequent Releases** fall on significant client milestones, and deliver production-ready software, which the client can choose to internally test or deploy.
- **Manage Iterations** follow a more typical application management paradigm with established Service Level Agreements, and a pattern of regular releases together with smaller development work as needed."[9]

The Sapient|Approach life-cycle model expects that different activities will happen in parallel, as shown in Figure 4.4, which is based on the ideas behind unified processes such as the Rational Unified Process (RUP®).

Another significant feature of the Sapient methodology is that it is not just a development methodology. It is heavily focused on business outcomes and also includes provisions for redefining and reengineering business processes and business process improvement that is integrated into the overall project with the systems development work that may be needed to support those initiatives.

Sapient also uses a modified "Scrum-of-Scrum" approach to scale the methodology for multiple development teams on larger, more complex projects as shown in Figure 4.5.

[9] "The Right IT Results Faster with Sapient|Approach," Sapient Corporation White Paper, 2005, p. 12

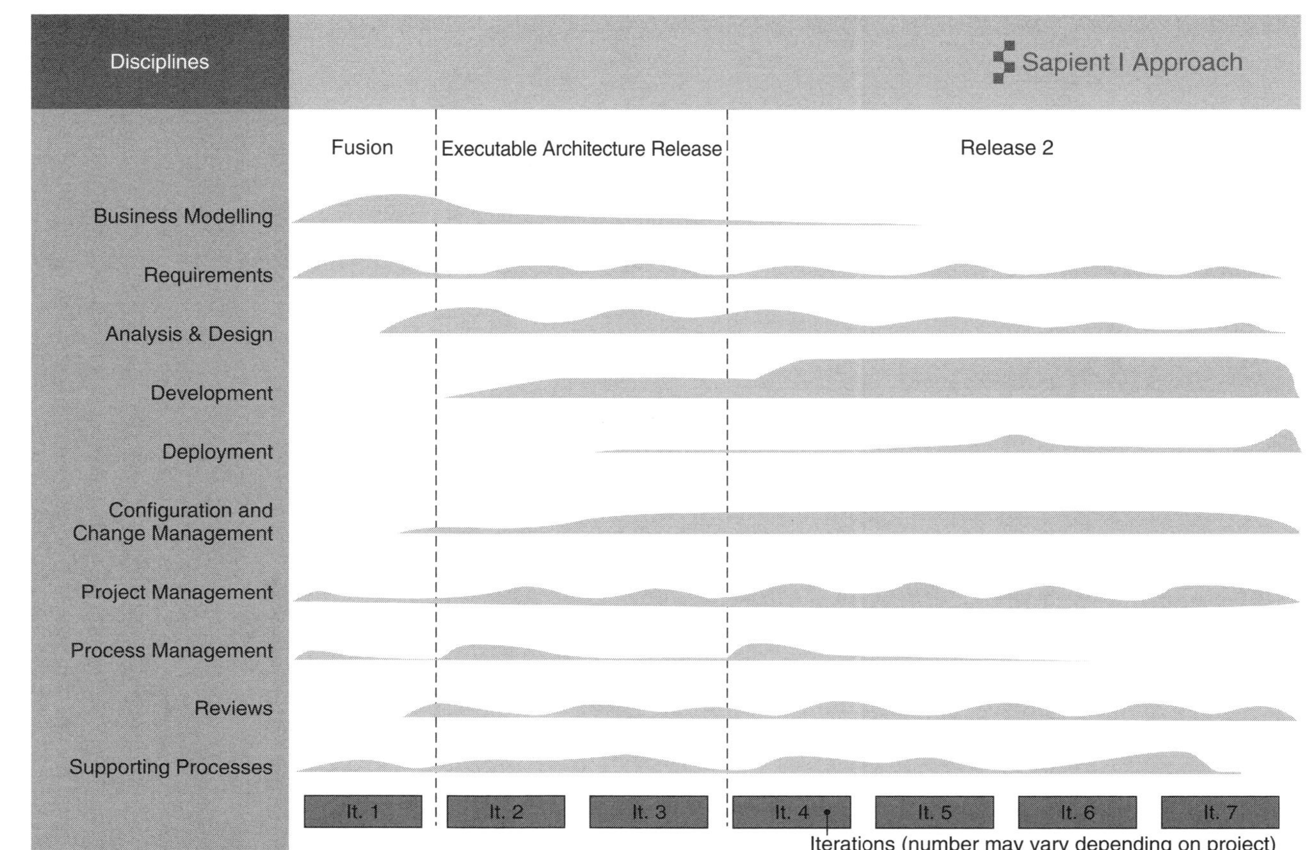

Figure 4.4 Sapient|Approach life-cycle showing interdependence of disciplines (Source: "The Right IT Results Faster with Sapient|Approach," Sapient Corporation White Paper, 2005, p. 13)

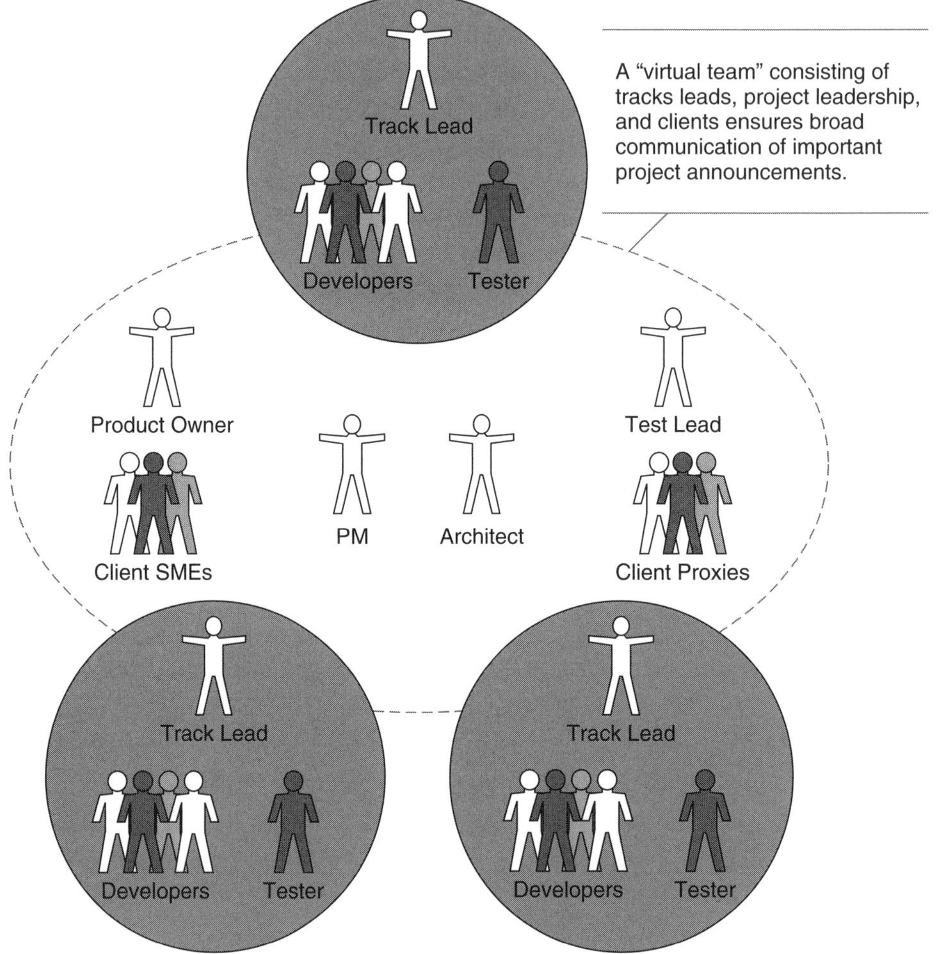

Figure 4.5 Sapient team structure

Another very interesting feature of the Sapient|Approach methodology is the way that it has incorporated Model-Driven Development (MDD), which is not normally considered an agile process, into the methodology.

> "We have formalized our approach to MDD as an integral element of our overall delivery model, known as Sapient|Approach (S|A). MDD as described in S|A centers on a triadic PIM (Platform-Independent Model) consisting of:
>
> - An entity model depicting the business entities and their relationships. Each entity is represented as a UML class with attributes for data fields.

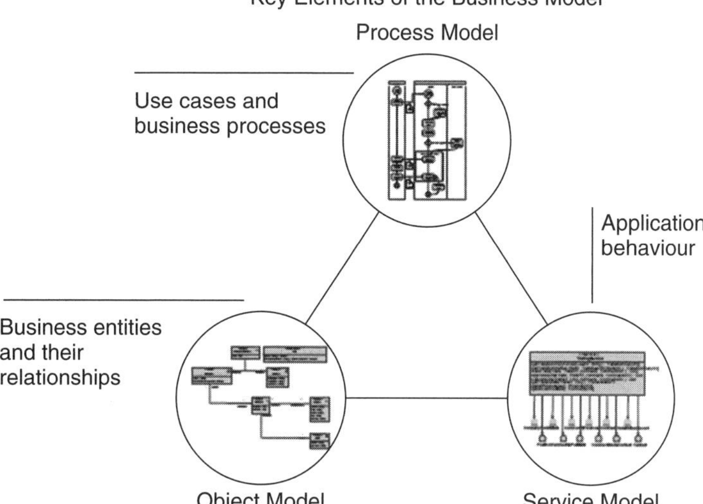

Figure 4.6 Sapient Platform-Independent Model

- A service model depicting the behavior of the application. Each service is represented as a UML class with methods that take entities as inputs and outputs. Service classes depend on the entities to get the job done.
- A process model depicting the use cases and business processes of the application. Each process is represented as an activity diagram with a start state, intermediate states, and one or more end states."[10]

The Triadic Platform-Independent Process Model (PIM) used by Sapient is shown in Figure 4.6[11]

Automated tools are then used to generate the structure of the working application from the Platform-Independent Model (PIM), as shown in Figure 4.7.

[10] Gottesman, Erik, "Model-driven Development Through the Agile Looking Glass," Agile India, 2006

[11] Gottesman, Erik, "Model-driven Development Through the Agile Looking Glass," Agile India, 2006

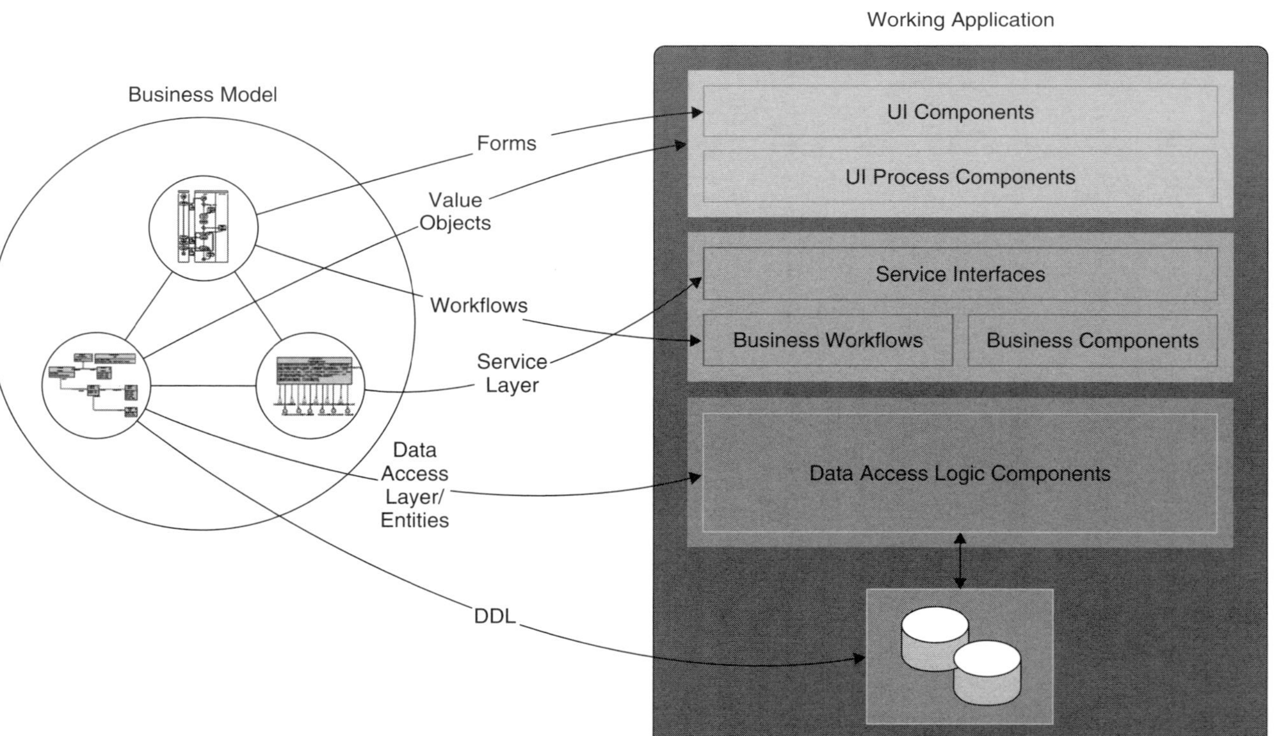

Figure 4.7 Sapient code transformation process

CHAPTER 5

PART I SUMMARY AND ACTION PLAN

OVERALL SUMMARY

The following is a summary of some key points that I believe are important from Part I of this book:

1. Avoid All-or-Nothing Thinking
   The word "agile" has come to be associated with specific agile methodologies such as Scrum and Extreme programming (XP). The implication that creates is that if you're not using those methodologies, you're not agile at all. There are a number of ways companies can become more agile without necessarily practicing Scrum and Extreme Programming (XP).

   There is a whole spectrum of different methodologies and variations on methodologies between the most pure forms of agile, such as Scrum and XP, at one end and the most traditional plan-driven forms of Waterfall at the other end. Choosing either end might result in severe tradeoffs for most companies, and it doesn't need to be an all-or-nothing decision. There are plenty of alternatives in the middle between those two extremes that offer a balance of control and agility that can be tailored to a company's business environment.

   Existing traditional plan-driven methodologies like the Waterfall are not dead, and there will still be a need for traditional plan-driven development projects as well as some that blend traditional plan-driven and agile methodologies. (See Figure 5.1 for a comparison of alternative approaches)
2. Avoid Jumping on the "Program du Jour" Bandwagon
   Agile is a hot area right now and, as in many other similar situations, everyone wants to jump on the bandwagon because it's a popular thing to do, and they may do it without an overall business strategy behind it and without fully understand the tradeoffs and issues associated with what they're jumping into.

   Agile has a lot of potential in suitable environments, but:

   - It needs to be consistent with the business and project environment it is applied to, and

- There is no free lunch—it takes a lot of work to fully implement agile methodologies; there are a number of risks and issues associated with it, and it definitely is not suitable for all business environments and all projects.

Developing a strategy on what level of agile product development is most appropriate for your business should be a major strategic decision for any company that does product development and relies on successful project management to effectively execute those projects.

3. Fit Methodologies to Your Business and Projects (Not vice-versa)
Many companies attempt to force-fit their business and projects to a standard methodology (either agile or non-agile). That almost always results in less than optimum results—the best approach is to define a strategy of what balance of control and agility is best-suited for your business environment and projects and then select and customize a broader range of methodologies, principles, and practices to implement that strategy. Force-fitting a project to Scrum or Extreme Programming (if it isn't appropriate for the project) can be just as bad as force-fitting a project to a traditional methodology.
4. Focus on Business Outcomes as Well as Costs and Schedules
The focus of any project methodology should provide a balance of flexibility and adaptability to achieve successful business outcomes as well as a sufficient level of control over costs and schedules and risks. Each project is unique and:
   - The risks and complexity of the project, as well as
   - The business goals, capabilities, and culture of the organization

   All of these factors should determine the methodology that is best suited for a given project.
5. Implement Methodologies Intelligently
Once a methodology is chosen, it should be implemented intelligently with an appropriate degree of tailoring and flexibility to adapt to change. No methodology should ever be considered to be absolute dogma. This, of course, implies that project managers and project teams are sufficiently trained to make responsible decisions that may be needed to customize and tailor methodologies to fit each project.
6. Major Organizational Change May be Needed Implementing a more agile product development strategy may have broad-based implications and may require a major organizational transformation in some cases to be successful. The magnitude of that effort will depend on the size of the gap between the company's current processes, culture, and capabilities and the desired end state. That transformation needs to be understood and planned, and an incremental transformation may be appropriate in some cases.

	"Extreme" Waterfall	"Hybrid" Agile	"Extreme" Agile
	Deterministic		*Evolutionary*
Project Management	■ **Detailed plan for entire project** ■ Scope-boxed phases ■ Track progress by tasks and milestones completed ■ Detailed documentation for all requirements	■ Short to medium length time-boxed iterations ■ Varying granularity plans ■ Track progress by value delivered ■ **Risk-driven requirements documentation**	■ 1-week timeboxed iterations ■ **Plan only current iteration** ■ Track progress by working code ■ Tests are only long-term requirements documentation
	Big up front design		*Just in time, quality focus*
Development Process	■ Design all before coding in complete detail ■ Periodic builds ■ **Integrate only once all code complete** ■ Partial unit test coverage	■ **Risk-and value-driven design choices** ■ Daily builds ■ Continuous functional testing, largely automated ■ 80% unit test coverage	■ Design all just in time-nothing up front ■ **Minimal design documentation** ■ Continuous integration builds ■ Test-driven development; 100% unit test coverage
	Low		*High*
Collaboration	■ Business involvement only at project start and completion ■ **"Throw it over the wall" requirements communication model** ■ Communication via periodic status meetings (monthly or greater)	■ **Frequent, regular business involvement** ■ Cross-group collaboration via frequent checkpoints ■ Cross-functional teams ■ Self-organizing teams ■ Daily "standup" meetings	■ **Continuous face-to-face business involvement** ■ Cross-functional teams ■ Pairing ■ Daily standup meetings

Figure 5.1 Comparison of agile and non-agile approaches (Source: "Enterprise Application of CMMI and Agile, "Sapient White Paper, March 2010)

DEVELOPING AN ACTION PLAN FOR YOUR BUSINESS

Moving to a more agile development strategy for your business can be either a major radical shift in the organization and its culture or only a minor shift in direction, depending on where you are today and where you want to get to. In any case, it is worth some level of planning, and that planning should include the following questions:

- What is the impact of agile on your business? What value will be gained from becoming more agile?
- Are you satisfied with your current product development process?
- What does the future look like?
- How ready is the company to make a transition to a more agile approach?
- How agile do you want to be and when do you want to get there?

Planning Questions

Each of these questions will be discussed in the following sections.

1. What Is the Impact of Agile on Your Business?
   - What is the relative impact of alternative agile approaches on providing business value?
   - How does a more agile approach align with the company's business strategy?
   - What are the tradeoffs associated with these approaches?
   - What approach seems to provide the most appropriate balance of control and agility for the business?
2. Are You Satisfied with Your Current Product Development Process?
   - What works well?
   - What doesn't work well? What are the "pain points" in the current process?
   - What do stakeholders and users think? What would they like to see?
   - Are projects meeting their business goals and objectives?
   - Where are the opportunities for improvement?
   - What are the highest priority issues to be addressed?
   - Are there any significant risk and regulatory factors that need to be considered?
3. What Does the Future Look Like?
   Are there any changes coming in the future that might require doing things differently?
   - Business changes?
   - Technology changes?

- Risk environment changes?
- Regulatory changes?
- Etc.

4. How ready is the company to make a transition to a more agile approach? The biggest factors in making a transition to an agile approach are not technical issues but cultural and organizational issues.
Sapient has developed a checklist of factors that organizations can use to assess their readiness for agile:

> **Overall Business Environment:**[1]
>
> - "Trust pervades the culture of the organization, the interactions between its people, and its clients.
> - Individuals demonstrate a high level of enthusiasm for or openness toward change.
> - Management empowers individuals to take risks without fear of repercussions.
> - Disciplined execution is representative of the organization's delivery practices or broadly viewed as a goal worth striving for.
> - Teams and management alike evidence the commitment and patience necessary to seeing through changes despite challenges and disappointments along the way.
> - A willingness exists to make reasonable investments in tools, training, coaching, and mentoring to facilitate successful adoption and sustained change."

> **Project Environment:**[2]
>
> - "Project Stakeholders are known and aligned around a unifying vision of the solution.
> - Product owners (customers) are able to commit the time required to collaborate frequently with teams providing feedback and direction.
> - Product owners are empowered by the business to make key decisions relating to scope and priorities.
> - Product owners are comfortable being exposed to work in progress and a heightened level of transparency with respect to quality and progress.
> - Team and organizational structures support cross-functional, multi-disciplinary collaboration.

---

[1] "Executive Brief | Are You Ready for Agile?" Sapient Corporate White Paper, www.sapient.com
[2] "Executive Brief | Are You Ready for Agile?" Sapient Corporate White Paper

> - The full team participates in daily status meetings, shared progress and resolving blocking issues through collaboration
> - Individual team members are self-directed and take initiative and ownership to help move the project forward.
> - People accept that speculation is wasteful and are thus tolerant of ambiguity.
> - People are comfortable giving and receiving feedback to one another.
> - Project management embraces change in a disciplined fashion, keeping the teams focused on tangible, short-term goals and shielding them from disruptive ad-hoc changes.
> - Project management makes decisions based on objective data.
> - Tools used to facilitate delivery processes are capable yet simple enough that they pose minimal overhead.
> - Simplicity is accepted as a fundamental design principle."

5. How Agile Do You Want to Be and When Do You Want to Get There? Many agile books will tell you to just start right away to develop a pilot project with Scrum and let it evolve from there. That approach may work in some companies, but going to a Scrum methodology is definitely not the right solution for everyone, and even if it is the right solution, it may take a long-term commitment and plan to achieve the kind of transformation that could be necessary to get there.

A hybrid approach might make sense in some companies for a couple of key reasons:

- It may not make sense for some companies to move to a pure agile approach because the nature of their products and services is fairly certain and predictable or they operate in a high risk or regulated environment that may require a more plan-driven approach.
- Some companies may have some significant cultural obstacles to overcome to move to a pure agile approach, and a change management approach is probably needed. It is well recognized that there are three factors that are essential to the success of any change management initiative:
  - **"Burning Platform"**—There has to be a sufficient level of "pain" with the current situation to motivate a significant change—if there isn't a sufficient level of pain to provide that motivation, the effort may not get very far.
  - **Vision and Strong Leadership**—Senior management needs to define a vision of where the company wants to go, explain why it's important to get there, and provide the overall leadership

- **Progress in That Direction**—The third element of a successful change management initiative is to show progress toward moving in that direction.

If there is no "burning platform" (i.e., no strong compelling reason why an agile transformation is important), it may be difficult to achieve the level of change that may be needed to make it successful. In some of these situations, a hybrid approach may make sense, at least as an interim solution, because of the difficulty of implementing a broad-based change management initiative.

For large companies that have a well-established approach built around traditional plan-driven development processes, this may not be an easy decision. Although the benefits of migrating to a more agile approach may be very significant:

- The level of effort to implement it may be also be very significant, many people in the organization may need retraining to migrate to agile, and some personnel changes may also be needed.
- It may bring about a fairly significant amount of change that might be disruptive to the company's business.
- The impact of the agile implementation on existing methods for project governance and managing project costs and schedules also needs to be considered and planned for.

Alternative Approaches

There are several approaches that might be considered:

1. **Incremental Improvements**—For companies that have very cumbersome traditional development processes but are not ready to make a significant change, there are a number of things that can be done to streamline and improve their development processes and incorporate some more agile practices. These changes can have a significant impact on improving the current process without requiring extensive organizational changes and will move the company further along towards an agile approach. The following are some examples:
   - Develop an organizational culture and leadership approach that is more agile based on:
     - Respect for people and empowerment of people
     - Cross-functional, collaborative teamwork across functional organizations
     - Collective ownership of project quality and business outcomes
   - Begin developing a more cross-functional team approach

- Provide training to everyone in the organization so that they are better prepared to accept the responsibility associated with implementing a more empowered approach.
- Streamline current development processes and build more flexibility into the processes. Many companies rigidly attempt to follow a single project methodology for all projects in order to maintain project control.
  - Use lean principles and perform a "value stream" analysis of the current process to eliminate waste
  - Review and streamline the documents and artifacts required for projects based on an assessment of the value they provide
  - Train and empower project teams to make good risk management decisions to tailor the life-cycle model as needed to develop an appropriate balance of control and flexibility for each project.
  - Create an increased level of focus on continuous improvement of processes and provide a mechanism to evolve the processes based on lessons learned.
  - If a Project Management Office (PMO) organization is in place, shift the role of the PMO from a process enforcement role to a value-added consulting role.
- Adjust the management and leadership style as well as metrics if necessary to provide an appropriate balance between control and agility and to be consistent with the preceding approach.

2. **Implement a More Iterative Approach**—If it is not feasible to migrate to a pure agile approach, a hybrid approach that is more iterative might be a good compromise:
   - Simply providing a choice between traditional plan-driven approaches and iterative approaches could be a major step forward, if it is combined with some of the organizational culture changes discussed under incremental improvements.
   - Developing a more iterative approach should also consist of increasing the level of engagement of business sponsors in the design and development effort.

   Implementing a more iterative approach would consist of:
   - Designing the life-cycle model(s) to support the approach—this might be either an iterative plan-driven approach or an iterative emergent approach, or some combination of both.
   - Selecting any tools that might be needed to support the approach.
   - Training personnel on the new process—project managers involved in the process need to understand how to tailor and use the process to fit their projects.

- Committing resources to project teams to begin implementing the process.

3. **Implement a Pure Agile Approach**—Many companies may choose to go directly to a pure agile approach for all or part of their development projects. There is no question that a pure agile approach has major benefits for projects and business environments that have high levels of uncertainty. For those companies that elect to make the transition to a pure agile approach, I recommend Mike Cohn's book *Succeeding with Agile—Software Development Using Scrum*[3] as a good resource to help develop a plan. He goes into detail on some of the factors that might need to be addressed in this plan such as:
   - Common activities in any successful Scrum adoption:
     - Building awareness and consensus that the current. process is not delivering acceptable results.
     - Creating desire to adopt Scrum as a way to address current problems.
     - Developing the ability to succeed with Scrum.
     - Promotion of Scrum throughout the company.
     - Transferring an understanding of the implications of Scrum to all the organizations that might be impacted.
   - Implementing an Enterprise Transition Community (ETC) to plan, initiate, and steer the implementation of Scrum in the company.
   - Setting up an Improvement Community to collaboratively improve the organization's use of Scrum.
   - Selecting and implementing pilot projects to begin actual implementation.

   Many times, a pure agile (e.g., Scrum) implementation will need to be combined with a broader project management layer and perhaps also a portfolio and/or program governance layer. Jim Highsmith's book *Agile Project Management—Creating Innovative Products*[4] is a good resource for designing and implementing a project management and portfolio management approach to wrap around a pure agile approach.

How Do You Get There?

After you've chosen an approach that makes sense for your business, the final question is "How do you get from where you are to there?" The answer to that is it depends on how big the transformation is that is needed and whether

---

[3] Cohn, Mike *Succeeding with Agile—Software Development Using Scrum*, New York: Addison-Wesley, 2009

[4] Highsmith, Jim, *Agile Project Management—Creating Innovative Products*, New York: Addison-Wesley, 2010

a more incremental approach for getting there is appropriate or a more radical transformation approach will work better:

- One school of thought is that organizations are at different levels of maturity, there is a progression of levels that you need to go through to get to the level of maturity needed to implement a pure agile approach similar to other maturity models such as CMMI,[5] and you just can't jump from level 1 to level 5 instantly. The level of maturity required to implement a pure agile approach should not be underestimated, and it can take time to move a large organization to a higher level.
- Another way of thinking is that if you really want to make a radical change, a more aggressive approach may be needed. This is similar to the difference between an incremental process improvement approach like TQM or Six Sigma and a more radical approach like business process reengineering (BPR). BPR taught us that sometimes it makes sense to toss out the current process and start over with a clean slate to really rethink the way thing are done to come through with breakthrough improvements.

There's some merit in both of these ways of thinking. There is a progression of maturity levels that companies need to go through to get to a pure agile approach and that can take time, but rather than attempting to bring the entire organization up to a higher level of maturity all at once, a pilot project that is limited to a smaller portion of the organization would be a way of demonstrating success quickly on a smaller scale. That approach would also avoid the disruption that a more widespread radical transformation might cause. The method for getting there will generally follow along the following lines:

- Improvements in organizational maturity may require planning of change management and training activities to bring about that kind of change.
- Incremental Improvements in existing development processes will generally use existing process improvement techniques, such as lean thinking and value stream mapping, to improve current processes.
- Moving to a more iterative development process will require more rethinking of current design processes and design of new iterative processes. In most cases, it is not just a matter of adopting standard, off-the-shelf iterative development processes like RUP. A considerable amount of thinking and work may be needed to adapt and customize these processes to fit the company's business environment.
- A move to a pure agile development methodology like Scrum is likely to require the greatest transformation and is more likely to resemble a business process reengineering type of transformation.

---

[5] "Capability Maturity Model Integration (CMMI)," www.sei.cmu.edu/cmmi

If you choose to go directly to a pure agile approach like Scrum, Ken Schwaber's book *The Enterprise and Scrum*[6] is a good resource to use. Ken Schwaber recommends three levels of transition teams:

- The **Enterprise Transition Team** is responsible for planning and managing the implementation of Scrum at an enterprise level. This would include defining and planning the scope of the Scrum implementation across the enterprise and defining and managing the enterprise-level activities that need to take place to successfully implement a Scrum that strategy. This effort would normally be driven by a cross-functional team of the company's senior management and should include any senior managers who are impacted by the implementation.
- **Scrum Rollout Teams** are responsible for doing the actual adoption work at a more tactical level to roll out the implementation. These teams would be responsible for planning and managing efforts that support multiple development teams such as customizing the methodology as needed to fit with the company's business environment, defining and, implementing any training that may be needed, and monitoring the progress of adoption by development teams.
- **Development Teams** would be responsible for applying the methodology to selected projects.

Treating the implementation of the overall enterprise transition as an agile project in itself has the advantage of engraining agile thinking at a number of different levels, including the most senior managers.

> "Adopting Scrum in an enterprise is like looking into the abyss, girding oneself for an epic journey, and then making the plunge. What will be discovered and have to be conquered is different in each enterprise; what is common is the courage to start and then persist." [7]

[6] Schwaber, Ken, *The Enterprise and Scrum*, Redmond, WA: Microsoft Press, 2007
[7] Schwaber, Ken, *The Enterprise and Scrum*, Redmond, WA: Microsoft Press, 2007

PART II
OVERVIEW

The following are the objectives of Part II of the book.

For project managers, the book is intended to provide a much deeper understanding of lean and agile principles, methodologies, and practices to enable project managers to develop a more agile project management approach. It also provides an understanding of how to blend and tailor both agile and traditional principles, methodologies, and practices to create an appropriate balance of control and agility to fit a business environment, as well as to the risks and complexities of any individual project. Key points include:

- How the project management role is changed in agile projects and what new skills and career directions may be needed to grow into agile project management roles
- How to develop a project management approach that is adaptive to agile as well as non-agile project environments, including how to integrate existing project management knowledge such as *A Guide to the Project Management Body of Knowledge* (*PMBOK® Guide*) with new and rapidly evolving agile principles, practices, and methodologies
- How to design and tailor the right combination of principles, practices, and methodologies (agile as well as non-agile) to provide a balance of control and agility to fit the needs of the business and the risks and complexity of projects rather than attempting to use a standard off-the-shelf methodology (either agile or non-agile) for all projects

The future direction of project management is changing rapidly as a result of agile methodologies. For many project managers, it will call for:

- New ways of thinking about the project management role
- New approaches and methodologies for implementing projects
- New skills for working in a very different environment

Bob Wysocki has created an analogy that I really like—he talks about the difference between a project manager acting as a "cook" or as a "chef":[1]

- A good "cook" may have the ability to create some very good meals, but those dishes may be limited to a repertoire of standard dishes, and

[1] Wysocki, Bob, e-mail comments, 6/4/2010

his/her knowledge of how to prepare those meals may be primarily based on following some predefined recipes out of a cookbook.

- A "chef," on the other hand, typically has a far greater ability to prepare a much broader range of more sophisticated dishes using much more exotic ingredients in some cases. His/her knowledge of how to prepare those meals is not limited to predefined recipes and, in many cases, a chef will create entirely new and innovative recipes for a given situation. The best chefs are also not limited to one kind of cuisine and are capable of combining dishes from entirely different kinds of cuisine.

That sums up what I believe is the key challenge for project managers fairly well. In the future:

- More project managers will need to be "chefs" rather than "cooks."
- Project managers will need to be able to select from a broader range of methodologies, practices, and principles (both agile and non-agile) that are much less well defined to create a project management approach that is well aligned with the needs of a business environment and then customize and tailor them to fit the risks and complexities of individual projects.

It requires a much higher level of skill to do that. It requires:

- Knowledge of a much broader range of methodologies and practices (both agile and non-agile)
- An understanding of the fundamental principles behind those methodologies and practices to know how to mix and match them and customize them as needed to maximize the success of a given project

Just as companies need to make decisions about how agile they want to be and when they want to get there, the project management approach needs to change to support that direction and project managers need to develop their own skills to support that approach, as shown in Figure P.1

In some cases, new roles may be needed for project managers to perform such as designing customized software development life cycle (SDLC) processes that provide a balance of control and agility. Part II of the book is designed to help project managers understand how the project management role may evolve in helping their companies become more agile.

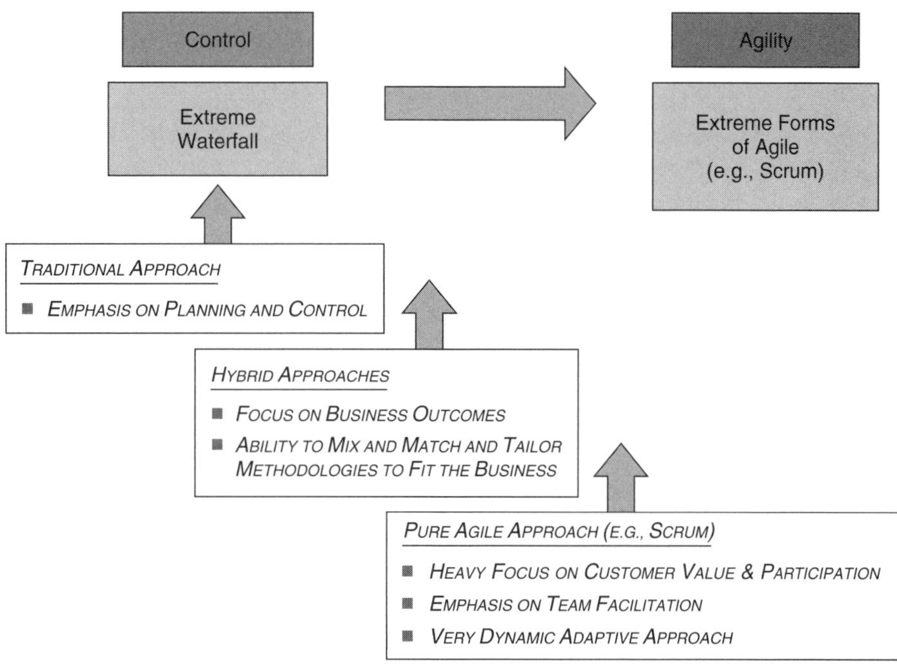

Figure P.1 Comparison of project management roles

CHAPTER 6

AGILE PROJECT MANAGEMENT

AGILE PROJECT MANAGEMENT ROLES

Agile methodologies are intentionally lean, they focus on fundamental principles, and they are also not prescriptive—that is by design. Agile methodologies do not specifically define a project management role or a business analyst role. The lack of definition of these roles has led to the perception that the project management and business analyst functions are no longer needed in agile projects.

The reality is that even though there may be no one with the formal title of "project manager" or "business analyst" on an agile project, some of the functions performed by project managers and business analysts are still required and need to be performed by someone on the agile team, even if there is no one with that formal title. That means that someone on the team needs to have the skills and knowledge required to perform those tasks.

Some traditional project management functions may not be needed or may be performed in other ways in a pure agile approach. Several factors create a very different environment on agile projects that dramatically impacts the need for project management and how it is performed:

- Many of the decisions are made collectively by the team, and the Scrum-Master plays a facilitative rather than a directive role.
- The team also uses a consensus-driven approach to come up with schedule estimates for the project and release plans.
- There is typically a much more limited amount of upfront planning and documentation on each project.
- There is also a much greater emphasis on taking a more flexible and adaptive approach to optimize business outcomes rather than a control-oriented approach that is focused on managing costs and schedules.
- The primary members of the team are usually assigned full time to the project, so there is less of a need for resource planning and securing commitments for resources to support the project from functional departments; however, there is much more of a need for the team to be self-managing without as much direct intervention by functional managers.

- The methods for reporting and tracking progress of the project are also built into the way the team operates and are typically less formal.

On small-scale projects, the ScrumMaster may perform the tasks that a project manager might normally perform; however, the ScrumMaster role is very different from most typical project management roles. A number of books have compared the role of the ScrumMaster to a "sheep dog" that guards and shepherds a flock of sheep. He/she keeps the sheep from straying too far out of the group and protects the flock from unwanted interference and obstacles. It is much more of a facilitative role than it is a directive role.

There are basically two levels of project management in a pure agile (e.g., Scrum) project:

- Within a Scrum team, the ScrumMaster typically performs many of the tasks that would normally be performed by a project manager such as leading and facilitating the team and tracking and managing progress of the project. It is done in an entirely different context, and it is a very different role from a traditional project management role, but some of the functions that the ScrumMaster performs involve some project management skills.
- In larger, more complex agile projects, an extra layer of management may be needed to coordinate and manage the work of multiple teams in addition to the role performed by the ScrumMaster within individual teams. That layer of project management can be implemented in a number of different ways (See discussion on project management practices), but it will also require an additional level of project management responsibility.

The pure agile approach (e.g., Scrum) relies heavily on self-organizing teams facilitated by the ScrumMaster to collectively perform most of the project management functions. Putting a lot of faith in self-organizing teams is a good idea, but it clearly has its limits:

- The success or failure of it is highly dependent on the skills of all the individuals on the team in following the Scrum process, and it only works if the individuals on the team are experienced enough and knowledgeable enough to take on that responsibility. Making a self-organizing team work effectively is also very dependent on developing a very collaborative approach both among all of the direct participants in the team and between the team and any external stakeholders.
- The self-organized team model isn't very scalable to larger projects, and it doesn't adequately address many of the typical higher-level project management planning and management roles that are essential to the success of projects, especially those requiring multiple teams.
- In situations that require a balance of agility and control, a hybrid project management approach might be needed that blends an additional level of planning and management with self-organizing teams as a foundation.

Comparison of Traditional and Agile Project Management Roles

The diagrams below show a comparison of the way roles that are typically implemented on traditional development projects and agile development projects. Figure 6.1 shows the typical role definitions found in traditional projects and Figure 6.2 shows the typical role definitions found in agile projects. Note that these diagrams only show the roles and responsibilities within single teams for agile projects—an additional layer of project management would normally be needed to coordinate the efforts of projects that require multiple teams.

The following is a summary of some key differences in an agile project:

- A Project Management Office (PMO) might not typically be involved in an agile project at all in many cases. If a PMO were involved at all, it might play much more of a value-added process consulting role rather than a process control function in an agile environment.
- The ScrumMaster replaces some of the functions of the project manager and plays much more of a "servant leader" role performing team facilitation and the team, as a whole, makes project decisions that might normally be made individually by the project manager. The idea of engaging the team in the decision-making process is a good technique that many project managers practice to some extent anyway on traditional projects.
- The Product Owner may replace many of the functions that might have been performed by a Business Analyst to provide the overall requirements

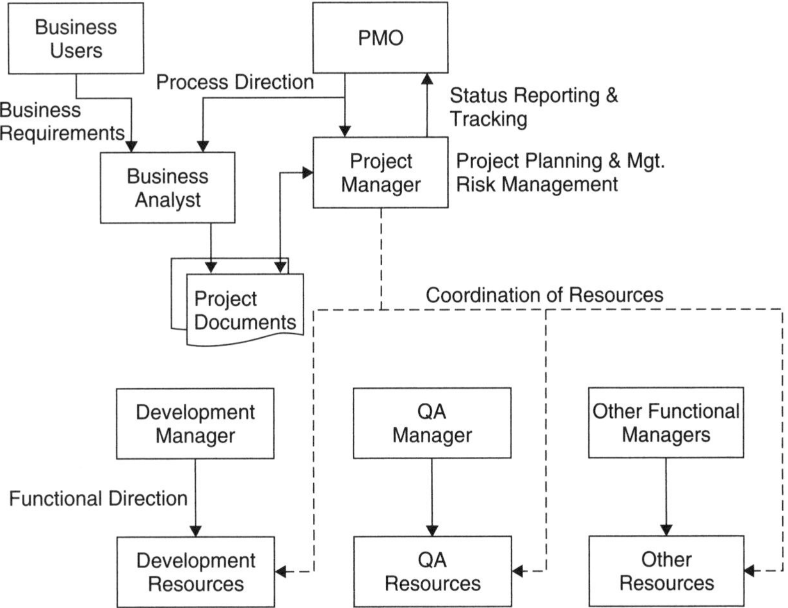

Figure 6.1 Typical role definition in traditional development projects

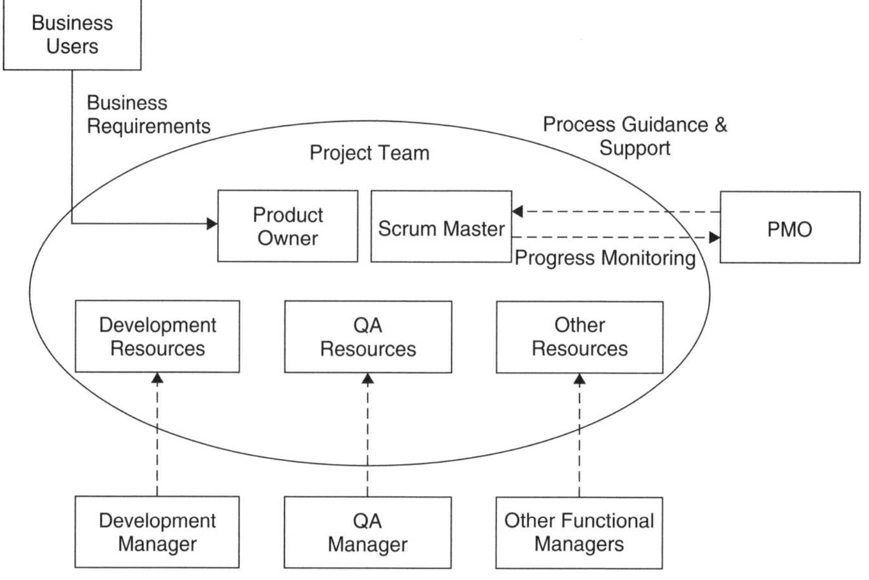

Figure 6.2 Typical role definitions in an agile project

definition for the project; however, that role is also considerably different from a Business Analyst role. The Product Owner is expected to be a subject matter expert, represent the interests of all the business stakeholders, and provide overall business direction to the project. It is very conceivable that a Business Analyst may also be needed on the team to assist the Product Owner in performing that role.

- The functional department managers such as the Development Manager and the QA Manager play a significantly reduced role and provide only very limited functional direction to the team—the functional members of the team are expected to provide most of their own functional direction. Naturally, that requires fairly highly skilled people to fill those roles.

The table below shows a comparison of the typical project management and governance roles in traditional, plan-driven projects and agile projects.

Responsibility	Traditional	Agile
Process Direction and Control	• The PMO provides process direction and control (standardize the utilization of processes).	• The Project Team (led and facilitated by the ScrumMaster) is responsible for defining, implementing, and continuously improving the process. • The PMO may play a value-added consulting or supporting role if necessary.

Responsibility	Traditional	Agile
Progress Tracking	• The Project Manager is responsible for tracking and reporting of project progress and control and management of overall costs and schedules. • The PMO may provide overall oversight and control for all projects.	• The Project Team (led and facilitated by the ScrumMaster) is responsible for tracking and monitoring of their own progress. • Progress reporting metrics such as the "burn down chart" are built into the process. • The PMO may play a consolidation role.
Functional Management Responsibility for Resources	• Functional managers (QA, Dev, etc.) provide direct management for all functional resources involved in projects. • The Project Manager is responsible for defining and assigning tasks to functional resources and obtaining commitments for task performance from functional managers as necessary.	• The Project Team (led and facilitated by the ScrumMaster) is responsible for functional management of team resources, including assigning tasks, obtaining commitments, and making any functional decisions that may be needed. • Functional managers may play a supporting role if necessary.
Coordination of Resources	• The Project Manager is responsible for coordinating the availability of resources from supporting departments.	• Most resources are assigned full time to the project; therefore, less resource coordination is needed. • The ScrumMaster will coordinate availability of shared resources from other departments.
Business Analysis and Require-ments Elicitation	• Requirements are documented and controlled. • Business Analysts work directly with the users to analyze, define, and document requirements.	• Documentation of requirements may be less formal and may be less controlled. • The Product Owner is dedicated to the team and is the representative of user requirements to the team. • The Product Owner might be trained as a Business Analyst or use Business Analysts to help if required
Change Management	• The Project Manager is responsible for controlling and managing changes to the project requirements as the project progresses.	• The Product Owner is responsible for continuously managing the Product Backlog in response to changes as the project progresses. The Product Owner may be assisted by the ScrumMaster in performing that role. • The Project Team (led and facilitated by the ScrumMaster) and the Product Owner are responsible for continuously updating release plans as necessary as the project progresses in response to changes in the Product Backlog.

Responsibility	Traditional	Agile
Risk Management	• The Project Manager is responsible for risk management on behalf of the business stakeholders.	• The Project Team (led and facilitated by the ScrumMaster) is responsible for risk management. • The Product Owner is expected to play a major role in risk management decisions on behalf of the Business Stakeholders.

Agile Business Analyst Role

The role of the Business Analyst is also not formally defined in agile projects. It is expected that the development team will work directly with the representative of the business users (Product Owner) to define many of the detailed requirements as the design progresses. Having developers work directly with the users has a lot of advantages, and it solves a number of problems that might occur in a typical project management approach such as:

- Documented requirements might not be understood by the development team and might be misinterpreted.
- The documented requirements might not really capture the true needs of the business users because the business users may not be able to articulate all the details of what is needed in writing (Sometimes prototyping of some functionality is the best way to further define detailed requirements).
- The business needs and requirements might change between the time the requirements are documented and the design is implemented, and traditional project management models are somewhat resistant to change.

On the other hand, the model of relying totally on the development team to elicit requirements directly from the users has some limitations:

- Developers are not necessarily trained to see things from a business process perspective, and an analysis of the business processes that the system supports often needs to be done prior to or concurrently with the design of the system.
- In more complex situations, a significant amount of business analysis skill may be needed to perform further analysis of the requirements to ensure that they are complete, accurately defined, and consistent with the business objectives that they are intended to achieve (traceability analysis).
- The typical agile project relies heavily on informal, face-to-face discussions between the development team and the business users to develop detailed requirements, and the details of these requirements discussions may not be well documented. From a supportability perspective, many times it is essential to have well-documented requirements to serve as a baseline for managing the system throughout its operational life cycle.

- As the complexity of the business requirements grows, the need for the Business Analyst role becomes even more significant. For example, there might be significant business rules associated with some of the requirements that need to be well documented so that they are consistently implemented and enforced by the system.

It has become fairly widely recognized that, as the complexity of business systems evolve and as business systems and the business processes that they are associated with become increasingly intertwined, it can take a lot of skill to elicit, analyze, and manage the requirements for these systems. There's a lot of similarity to the Project Management role—just as the typical Project Manager role may need to go through some significant rethinking to work effectively in an agile environment, the Business Analyst role must also go through some rethinking to become more agile, but the need for both of those skills certainly doesn't go away.

AGILE PROJECT MANAGEMENT APPROACH

Project Management Mindset

To succeed in an agile environment, some Project Managers may need to adopt new ways of thinking. There are several important shifts in thinking that may be needed.

Systems-Thinking Approach

Here's an excellent quote from Erik Gottesman of Sapient on the difference between a traditional and agile project management approach:

> "When I think about the distinctions between traditional and agile project management, the shift from one to the other and the "deprogramming" involved, I always feel that the change is minimally technical. While there are differences in process that need to be learned and practiced, the change is more substantially attitudinal—a shift from command-and-control thinking to systems thinking, characterized by a greater focus on measuring process output versus person output. I can still employ many of the traditional project and program management skills I've developed, but I look at them through a different lens."[1]

What is "systems-thinking"? "Systems-thinking" means being able to see the "whole" rather than just the components of a system or process and being able to understand how the components function and interact with each other to make the overall system function. From a project management perspective, it means not getting lost in the mechanics of how a particular methodology (agile or non-agile)

---

[1] Gottesman, Erik, E-mail comments on book review

works, being able to see the "big picture," and being able to understand the principles and practices that are behind methodologies at a deeper level. It also means seeing the dynamics of how those principles and practices work together and interact with each other in a methodology to produce an overall result as a system rather than seeing the methodology as a more mechanical, step-by-step process.

When you take a "systems-thinking" approach, you see things in an entirely different perspective and begin to see beyond the mechanics of each of these methodologies. Here's an example: "Respect for people" is a principle that is very important in many agile methodologies like Scrum. If you believe the stereotypes about traditional project management, the principle of "respect for people" may not seem to be very compatible with the typical perception that is associated with a "command-and-control," traditional project management approach. However, if you understand the methodologies at a deeper level and see beyond many of these stereotypes, you begin to realize that all methodologies incorporate "respect for people" to some degree—the thing that may be different is the amount of empowerment and delegation of responsibility that is incorporated into the methodology, and there may be good reasons why the level of empowerment may need to be different, including:

- Risk and regulatory requirements require a higher level of control.
- The people performing the process are not well trained enough to take on more responsibility.
- The organizational culture and management style of the company isn't consistent with high levels of employee empowerment.

Of course, there are many situations where project managers do fit the traditional stereotype and don't incorporate respect for people into a "command-and-control" project management approach for no good reason, but that's not necessarily a fault or limitation of the methodology; it's just poor or ineffective implementation.

Focus on Customer Value

Agile methodologies require a more flexible approach designed to maximize customer value in addition to maximizing control and predictability.

> "... in too many organizations project management has become focused on administrative excellence rather than technical excellence.... Project leaders must champion technical excellence because therein lies the key to adaptability and low-cost integration that drive long-term product success."[2]

[2] Highsmith, Jim, *Agile Project Management—Creating Innovative Products*, New York: Addison-Wesley, 2010, pp. 38–39

There are two key changes that may be needed:

- **Balance of Control and Agility**—In addition to the traditional project management emphasis on controlling costs and schedules, Project Managers need to focus on developing a balanced approach that blends the right level of control with a sufficient level of agility to also successfully deliver business outcomes. Of course, the right balance of control and agility for a particular project will depend on a number of factors, including the culture of the company and the need for control, the level of uncertainty in the requirements for the project and the need for direct user involvement, and the risks and complexity of the project.
- **Flexibility and Adaptability**—Instead of rigidly implementing a given standard project management methodology (either agile or non-agile) "by the book," Project Managers need to be able to craft a project management approach that is tailored to an individual project and to the business environment that project is associated with. Robert Wysocki sums this up well in his book *Effective Project Management—Traditional, Agile, Extreme*:

> "The PMBOK® definition of Project Management is crisp, clean, and clearly stated. It has provided a solid foundation on which to define the process groups and processes that underlie all project management. But I think there is another definition that transcends the PMBOK® definition and is far more comprehensive of what Project Management entails. I offer that definition as nothing more than organized common sense. Projects are unique, and each one is different than all others that have preceded it. That uniqueness requires a unique approach that continually adapts as new characteristics of the project emerge. These characteristics can and do emerge anywhere along the project life cycle. Being ready for them and adjusting as needed means that we must be always attentive to doing what makes good sense given the circumstances. Hence, Project Management is nothing more than organized common sense....
>
> We are not in Kansas anymore! The discipline of project management has morphed to a new state.... what does all of this mean to the struggling Project Manager?
>
> To me the answer is obvious. You must open your minds to the basic principles on which project management is based so as to accommodate change and avoid wasting dollars and wasting time. For as long as I can remember, I and my colleagues have been preaching that one size does not fit all."[3]

[3] Wysocki, Robert, *Effective Project Management—Traditional, Agile, Extreme*, pg xlvii, Hoboken, NJ: Wiley, 2009

Adapting Methodologies to Fit the Project and the Problem

Many project managers are heavily trained in a particular methodology and tend to use that approach for all projects because that's what they're most comfortable with. Using the same approach over and over again with a high level of repeatability is a good way to provide process predictability. It's similar to manufacturing standard parts on an assembly line, and it maximizes the efficiency of the process to standardize it and make it repeatable, but that approach doesn't lend itself to more agile environments that require customizing the process and the results to fit different customer needs.

The shift in thinking that is needed is, instead of force-fitting the project to any particular methodology (agile or non-agile), fit the methodology (or combination of methodologies) to the project. It takes much more skill and a broader and deeper understanding of a number of different methodologies, principles, and practices to do that:

1. Agile methodologies are, by design, loosely defined and meant to be tailored and customized to fit the situation. They are also meant to be building blocks that need to be assembled in the right combinations to fit the business and project environment that they are used in. For example:
   - Scrum doesn't specify what development methodology to use with it. Extreme Programming (XP) is commonly used with Scrum as a development methodology, but that is not always the case, and even if XP is used, it is often modified or tailored as needed to fit the capabilities and style of the organization as well as other factors.
   - Scrum doesn't say anything explicitly about project management—within a Scrum team at the iteration level, there is no project management role and the project management functions are performed by a combination of the ScrumMaster and Product Owner roles. That doesn't necessarily mean that project management is not required for larger more complex projects that require multiple teams, but Scrum doesn't specify how that should be done. Some people have used a "Scrum of Scrums" approach to extend the Scrum methodology to multiple teams, but that isn't necessarily the only way to provide that level of project management.
2. Agile methodologies also don't specify how everything should be done and don't necessarily replace all existing methodologies and practices. A good example of that is requirements elicitation: Scrum doesn't provide much explicit guidance on how to elicit requirements, and some existing practices for requirements elicitation and analysis still may be appropriate.

The key point is that agile methodologies intentionally leave a lot to be defined about exactly how the methodology is implemented. In some cases, the absence of definition has been interpreted to mean that the missing practices are not required and that is not the case at all. Good judgment and common sense are needed to define and tailor the process for each project.

Project Management Skills

Some people have the narrow view that project management is primarily an administrative function associated with estimating and managing project costs and schedules. That is a function that many Project Managers are required to perform, and it is an important area that they are measured on, but in most cases, project managers have a fairly broad range of skills that go well beyond those basic project management functions. Agile methodologies will probably accelerate that trend for project managers to develop more emphasis on broader and deeper skills that go beyond basic project management. A broader and deeper range of skills beyond basic project management skills may be required in an agile environment:

- **Technical Skills**—In a traditional plan-driven Waterfall environment, the development effort may have been managed as a separate activity within the overall project with functional direction from a Development Manager. In an agile environment, it becomes much more difficult to separate the development effort from the rest of the project, and the team (led and facilitated by the ScrumMaster) is expected to provide its own direction for most functional decisions rather than relying heavily on functional direction provided by functional managers. The ScrumMaster and/or Project Manager needs to be at least technically knowledgeable to participate in the decision-making process and gain credibility in facilitating and managing technical teams.
- **Business Analyst Skills**—In the past, the requirements definition process may have been performed separately by a Business Analyst who might have been responsible for completing the definition of requirements documents prior to starting the actual development effort. In an agile development environment, it is also difficult to separate the requirements definition function as a separate effort. There may be some Business Analyst work performed upfront prior to the beginning of the project, but the majority of the detailed requirements development effort is probably going to be performed collaboratively as the development progresses. In many cases, there may not be a formal Business Analyst role and the Product Owner is expected to represent the user stakeholders' interests on any requirements. The ScrumMaster has to be at least knowledgeable enough about the Business Systems Analysis process to ensure that the requirements definition effort is complete and sufficient and someone on the team performs whatever functions might be required.
- **People Management and Leadership Skills**—In the past, a Project Manager may or may not have played an actual people management role: In many traditional plan-driven development projects, the projects

use resources from different organizations that are loosely knit to form a project team and Project Managers lead by influence. The primary functional direction to those people on the team may come from the functional department that they report into (e.g., development or QA). In an agile environment, the team is cross-functional and dedicated to the project—that requires much stronger leadership skills to build highly cohesive and collaborative teams. It also requires a very facilitative management and leadership style. The most effective Project Managers, in many cases, are excellent leaders with the wisdom/maturity to provide leadership appropriate to the situation.

- **Process Design Capabilities**—In the past, a Project Manager may have been able to simply take an established, off-the-shelf SDLC process and execute it. In an agile environment, a much deeper understanding of the principles behind a number of different SDLC processes may be needed in order to choose the right process for a given project and tailor it as necessary to fit the needs of the project.

> "Agile development and project management are built on the underlying premise that individual capability is the cornerstone of success and furthermore, that individuals are unique contributors. It follows from these premises that rather than molding people to a set of common processes and practices, processes and practices should be molded to the team itself. Although an organization might insist that project teams follow a guiding framework, there should be flexibility in what individual practices are used to meet the needs of each phase. The team should discuss what practices will be used and not used. Just because a practice is a good one doesn't mean it needs to be used on every project. With individual practices, each team will tailor them in different ways according to the capabilities of the team members, the size of the project, the number of customers, and many other factors."[4]

AGILE PROJECT MANAGEMENT PRACTICES

A basic project management approach is built into Scrum at the iteration level and at the release planning level. The approach for providing project management above that level is not defined as part of the methodology. It is up to the organization implementing the project to define how (and if) any additional project management role will be performed:

- In the simplest case, whatever project management tasks that might be required will be performed by the ScrumMaster and the Product Owner.

[4] Highsmith, Jim, *Agile Project Management—Creating Innovative Products*, New York: Addison-Wesley, 2010, p. 125

- On larger more complex projects requiring multiple teams, there may be a need for more of a higher-level methodology that includes a project management approach that is not defined by Scrum.

You won't find much prescriptive direction to define how agile project management should be performed. It would be inconsistent with agile to define a project management approach that was overly prescriptive. The approach that is typically taken with agile methodologies is to focus on understanding the principles and leave it somewhat up to the individual implementing the principles to interpret how those principles should be implemented in a given situation.

Agile Project Management Principles

There are a number of principles of an agile project that dramatically change the project management role. Many of these principles can also be used in a hybrid agile approach to enhance project agility.

Rolling Wave Planning

Most agile methodologies emphasize the concept of taking a "just-in-time" approach to planning and don't attempt to do most of the planning at the front end of the project. The front-end planning that is normally done is somewhat minimized and a lot of the planning that might normally be done in the front end of the project is deferred until later in the project and done collaboratively by the team. The level of detail in agile planning may also be at different levels of detail based on the time horizon and level of risk associated with the effort being planned.

General Rules

The following practices can be applied to any project (either agile or traditional):

1. Instead of doing a completely detailed plan upfront in the project, limit the upfront planning to the minimum effort required to define and plan the project.
   - Use a risk-and-value-based approach to determine what level of upfront planning is appropriate. Ask the question "What's the risk in deferring some planning until later in the project and what's the value to be gained by doing it upfront versus deferring that planning and decision making?"
   - The decision to choose an appropriate level of planning for the project should be made jointly with the project sponsors and stakeholders. Project sponsors and stakeholders should agree that the planning approach is acceptable.

2. Break up the functionality in the project as much as possible into iterations and prioritize the requirements to ensure that the most important functionality is addressed as early as possible. Defer detailed planning for each iteration as much as possible and use a just-in-time planning approach for each iteration as the project progresses.

Customer Collaboration

Agile methodologies are heavily based on customer collaboration and expect the customer to play a very active role in defining and managing the project requirements as the project progresses, and the customer should feel just as responsible for producing a successful result as the development team. In a Scrum project, for example, the role of the Product Owner represents the voice of the customer and is expected to provide overall direction to guide the project toward producing the value to satisfy customer needs.

General Rules

The following practices can be applied to any project (either agile or traditional):

1. Design the project methodology to include as much customer collaboration as possible. The actual amount of customer collaboration will depend on several factors:
   - The need for ongoing customer collaboration as the project progresses, which will generally be a function of the uncertainty in the requirements
   - The willingness and ability of the customer to provide ongoing collaborative input and to share responsibility for project direction
2. Define the approach for planning, requirements definition, and change management to be consistent with the level of customer collaboration.

Collective Ownership

Agile methodologies emphasize empowered, self-organizing teams and "collective ownership":

- In traditional development models, responsibility is typically split among multiple functional organizations (development, QA, etc.) with a project manager who is responsible for coordinating and integrating the overall effort.
- In an agile model, people are assigned to the team for the duration of the project, and the team as a whole is expected to take collective ownership of delivering the solution.

The role of the project manager shifts to more of a facilitation role than an authoritative, ownership role, with a much higher level of delegation of responsibility to the team.

General Rules

The following practices can be applied to any project (either agile or traditional):

1. Use as much empowerment as possible to develop a sense of collective ownership by the project team based on a number of factors:
   - The need for project control
   - The organizational culture of the company
   - The capability of the team to take an active role in decision making
2. Create strong teamwork among everyone on the development team and try to preserve the continuity of the individuals assigned to the team as much as possible.

Emphasis on Validation over Verification

For many years, the project management and quality management professions have differentiated "verification" and "validation" of customer requirements:

- **Verification** means that the product has been determined to meet all documented requirements and specifications—"Is the product right?"
- **Validation** means that the product meets the customer need that it was intended to fill—"Is it the right product?"

Traditional project management approaches have put a heavier emphasis on "verification" as opposed to "validation." In many traditional projects, there is extensive verification testing against documented requirements, but validation testing is normally limited to beta testing and/or acceptance testing, which is typically done just before the product is ready for final release. Finding out that the product doesn't really meet user needs at that point can be disastrous. Agile methodologies avoid this problem by putting a much higher level of emphasis on validating that the product meets user needs much earlier in the development cycle by engaging the user much more directly in the design and development effort as it progresses. A limited acceptance test of each feature is normally performed by the Product Owner at the end of each iteration.

This shift in emphasis significantly changes the approach to project management to put more emphasis on satisfying customer needs early in the project rather than relying heavily on traditional forms of beta testing and acceptance testing at the very end of the project to validate that the product meets customer needs.

General Rules

The following practices can be applied to any project (either agile or traditional):

1. Use an iterative approach for developing functionality incrementally to get user feedback and input as early as possible and develop an emphasis on

early validation of product functionality based on active user collaboration and engagement as much as possible.

2. Plan for and gain support from the user community for active participation in the project as it progresses to provide validation of functionality as it is produced if possible.

Fail Early, Fail Often, and Continuous Improvement

Agile approaches are based on the philosophy of "fail early and fail often" from the Toyota Production System. Breaking up the project into short iterations, developing and implementing highly automated tests as the project progresses, and using continuous integration to ensure that all software is compatible makes it possible to detect problems and take corrective action as early as possible. The iterative approach also makes it possible to experiment with different approaches to satisfy customer needs in environments with high levels of uncertainty.

All agile methodologies also put a strong emphasis on continuous improvement, and that is one of the real benefits of agile methodologies:

- Because the development cycles are short, learning and adjustments to the process can happen rapidly as the project progresses rather than waiting till the end of the project for a postmortem.
- Also, because the processes are more flexible and adaptive, changes to the development and project management processes in response to lessons learned can also happen quickly.

General Rules

The following practices can be applied to any project (either agile or traditional):

1. Avoid the use of rigidly defined processes that do not provide a capability for customizing and improving the process.
2. Use short iterative processes as much as possible to recognize problems early and take corrective action.
3. Create a "learning environment" with an emphasis on continuous improvement. Emphasize transparency to openly recognize problems and opportunities for improvement as they occur, and use root cause analysis as needed to develop systemic solutions to prevent problems from recurring.
4. Encourage project teams to customize processes as needed to fit their projects and to continuously improve the processes. (Fit the process to the project rather than forcing the project to fit the process)
5. Train project teams as needed to provide them with a sufficient level of skill to continuously improve processes and provide coaching and mentoring as needed to help successfully implement this approach.

Agile Project Management Techniques

This section discusses some commonly used agile project management techniques that can also be applied to a hybrid project management approach.

Daily Standup Meetings

A technique commonly used in many agile methodologies is daily standup meetings. These are typically very quick and focused status meetings for everyone on the team to check in with each other. They are typically limited to the direct project team only, and each member of the team answers several questions such as:

- What did I accomplish yesterday?
- What will I do today?
- What obstacles are impeding my progress?

The daily standup meetings are typically done standing up so that they will be short in duration. Limiting the focus of these meetings to only a few key questions also keeps the meetings very focused and short. These meetings also serve to build and sustain the unity of the team.

Daily standup meetings are a good practice that can be applied to any project (agile or traditional):

- They are a good way of developing a very fast-paced approach for making progress quickly.
- They provide a good way of keeping everyone in the project engaged and focused on results.
- They are also excellent for team building.

Consensus Building

Agile methodologies are based heavily on facilitation and consensus building among the team on a particular topic. Getting real consensus is important and requires some skill. Many times, a project manager will ask for agreement and not really get a sense of real commitment. How often have you seen people nod or say nothing in a meeting and everyone assumes that implies complete consensus? Agile approaches put an emphasis on developing solid, unequivocal consensus among everyone on the team.

A commonly used technique that I like is called the "fist of five" approach. A facilitator leads the discussion and asks for consensus among the members of the team. Each person on the team holds up some number of fingers to indicate consensus. The following is one variation of the meaning of hand signals used. (There are many other variations):

1. "One finger = serious concerns that have not been heard or addressed
2. Two fingers = still have unaddressed concerns

> 3. Three fingers = consent with major reservation
> 4. Four fingers = consent with slight reservation
> 5. Five fingers = full consent
>
> Holding up zero fingers constitutes a Fist Block which is the strongest form of dissent"[5]

If the group is not entirely in consensus (everyone holding up five fingers), the facilitator then leads further discussion to attempt to reach full consensus. This is also a good approach that can be used for consensus building on any project (either agile or traditional).

Timeboxing

Many agile methodologies advocate "timeboxing." Timeboxing is the practice of fixing the end date of an iteration and not allowing it to change. The lengths of timeboxes are set based on the velocity of the team and are not necessarily equal, although fixed iteration lengths are generally promoted.

Rather than setting the length of an iteration based on implementing a certain amount of functionality in the iteration (scopeboxing), the timeboxing technique fixes the length of the iteration and the team determines how much functionality can be delivered in that fixed length of time. Once the functionality to be included in a given iteration is determined, it will not normally be changed; however, the detailed requirements associated with the functionality will be defined as the iteration progresses.

> "There are many advantages to timeboxing. These include:
>
> - Focus—So many of us struggle with focus. We lose focus, we get interrupted, and we make lists and plan out our weekends instead of work. All this lost focus when we should be working. The great advantage of timeboxing is you learn how to focus your attention on the job at hand for the specified period of time. If this is a challenge, you can start small (say, 10 minutes of focused work) and work up to 30 minutes blocks of time or whatever will work for you. Once you gain the focus, you find that your productivity increases ten-fold.
> - Increased productivity—When you are working on an open-ended job, using the timeboxing concept will increase your productivity in ways you never imagined. When you set a timer and work diligently and in a focused manner on only the task you have identified, you work smarter and harder, and you get more done.
> - Realization of time spent—When you use time blocking to get a job done, you realize how much time you might normally waste when

---

[5] "Fist of Five," http://cgi.stanford.edu/~group-synergy/pmwiki/index.php?n=Main.FistOfFive

> working. If you set a timer for 5 minutes, and work hard for only those 5 minutes, you might get the same amount of work done that you might previously have done in 20 minutes.
>
> - Time available—Timeboxing makes you consciously aware of something you previously weren't consciously aware of—how much time you can give to a particular project. Once you get comfortable with the concept, you realize you have more time than you thought. You get more done. And that brings us back to the point—your productivity increases.
>
> Using timeboxing can help workers focus more on the job at hand, get more done and ultimately feel more accomplished at what they are doing"[6]

Timeboxing addresses two common productivity issues:

- **Parkinson's Law** says that *"Work expands so as to fill the time available for its completion"*[7]. Fixing the time allowed eliminates wasted slack time that might be built into a scope-boxing approach
- **The Student Syndrome** "refers to the phenomenon that many people will start to fully apply themselves to a task just at the last possible moment after a deadline. This leads to wasting any buffers built into individual task duration estimates."[8]

Timeboxing can be applied to traditional projects as well as agile projects—it's a good development practice to keep a sustained pace of effort, but it is highly dependent on the culture and style of the organization.

Agile Project Management Models

A project management model for agile methodologies is needed in many cases to wrap around the lower-level technical practices and iteration management layers to provide a more robust way of delivering large, complex solutions particularly those involving multiple agile teams. There are a variety of ways of providing this functionality.

Scrum-of-Scrums Approach

One approach for managing projects requiring multiple teams is a "Scrum-of-Scrums" approach. A "Scrum-of-Scrums" is a master overall Scrum team that coordinates the work of a number of other teams. It is made up of representatives

---

[6] "Timeboxing," www.agilehardware.com/pages/Timeboxing.html

[7] "Parkinson's Law," http://en.wikipedia.org/wiki/Parkinson's_Law

[8] "Student Syndrome," http://en.wikipedia.org/wiki/Student_syndrome

from each of the other teams. There are different approaches for determining who should represent each individual scrum team in the Scrum-of-Scrums meeting:

> "Since the Scrum team is facilitated by the ScrumMaster, you would expect the ScrumMaster to attend the Scrum of Scrums meeting or, in his absence, the Product Owner. Well, the advice is different—a member of the team should attend the Scrum on behalf of the team, and this can be any team member. It follows from the above that since any team member can attend, the member who is attending the Scrum of Scrums can keep on changing after every few meetings. However, it is not a total free for all, sending the person who will be best able to project the current position of the team; such as a tester when the team is in the testing phase; or a designer when the project is in the initial design phase. This also means that the Scrum of Scrums can be attended by the ScrumMaster as well."[9]

An overall ScrumMaster acts as the facilitator for the Scrum-of-Scrums meeting. The frequency of the Scrum-of-Scrums meetings is also a variable. The individual scrum teams meet daily; however, it may not be necessary for the scrum-of-scrum meetings to also happen daily. The Scrum-of-Scrums approach provides a basic coordination mechanism for overall project planning and management and resolving any cross-team issues and dependencies that need to be resolved; however, it may need to be extended to include other project management practices on large complex projects.

Agile Project Management (APM) Model

Jim Highsmith[10] has proposed an Agile Project Management (APM) model as shown in Figure 6.3.

Each of the phases in the APM model is described in the following sections:

1. Envision

   The objective of the Envision Phase is to determine the product vision and product objectives and constraints, the project community, and how the team will work together. In many cases, it is useful to document the results of this effort in a "Project Vision" document:

   > - "What is the customer's product vision?
   > - What are the key capabilities required in the product?
   > - What are the project's business objectives?

---

[9] "Scrum of Scrums—A Brief Explanation and Some Details", http://learnsoftwareprocesses.com/2010/03/02/scrum-of-scrums-a-brief-definition-and-some-details/

[10] Highsmith, Jim, *Agile Project Management—Creating Innovative Products*, New York: Addison-Wesley, 2010, p. 82

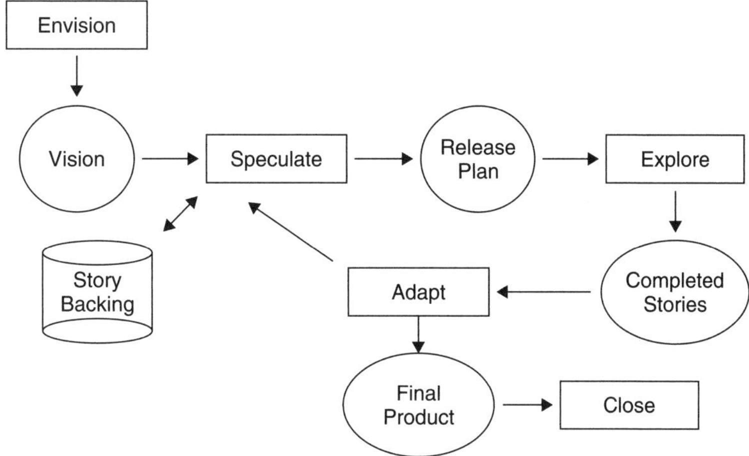

Figure 6.3 Agile Project Management (APM) model

> - What are the product's quality objectives?
> - What are the project constraints (scope, schedule, cost)
> - Who are the right participants to include in the project community?
> - How will the team deliver the product (approach)?"[11]

2. Speculate
The objective of the Speculate Phase is to develop a plan for how the vision will be delivered. The plan might be based on releases, features, or capabilities. The features and capabilities might be expressed in a variety of different forms such as user stories but will typically be limited only to high-level descriptions sufficient to identify what is required and develop a rough estimate of the level of effort associated with it. These features and capabilities will normally become the "Product Backlog" and will be elaborated into further detail later. This phase is equivalent to release planning in Scrum, and it will be revisited after the completion of each iteration (Explore/Adapt Phase) to redefine and reprioritize the Product Backlog and Release Plan based on the results of the previous iteration:

> "The Speculate Phase consists of:
> - Gathering the initial broad requirements for the product
> - Defining the workload as a backlog of product features
> - Creating a iterative, feature-based release plan

[11] Highsmith, Jim, *Agile Project Management—Creating Innovative Products*, New York: Addison-Wesley, 2010, p. 83

> - Incorporating risk mitigation strategies into the plan
> - Estimating project costs and generating other required administrative and financial information"[12]

3. Explore
   The objective of the Explore Phase is to plan and deliver running, tested features (stories) in a short iteration. That effort consists of further defining the detailed requirements associated with each feature or story as well as designing developing, and testing, the functionality required.
4. Adapt
   The objective of the Adapt Phase is to review the delivered results, the current situation, and the team's performance and adapt as necessary. The key questions to be asked in the Adapt Phase are:

   > - "Is value, in the form of a releasable product being delivered?
   > - Is the quality goal of building a reliable, adaptable product being met?
   > - Is the project progressing satisfactorily within acceptable constraints?
   > - Is the team adapting effectively to changes imposed by management, customers, or technology?"[13]

5. Close
   Conclude the project, pass along key learnings, and celebrate.

The APM model has some elements of a traditional plan-driven model wrapped around an agile approach:

1. The level of upfront planning is very limited similar to Scrum but goes beyond what would normally be found in some other agile approaches like Extreme Programming (XP). For example:
   - The first phase is called "Envision," which is similar to a concept phase or charter definition phase of a traditional project. It goes beyond the level of planning that might be found in many agile projects; however, the approach for performing this effort may not be as formal and complete as a traditional development methodology.
   - The goal of this phase is limited to providing a vision for the product and the project to a sufficient extent for the project to move forward. It addresses only the important elements that are essential to define upfront and defers further detailed planning until later in the project. In a traditional project methodology, the goal of this phase might be to gain

---

[12] Highsmith, Jim, *Agile Project Management—Creating Innovative Products*, New York: Addison-Wesley, 2010, p. 84

[13] Highsmith, Jim, *Agile Project Management—Creating Innovative Products*, New York: Addison-Wesley, 2010, p. 84

formal approval for starting the project; in a more agile environment, the goal might be more of doing a sufficient level of due diligence to define the product vision and product approach to get everyone on the team on board and engaged in the effort.

- The second phase is called "Speculate," and that word was intentionally chosen to indicate that a lot of what is done at that point is "speculation" and is subject to further refinement and change as the project progresses. This phase might be compared to a requirements definition phase of a traditional project with a couple of very important differences:
  - Requirements definition is limited to high-level requirements only, and more detailed requirements are deferred till a later stage in the project.
  - It is understood that the requirements are subject to change as the project progresses.

  A traditional development process might attempt to define rock-solid, detailed requirements upfront that are not subject to change, but that approach is just not realistic in many cases. Agile methodologies accept the futility of attempting to do that and openly acknowledge that the requirements are volatile and subject to change. Of course, that might mean that it is more difficult to accurately define the costs and schedule for the project upfront, but that might be an acceptable tradeoff.
- The third phase is called "Explore," which is also aptly named to provide the sense that detailed requirements will be based on an "exploration" process, and might involve some trial-and-error experimentation. This phase is very similar to an iterative development approach that would be found in an agile project, and it also accepts the notion that it might be difficult to define the exact detailed requirements for the development effort prior to starting the design.

2. The phases in the life-cycle model are not as crisply defined as a traditional life-cycle model, the level of formality associated with phase transitions may not be as formal, and it is understood that phases might be repeated if necessary.
3. There is more adaptivity built into the process than in a traditional development process. It accepts the notion that the process will be somewhat fluid and will be adapted as it progresses and that the product design will also be adapted as the project progresses to ensure that it meets the user needs.

Further details on this life-cycle model can be found in the Jim Highsmith's book[14].

[14] Highsmith, Jim, *Agile Project Management—Creating Innovative Products*, New York: Addison-Wesley, NY 2010

AGILE AND *A GUIDE TO PROJECT MANAGEMENT BODY OF KNOWLEDGE (PMBOK® GUIDE)*

Many project managers may be wondering "Where does *A Guide to Project Management Body of Knowledge* (*PMBOK® Guide*) fit into all of this?" The *PMBOK® Guide* is a well-recognized source of knowledge regarding Project Management practices and processes. The latest edition of the *PMBOK® Guide* carefully states how it is intended to be used:

> "The *PMBOK® Guide* provides guidelines for managing individual projects. It defines project management and related concepts and describes the project management life cycle and related processes.... As a foundational reference; this standard is neither complete nor all-inclusive. This standard is a guide rather than a methodology. One can use different methodologies and tools to implement this framework."[15]

Most of the practices described in the *PMBOK® Guide* are general enough to be applied to any project (agile or traditional) but the *PMBOK® Guide* has its roots in traditional plan-driven development processes and typically has been interpreted in that context. It probably needs much more interpretation to apply to an agile project.

Brian Bozzuto gave an interesting presentation at the PMI® Global Conference in Orlando in 2009 on how agile principles relate to the practices and processes defined in the *PMBOK® Guide*. Brian characterizes a perceived disconnect between the two as "dwelling on stereotypes." He presents a commonly held stereotype perception of the *PMBOK® Guide* project management style as:

> - "Too much paperwork
> - Lots of checklists
> - Cumbersome processes
> - The process manages you instead of you managing the process"[16]

He presents a commonly held stereotype perception of agile as the exact opposite:

> - "Throw process out
> - Chaotic, no control

[15] Highsmith, Jim, *Agile Project Management—Creating Innovative Products*, New York: Addison-Wesley, 2010

[16] *A Guide to the Project Management Body of Knowledge*, Fourth Edition, Newtown Square, PA, PMI, 2008, pp. 3–4,

- Won't work for complex projects
- Unprofessional"[17]

Brian is right, these are mostly stereotypical perceptions; however, in each of these stereotypical perceptions, there is some reality. There are a number of factors that have probably contributed to these stereotypical perceptions:

1. Implementation versus Intent
   To understand these differences in perception, we need to separate the principles and practices behind PMBOK® from how they are actually implemented in practice. Methodologies and practices sometimes get a bad reputation because of faulty implementation and, in many cases; it's the implementation that's at fault and not necessarily the intent of the methodology or practice itself. Both traditional plan-driven and agile methodologies have gotten a bad reputation in some situations because of poor implementation:
   - Traditional plan-driven methodologies have gotten a bad reputation in some cases because people have gone overboard with documentation and bureaucratic controls instead of taking an intelligent approach to tailor the level of documentation and control to the project and business environment. There's nothing about traditional plan-driven methodologies that prevents doing sensible things to limit the amount of control and documentation to reasonable levels.
   - At the other extreme, agile methodologies have gotten a bad reputation in some cases because people have tried to jump too quickly into execution of the project with little or no upfront planning. Again, there is nothing in most agile methodologies that prevents using good judgment to determine what amount of upfront planning is reasonable.

   In both of these cases, the fault may be more in the implementation than it is with the methodology, principles, or practices, but sometimes people blame the methodology, principles, or practices nonetheless. The *PMBOK® Guide* principles and practices have taken on a strong association with traditional methodologies and in some cases those principles and practices have been poorly implemented.
2. Difference in Generative versus Prescriptive Approaches
   Agile principles and practices and PMBOK® are based on two very different philosophies. Agile typically provides some very simple value-oriented principles without being prescriptive and leaves a lot up to the person implementing the methodology to determine how it should be applied in

[17] Bozzuto, Brian, "Aligning PMBOK Agile," PMI Global Conference, Orlando 2009, http://agile.vc.pmi.org/Community/Spotlight/tabid/876/vw/1/ItemID/122/Default.aspx

a given situation. It expects the person implementing the methodology to "tailor it up" by adding additional layers that may be needed in a given situation. The whole methodology is designed to be very flexible and adaptive.

> "One of the key concepts of agile project management is that the practices, when driven by guiding principles, are generative, not prescriptive. Prescriptive methodologies attempt to describe every activity a team should do. The problem with prescriptive methodologies is that people get lost. They have much to choose from and so little guidance as to applicability that they have trouble eliminating extraneous practices from their projects.
>
> A set of generative practices is a minimal set that works well as a system. It doesn't prescribe everything a team needs to do, but it identifies those practices that are of high value and should be used on nearly every project.
>
> Starting with a minimal set of practices and judiciously adding others as needed has proven to be more effective than starting with comprehensive prescriptive practices and attempting to streamline them down to something usable (Boehm and Turner 2003). Agile methods don't attempt to prescribe everything that any development effort might need in thousands of pages of documentation . . . "[18]

In contrast, many traditional plan-driven methodologies and practices use a "tailor down" approach. The *PMBOK® Guide* is an example—you're expected to "tailor it down" by only taking the parts of it you need for a particular project and adapting those parts to the project as necessary. It errs on the side of overspecifying what to do where agile approaches typically err on the side of underspecifying what to do—version 4.0 of the *PMBOK® Guide* is almost 500 pages long. It is clearly intended only as just a set of tools, and you're free to use those tools as just guidelines and apply your own interpretations to them as necessary; however, the way the *PMBOK® Guide* is written, it is very easy to interpret it as a very authoritative and prescriptive reference source, which it was not intended to be.

> "When agile methods employ documentation, they emphasize doing the minimum essential amount. Unfortunately, most plan-driven methods suffer from a "tailoring-down" syndrome, which is sadly reinforced by most government procurement regulations. These plan-driven methods are developed by experts, who want them to

[18] Bozzuto, Brian, "Aligning PMBOK Agile," PMI Global Conference, Orlando 2009, http://agile.vc.pmi.org/Community/Spotlight/tabid/876/vw/1/ItemID/122/Default.aspx

> provide users with guidance for most all foreseeable situations. The experts make them comprehensive, but "tailorable-down" for less critical or complex situations. The experts understand tailoring the methods and often provide guidelines and examples for others to use.
>
> Unfortunately, less expert and less self-confident developers, customers, and managers tend to see the full-up set of plans, specifications, and standards as a security blanket... and the least-expert participant generally drives the project to use the full-up set of documents rather than an appropriate subset. While the non-experts rarely read the ever-growing stack of documents, they will maintain a false sense of security in the knowledge that they have followed best practice to ensure project predictability and control. Needless to say, the expert methodologists are then frustrated with how their tailorable methods are used—and usually verbally abused—by developers and acquirers alike."[19]

Agile methodologies such as Scrum have been criticized for being "flaccid" and lacking substance in a number of important areas, particularly relating to higher-level project management practices.[20] On the other hand, the *PMBOK® Guide* and many traditional plan-driven practices and methodologies have been criticized as being too prescriptive. The ideal approach is generally always in the middle of these two extremes.

3. Humanistic Value Orientation versus Process Orientation
Another key difference is in the orientation toward humanistic values versus a process orientation. the *PMBOK® Guide* does not dwell heavily on the softer side of project management while agile principles are much more direct about addressing the softer, human side of people management. For example:

- Chapter 9 in the *PMBOK® Guide* talks about "Project Human Resource Management." This is a subject that should legitimately rely heavily on principles and training and is very difficult to get across with a detailed, step-by-step process view of how to do "human resource management."
- The *PMBOK® Guide* version 4.0 has added Appendix G, "Interpersonal Skills," to address some of topics in this area; however, it is a much more integral part of the agile approach as opposed to being added on as an appendix.

Of course, a good project manager knows enough to implement a people-oriented style of management even if the *PMBOK® Guide* doesn't say

[19] Highsmith, Jim, *Agile Project Management—Creating Innovative Products*, New York: Addison-Wesley, 2009, p. 7

[20] Boehm, Barry and Turner, Richard, *Balancing Agility and Discipline—A Guide for the Perplexed*," New York: Addison-Wesley, 2003, pp. 36–37

anything specifically about it, but agile principles have gone much further in specifying that as a key value behind the Agile Manifesto:

> "Build projects around motivated individuals. Give them the environment and support they need, and trust them to get the job done"[21]

The difference behind these two approaches is:

- The *PMBOK® Guide* started out with a strong process orientation and has begun grafting and integrating a more humanistic, people orientation with the process orientation, but the emphasis is still primarily on process with a secondary emphasis on people.
- The agile principles have started out with a strong humanistic people orientation as the central foundation of the agile movement—one of the key elements of the original Agile Manifesto was valuing "individuals and interactions over processes and tools."

These two approaches are beginning to converge, but it will take time to fully merge these ideologies:

- Agile approaches have matured significantly over the past 5–10 years and have increasingly recognized the need to adopt a strong process discipline on top of a strong people orientation
- The *PMBOK® Guide* has progressively begun to build more of a recognition of the softer side of project management and a people orientation into the PMBOK® principles and practices (Appendix G, which has recently been added to the latest version of the *PMBOK® Guide* is an example).

4. Emphasis on Upfront Planning and Control versus Responsiveness to Change

Another major difference between the *PMBOK® Guide* practices and agile methodologies is that the *PMBOK® Guide* has historically been heavily associated with a plan-driven orientation with an emphasis on control and naturally puts a lot of emphasis on controlling and managing the scope of a project. This emphasis on planning and control is not necessarily inherent in the *PMBOK® Guide*, but it is a common interpretation of how it is applied in practice. Controlling the scope of a project is not a critical part of an agile project—agile approaches are based on openly encouraging and welcoming change from stakeholders during the course of the project. That is a fundamental difference in philosophy.

- When business requirements are very uncertain and very subject to change as the project progresses, control is probably a "mirage"—even the best planned projects may appear to be under control but might

---

[21] Schwaber, Ken, Presentation to Open Space 2010, Boston, MA, April 2010

change so frequently that any semblance of real control is illusory. In these situations, it may be futile to attempt to achieve a high level of control and a balanced approach may be needed that mixes the right amount of control to manage against a plan with the right amount of agility to adapt to new and changing business requirements as the project progresses.

Achieving that kind of balance may require some rethinking, and there are clearly some tradeoffs that need to be considered. For example, successfully achieving business outcomes might mean developing a more collaborative approach throughout the development effort and allowing more business input to the development effort as it progresses—that may impact predictability and control of cost and schedule goals, but that may be a very acceptable tradeoff. There is nothing in the *PMBOK® Guide* that prevents you from making those tradeoffs but, on the other hand, there is not much that specifically encourages doing it either.

- At the other extreme, agile methodologies may encourage project teams to jump very quickly into executing projects with only a very limited amount of upfront planning and that can lead to an entirely different set of problems:
  - Because of the limited upfront planning, the initial cost and schedule estimates for completing the project may not be very reliable until the project is relatively far along, and that can lead to very major and unexpected surprises.
  - Because an incremental and iterative approach is typically used with agile methodologies to define the solution, the architectural approach sometimes isn't completely defined upfront and evolves throughout the duration of the project. As a result, extensive rework might be required.

In many of these situations, the failure wasn't so much the fault of the methodology or practices as it was just poor implementation. There's absolutely nothing about agile or non-agile methodologies that prevents using good judgment to tailor the methodology to the business environment as well as the risks and complexity of the project. For example, there is nothing that says a Scrum project can't include:

- A reasonable level of upfront planning to estimate costs and schedules to whatever level of accuracy that is desired as well as ongoing revisions of those estimates as the project progresses; however, many extreme proponents of agile methodologies have made the assumption that planning and management of costs and schedules is no longer relevant.
- A reasonable level of architectural planning where that makes sense and also revising and refining that architectural plan as the project progresses.

Merging PMBOK® Thinking and Agile Thinking

On the surface, the processes and practices in the *PMBOK® Guide* and agile principles and practices may seem like "oil and vinegar"—it's not obvious how you mix them together, but they actually can be complementary to each other. It will take time to figure out how to really blend these different approaches together. In the meantime, it will be up to individual project managers to be aware of these two different ideologies and use their own judgment to blend them together in the right proportions to fit the needs of the projects they are managing. Michelle Sliger's book *The Software Project Manager's Bridge to Agility*[22] provides a much more detailed analysis of comparing the sections of PMBOK against agile methodologies.

---

[22] "Principles Behind the Agile Manifesto," http://agilemanifesto.org/principles.html

CHAPTER 7

FUNDAMENTAL PRINCIPLES BEHIND SDLC MODELS

Some project managers make the mistake of taking a particular methodology and applying it mechanically "by the book." They might get lost in the mechanics of implementing a particular methodology (e.g., Scrum, Waterfall) and lose sight of the basic principles that underlie most software development methodologies.

> "Principles are guiding ideas and insights about a discipline, while practices are what you actually do to carry out principles.[1]
>
> Principles are universal, but it is not always easy to see how they apply to particular environments. Practices, on the other hand, give specific guidance on what to do, but they need to be adapted to the domain. We believe that there is no such thing as a "best" practice; practices must take the context into account. In fact, the problems that arise when applying metaphors from other disciplines to software development are often the result of trying to transfer the practices rather than the principles of the other discipline....
>
> Practices for one domain will not necessarily apply to other domains. Principles; however, are broadly applicable across domains as long as the guiding principles are translated into appropriate practices for each domain."[2]

Understanding the principles behind the methodology at a deeper level allows a project manager to:

- Select the right methodology for the project and business environment
- Apply the methodology more intelligently and customize it as needed to fit the risks and complexity of the project

There is a concept called "Shu Ha Ri" that originated in aikido martial arts that has been used very widely to illustrate this learning progression:

> "**Shu -** Imitation. You do something by copying someone else. You don't question it. The teacher gives you a prescriptive solution to a problem

[1] Senge, Peter, *The Fifth Discipline*, New York, NY, p. 373

[2] Poppendiek, Tom and Mary, *Lean Software Development—An Agile Toolkit*, New York: Addison-Wesley, 2003, pg xxiv

> that covers most of your needs. It may not be the most efficient or best solution, but it is simple to learn and covers most of the situations you encounter."
>
> "**Ha** - Understanding. You start to see the reason behind what the teacher taught you. You modify it to still fit the core philosophy, but streamline it for you. You also start to see that the solution doesn't solve every problem and therefore seek your teacher for new ideas and solutions, or you might even seek other teachers for solutions."
>
> "**Ri** - Mastery. You take everything you learn and apply it at will. You solve problems by blending solutions without even thinking. When someone asks what you just did is called, there is no name because you adapted a new solution on the fly. It just worked in that situation. Your own experiences outweigh your formal teachings."[3]

This chapter discusses some of those fundamental principles behind selecting and optimizing a methodology for a project. These principles apply to both agile and traditional methodologies.

This is not meant to be a complete and comprehensive coverage of all of the principles and factors that impact the design, selection, and customization of a software development life cycle (SDLC). The important thing is to adopt a "systems thinking" approach to begin to see the principles and factors that influence those decisions. It is also important to recognize that many of the principles and factors discussed in this section are not independent and interact with each other. For example, if you only considered an optimum method for developing requirements, you might choose to use a more adaptive model that delays the definition of detailed requirements until later in the development effort; however, from a risk management perspective, that may or may not be the best decision.

The use and selection of these principles and factors is fairly subjective and requires a lot of judgment, and the material in this chapter is highly simplified to make it easier to use. There are also different levels of principles. For anyone interested in a deeper study of these factors and principles, Don Reinertsen's book *The Principles of Product Flow* has a very detailed and quantitative model of principles to be considered in optimizing a product development process.[4]

GENERAL SOFTWARE DEVELOPMENT LIFE CYCLE (SDLC) CONSIDERATIONS

Some people have a misconception of what a software development life cycle (SDLC) is. When you say the word "SDLC" to some people, the first thing that

---

[3] "What is Shu Ha Ri?", http://agile-commentary.blogspot.com/2008/10/what-is-shu-ha-ri.html

[4] Reinertsen, Don, *The Principles of Product Development Flow*, Redondo Beach, CA: Celeritas Publishing, 2009

comes to their mind is a rigidly defined model for executing a project, such as the Waterfall model. For that reason, there is a tendency to do one of two things:

- Attempt to implement a standard "textbook" life-cycle model by the book and follow it rigidly, or
- Reject the life-cycle model as being too rigid and complex and use no life-cycle model at all

Those two approaches can be equally problematic. It takes a lot more experience to understand the principles behind an SDLC, pick the right SDLC for a particular project, and then tailor it, if necessary, to fit the risks and complexity of the project. This section discusses some of the most important principles to consider.

Flexibility versus Rigidity

Here are a couple of important principles:

1. **An SDLC process does not have to be rigidly defined**—An SDLC can be as flexible as you want it to be, but *even a flexible SDLC is a lot better than no SDLC at all*. Some companies make the mistake of defining an SDLC that is too rigid or unrealistic for people to really implement. It exists on paper, but no one really follows it. That situation isn't much better than having no SDLC at all.
2. **Even the milestones and deliverables inside of an SDLC process don't have to be rigidly followed**—Any SDLC should be implemented intelligently. For example, the project team might decide to skip completing a required artifact that might not be needed in a particular situation. There's nothing wrong with making that kind of decision if it is done based on an assessment of the risks and impact to the project and the appropriate stakeholders agree to that decision.

   Naturally, it takes some sophistication on the part of the project team to make good decisions like that—it requires an understanding of the principles behind the methodology and the purpose served by artifacts and other methodology requirements. There's a big difference between:

   - Pausing to make those decisions consciously and intelligently based on a good assessment of the risks and the impact of the decision with an appropriate level of review and approval and
   - Just "winging it" and skipping process requirements without giving it the appropriate level of thought

In general, there is a relationship between the rigidity of a process and the level of training required to perform the process. For example, you can create either:

- A very well-defined process that is intended to be followed by the book and doesn't require too much judgment and training, or

- A more loosely defined and/or flexible process that requires much more judgment and training to make the right decisions about how to implement the process

Training and process design should be consistent—for example, it would be a mistake to implement a very flexible and loosely defined process and not provide an appropriate level of training with it.

Repeatability is important and valuable; however, it has a direct relationship to the level of flexibility in a process:

- Having a defined process that is repeatable is valuable—an SDLC process that it is used effectively becomes a repository for preserving lessons learned on previous projects. If an SDLC process has proven successful on similar projects in the past, there is a higher probability that similar projects using the same process will also be successful
- However, the uniqueness of each project should always be considered. Here's an excellent quote from Robert Wysocki on this subject:

> "For years I have advocated that the approach to the project must be driven by the characteristics of the project. To reverse the order is to court disaster. I find it puzzling that we define a project as a unique experience that has never happened before and will never happen again under the same set of circumstances, but we make no assertion that the appropriate project management approach for these unique projects will also be unique. I would say that the project management approach is unique up to a point. Its uniqueness is constrained to using a set of validated and certified tools, templates and processes. To not establish such a boundary on how you can manage a project would be chaotic. Plus the organization could never be a learning organization when it comes to project management processes and practices."[5]

The key point is that the business culture and environment as well as the characteristics of the project should drive the methodology—it is a good thing to use a repeatable process, but you don't want to use a standard methodology without tailoring it or customizing it to fit with the project as needed. The level of customization and tailoring of projects will be dependent on several factors including:

- The organization's culture and need for control
- The level of training and sophistication of the project teams to make process customizations
- The need for customization based on differences in business environment and other unique factors associated with each project

---

[5] Wysocki, Robert, *Effective Project Management—Traditional, Agile, Extreme*, Hoboken, NJ: Wiley, New York, 2009, p. 304

It requires a balance—different organizations have different tolerance levels for "order versus chaos," and finding the right balance requires some skill:

- Too much order and lack of flexibility (forcing projects to fit repeatable methodologies when they don't really fit) can create an environment that stifles creativity and is too resistant to change.
- On the other extreme, a pure agile approach might tend more toward working on the "edge of chaos":

> "Agile project leaders help their team balance at the edge of chaos—some structure, but not too much; adequate documentation, but not too much; some upfront architectural work, but not too much. Finding these balance points is the 'art' of agile leadership. Although books like this can help leaders understand the issues and identify practices that help, only experience can refine a leader's art."[6]

Agile methodologies are also typically much less structured:

> "The idea of enough structure, but not too much, drives agile managers to continually ask the question, 'How little structure can I get away with?' Too much structure stifles creativity. Too little structure breeds inefficiency."[7]

Some organizations will have difficulty with the idea of working on the "edge of chaos" with a bare minimum of structure and control. Finding the right balance point is an important strategic decision for a company and, within an individual company, there may be some areas of the business that warrant a more agile approach and some areas that require a more controlled approach. Trying to use a standard methodology for all companies or even different business areas within the same company may overlook those needs for developing a more customized approach to better fit with the business environment.

Relationship of Training and Process Design

As previously mentioned, SDLC processes should be consistent with the skill level of the people who execute the process. In any SDLC process, there is a tradeoff between designing:

- A fairly well-defined process that doesn't require a high level of skill to execute, and
- A less-defined process that relies heavily on the person following the process to use good judgment to adapt it to a particular situation

---

[6] Highsmith, Jim, *Agile Project Management—Creating Innovative Products*, New York: Addison-Wesley, 2010, p. 50

[7] Highsmith, Jim, *Agile Project Management—Creating Innovative Products*, New York: Addison-Wesley, 2010

The first alternative requires less training and sophistication from the people who execute the process, while the second alternative relies very heavily on training and skills of the people performing the process to do the right thing without necessarily having explicit and well-defined direction.

Agile product development processes are much more adaptive and loosely defined, but naturally, that means that they rely heavily on a very highly skilled project team to use good judgment to execute the process effectively. That's a big dependency that needs to be understood—most agile methodologies are not likely to be successful if an attempt is made to apply the methodology with project teams that don't have the knowledge or skill to execute the project methodology effectively. It can take a significant amount of training, coaching, and mentoring to get an agile project team to a full level of proficiency.

The tradeoff is between:

- Making a significant investment in training, and, in return, developing very-high-performance teams that are highly adaptive and effective in a broad range of situations without requiring very explicitly defined processes and documentation
- Using less skilled teams and relying more heavily on detailed process requirements to ensure that the process is executed effectively

For example, a less-skilled team might require more detailed documentation as well as project reviews to validate the work that is being done while a higher-skilled team might be expected to take much more responsibility for more broadly defined tasks with less documentation and a more limited level of oversight and review. Another important consideration in agile projects is that agile project teams rely heavily on "collective ownership," where the team as a whole takes responsibility for its performance. That reduces the dependence somewhat on the skill of any one individual but also introduces some new skill requirements related to teamwork and collaboration.

Reliable versus Repeatable Processes

Very closely related to the role of training is the distinction between a reliable and a repeatable process. A repeatable process is typically not very adaptive and might have a very well-defined process associated with it. Success of the process is more dependent on the design of the process than it is on the skill of the individuals performing the process.

> "A repeatable process is one in which doing the same thing in the same way produces the same results. One that is reliable delivers regardless of impediments thrown in the way—reliability means constantly adapting to meet a goal."[8]

---

[8] Highsmith, Jim, *Agile Project Management—Creating Innovative Products*, New York: Addison-Wesley, 2010, p. 12

A repeatable process can be reliable provided that the impediments and adaptations that are required are limited, but when a significant number of impediments and adaptations are required, a repeatable process starts to break down and becomes unreliable, because it doesn't have the flexibility and adaptability designed into the process to handle that is needed for that kind of environment.

> "Confusion about reliable and repeatable has caused many organizations to pursue repeatable processes—very structured and precise—when exactly the opposite approach—mildly structured and flexible—works astonishingly better for new product and service development. If your goal is to deliver a product that meets a known and unchanging specification, then try a repeatable process. However, if your goal is to deliver a valuable product to a customer within some targeted boundaries, when change and deadlines are significant factors, then reliable agile processes work better."[9]

Traditional plan-driven methodologies are more repeatable and have a place where the level of uncertainty in the project is low and when the requirements can be defined with a high level of certainty early on in the project, but a much more adaptive approach is needed when the level of uncertainty is high and it's more difficult to define the requirements upfront:

- Using a repeatable process (where it is appropriate) has advantages—if the level of uncertainty is low, it can significantly reduce a number of risks in the project to follow a repeatable process that is well defined. It also can provide higher levels of efficiency where process adaptability and flexibility are not required.
- On the other hand, the level of uncertainty associated with projects can vary widely, and if the level of uncertainty in a project is high, a process that is more flexible and adaptive is typically a much better solution.

Reliability in an agile process comes primarily from the fact that the process is designed to be much more self-correcting. Because of the adaptive and iterative nature of agile methodologies, there is no assumption in an agile project that requirements are correct until they are actually validated with the user and that validation happens much earlier in the project at the end of each iteration. Traditional plan-driven methodologies make the assumption that requirements correctly and completely represent user needs as soon as they're signed off and that assumption may not be validated until the very end of the project when user acceptance testing is performed.

---

[9] Highsmith, Jim, *Agile Project Management—Creating Innovative Products*, New York: Addison-Wesley, 2010, p. 12

INTERRELATIONSHIP OF LIFE-CYCLE MODEL SELECTION FACTORS

The choice of a given type of SDLC is influenced by a number of interrelated factors as shown in Figure 7.1. Here are a few examples of these interrelationships:

- Project criticality and project risk impact the selection of a risk management approach (project risk is also impacted by the organizational culture and capabilities).
- The risk management approach, in turn, impacts the planning approach of whether the planning is done upfront or deferred.
- The planning approach is one of the factors that impact the selection of a life-cycle type.

The interaction of these various factors can be complex, and the interrelationships might change depending on the nature of the project and other factors. Each of these factors is discussed in more detail in the sections that follow.

REQUIREMENTS DEFINITION AND MANAGEMENT APPROACH

The method for capturing requirements probably has one of the biggest impacts on the choice of a particular SDLC. A key decision has to do with the level of uncertainty in the requirements and the tradeoffs associated with capturing some or all of the requirements upfront versus deferring some level of requirements definition until later in the project. For example, the Waterfall process attempts to define a significant portion of the requirements upfront prior to the start of any development effort and, in some cases, that may not be realistic.

> "Customers have a very difficult time visualizing from documents how a product will function, which is why in industry after industry companies have embraced modeling, simulations, and prototyping to improve the feedback loop from customers to the development teams."[10]

Even if it is realistic to do that,

- It may take a long time to do define all the requirements, and the sequential nature of the process will delay the start of any development until all requirements are defined. A more iterative process would allow breaking up the project into chunks and starting the development of some requirements much more quickly.

---

[10] Highsmith, Jim, *Agile Project Management—Creating Innovative Products*, New York: Addison-Wesley, 2010, p. 36

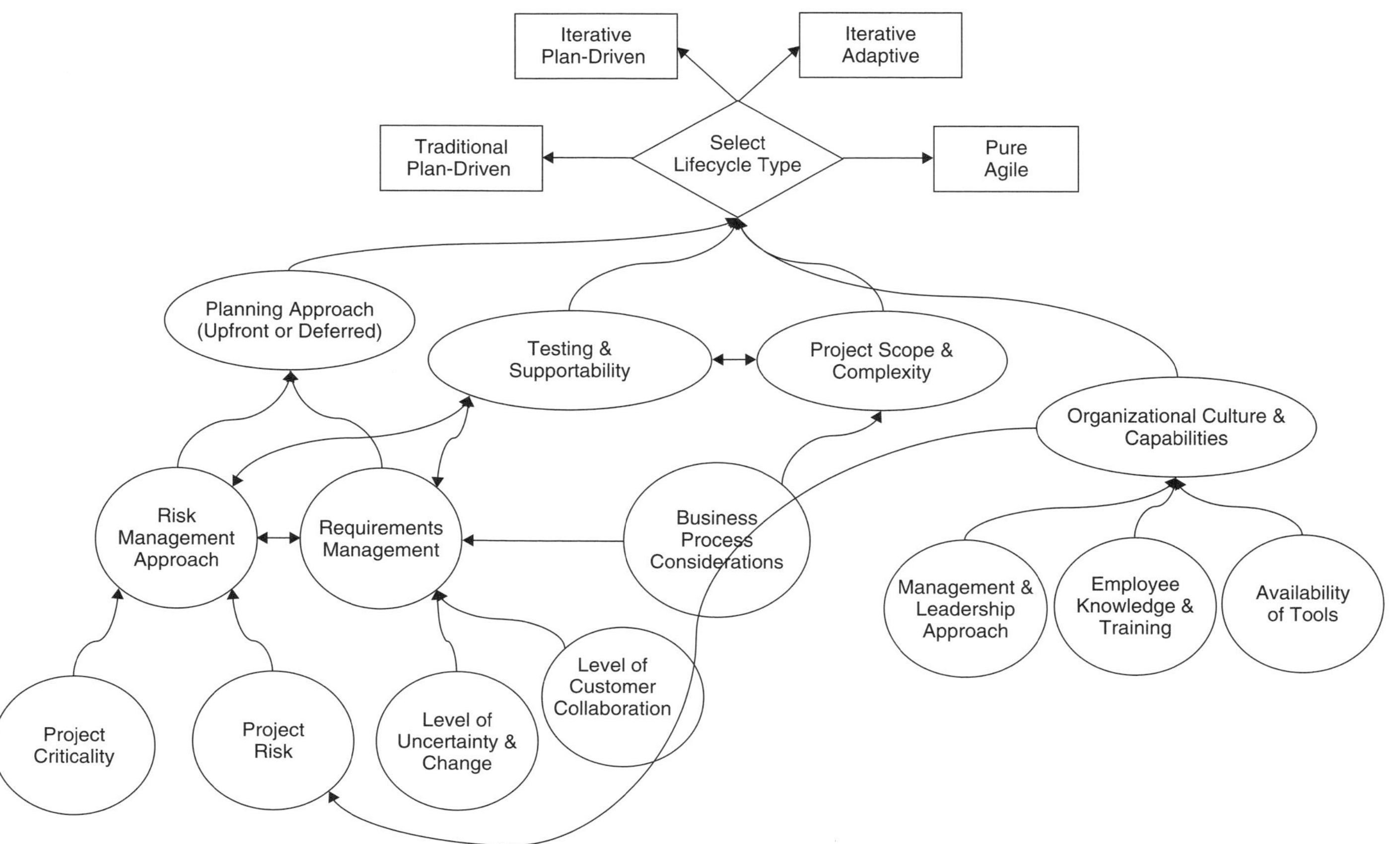

Figure 7.1 Interrelationship of life-cycle model selection factor

- Limited interaction with the development staff during the requirements definition process might lead to misunderstandings of the requirements and/or requirements that are not realistic to implement. More direct discussion with between the developers and the users as the product is being developed might eliminate some of these miscommunications.
- Speculation associated with attempting to define requirements that might be very uncertain might lead to unnecessary rework because sometimes that speculation will be wrong or inaccurate. Taking more of a just-in-time approach of defining the requirements closer to the point they are needed is likely to improve the reliability and accuracy of the requirements definition effort considerably.
- Changes in requirements while the project is in progress may cause a lot of unnecessary rework and replanning of the project to try to adjust to changes.

The big advantage of defining the requirements upfront (if it can be done) is that:

- It more clearly defines the scope of the effort, which may lead to more accurate plans and cost and schedule estimates, and it provides a better framework for defining what the architecture should be to fulfill those requirements.
- It also provides a much better capability to analyze the requirements for completeness and consistency prior to starting the design and that can be a very important factor in high-risk projects, where requirements traceability is an important consideration.

A compromise would be to define some (or most) of the high-level and more critical requirements upfront and defer completion of some of the more detailed requirements to the development effort.

- Agile approaches typically define only very high-level requirements upfront (vision and product backlog), define user stories for the product backlog prior to each release or iteration, and rely heavily on elaboration of the details of the user stories as they're developed in each iteration.
- Iterative approaches define more high-level requirements upfront and defer the definition of more detailed requirements for each iteration until they are required for that iteration.

Requirements elicitation and management is an art that can require a significant amount of skill to plan an approach that will be effective for capturing, analyzing, and managing the business requirements for a project. A good approach is to identify the best method for defining the requirements based on the uncertainty and complexity of the requirements and that will then become a major factor in determining the planning and overall project management approach for the overall project.

Business Process Considerations

An important factor to consider in requirements management is the interrelationship of the requirements to the business processes that the requirements support. In many cases, development of a new software application is an opportunity to redefine the business processes that are associated with the application. Sometimes companies fail to take the time to analyze requirements and processes to see if there's a better way of doing things from a business process perspective before starting the design of a new solution. Michael Hammer used to talk about "paving over the cow paths"—taking inefficient processes and simply automating them rather than using information technology to completely redefine and/or enable new ways of doing things.

One danger in agile methodologies is in jumping too quickly into the micro-level requirements and design without doing a sufficient level of upfront analysis of the business process and also identifying organizational changes that might be required to effectively implement a new system.

> "In looking at the focus of many agile methodologies, we may forget important history lessons from the dreaded traditional development and blithely aid our clients and customers by paving more cow paths. While the agile principle of early delivery of working software has created enormous benefits for many companies, there is an underlying assumption in many agile methods that customers and users have done their homework; that they:
>
> - Understand their business process,
> - Have done the necessary business process analysis and rationalization, and
> - Understand how automation might change their process.
>
> ... I am in no way advocating a return to the huge up-front requirements definition disasters of prior years, but I do believe that many development efforts could benefit from better business process (or product) understanding by the development team. Some degree of business process understanding, rationalization, and automation potential needs to be anticipated in early planning so that the later details, like features and use cases, can be put into context. Furthermore, business process design should be evolutionary, just like the software design: develop an initial business process framework or skeleton, implement both the software and the improved business processes incrementally, and then adapt both the process and the software."[11]

[11] Highsmith, Jim, "Paving Cowpaths," www.stickyminds.com/sitewide.asp?ObjectId=9226&Function=edetail&ObjectType=COL

It is always worthwhile to stop and question how much change in business processes might be associated with the development of a new application before getting too far into the development effort. If a substantial amount of business process reengineering is associated with the design and implementation of an application, it probably would be best to get that defined upfront for a couple of reasons:

- Attempting to do business process reengineering during the design and development process might lead to unnecessary churning, confusion, and rework for the development team.
- If the business leaders and the development team jump too quickly into the details of how the application is designed, they might overlook the big picture and miss opportunities for doing things completely differently from a business process perspective.

Requirements Complexity Considerations

In many cases, the importance, scope, and complexity of requirements may dictate that a more rigorous approach to requirements management is needed. Here are a couple of examples:

- It may be important to implement requirements traceability to ensure that the requirements are complete, sufficient, and consistent with the business objectives that they are intended to fulfill. It would be difficult to perform that kind of traceability analysis if the requirements were not at least well documented, and a requirements management tool may be needed to support that effort.
- Business rules are a type of requirement that may be overlooked if a sufficient level of requirements analysis is not performed. In many cases, there are business rules associated with requirements that must be enforced and the interrelationship of those business rules to the requirements also needs to be understood. That may also require a more rigorous requirements management approach to ensure that all business rules are captured and integrated into the design of the application.

Another value of requirements traceability is that it can help locate unnecessary requirements—requirements that have no relationship to fulfilling the business objectives of the system—"orphan" requirements that have become disconnected from a user need.

Testing Considerations

The strategy for testing of the application is also an important consideration in determining the requirements management approach. Without detailed requirements, it may be difficult to plan and implement test cases to validate that the requirements are met. This can be a very important factor in regulated environments that might require rigorous testing and documentation.

Agile methods and traditional plan-driven methods both have their strengths and weaknesses from a testing perspective:

1. Multilevel Testing Considerations
   Agile methodologies put a strong emphasis on testing the code as it is developed, but the emphasis is heavily on the testing of individual requirements at a unit test level and the documentation of requirements may be limited to the test cases in some situations:

   > "Agile methods address this problem by organizing the development into short increments, and by applying pair programming or other review techniques to remove more code defects as they are being generated. They also develop executable tests to serve in place of requirements and to enable earlier and continuous regression testing. Automated testing support is recommended by most agile methods."[12]

   Integrating the requirements into the testing effort has some clear advantages, but it's dangerous to assume that writing test cases for each requirement completely obviates the need for having requirements documented in some form for other purposes. For example, in most projects, multiple levels of testing are required that go beyond the unit test level that is performed within each iteration.

   That higher-level complete system testing goes beyond the level of testing in each individual iteration and may require a different kind of test planning that might be very difficult, if not impossible, to do without having well-defined and documented requirements. Traditional plan-driven methodologies put a higher level of emphasis on tracking and managing well-defined and documented requirements as well as multilevel test planning.

2. Test Management Considerations
   Agile methodologies integrate the testing resources into the team, while traditional plan-driven methodologies typically rely on a separate organization (QA) to manage those resources and the testing is many times done somewhat independently of the development team. There are advantages and disadvantages to both approaches:

   - Centralizing the management of the test resources provides functional direction to the testing effort to ensure that it is complete and consistently implemented across all projects. It also ensures some level of

[12] Boehm, Barry and Turner, Richard, "*Balancing Agility and Discipline—A Guide for the Perplexed,*" New York: Addison-Wesley, New York, 2003, pp. 43–44

objectivity in the testing process by having the testing performed by a separate organization.

- On the other hand, separating the testing resources from the development team has some significant disadvantages:
  - The sequential nature of the design and testing efforts probably delays the completion of the overall development effort.
  - Separation of the testing effort from the design team and the business user can lead to misunderstandings and potentially incomplete testing if the customer needs and requirements are not very well defined and clearly understood.
  - Plan-driven methods may create a testing bureaucracy that can be entirely divorced from developer and customers, have a somewhat adversarial relationship with the project team, and may focus heavily on determining if the product matches the letter of the specifications rather than the operational intent and customer need.

In many situations, these two approaches (agile and traditional plan-driven) are not mutually exclusive and some combination of both of these approaches may be the best choice. There is certainly a lot of value in having testing resources directly involved in the requirements definition effort and integrating a large part of the testing with the design effort, but there is also value in the plan-driven approach of having well-defined and documented requirements and a well-thought-out multilevel test planning effort. A compromise approach would be to create "communities of practice" to retain a focus on functional areas such as QA, while embedding the specialized resources associated with that function into project teams.

Supportability Considerations

The strategy for requirements management should not be limited to just the design and development effort—it should consider the full life cycle of the product. Supportability requirements frequently get overlooked in the design effort, and I've seen a number of applications that became extremely difficult or impossible to support once they were introduced into production because:

- The requirements of how the application was originally designed were not well documented.
- There was an inadequate capability for providing ongoing regression testing and configuration management once the application was introduced into production.

If the requirements and rules of how the application must operate are not well documented and are just embedded in the code, it can become a nightmare to support the application and/or replace and upgrade it whenever it needs replacement or upgrades.

Prioritization of Requirements

A requirements management approach should include a way of prioritizing requirements. Agile approaches, in particular, typically put a lot of emphasis on prioritizing requirements and using an iterative approach to develop the most important requirements first to deliver the most important value to the customer as early as possible.

"Just Barely Good Enough" Thinking

An important idea in any development effort (agile or non-agile) is the principle of "Just Barely Good Enough" (JBGE) requirements. Scott Ambler has done a nice job of capturing this idea in his work on agile modeling[13]. Many software applications become bloated with too many features that no one ever uses, which just makes the application complex, confusing, and difficult to use. Scott makes the point that:

> "For some reason people think that JBGE implies that the artifact isn't very good, when in fact nothing could be further from the truth. When you stop and think about it, if an artifact is JBGE then by definition it is at the most effective point that it could possibly be at."[14]

His point is that, beyond a certain optimum point, adding additional features has diminishing value and just adds complexity to the application and, of course, significantly extends the development effort. This is an important consideration in any software development effort, and it often requires close collaboration with the users to determine where this optimum point is.

Differentiate Wants from Needs

Another principle that is similar to "Just Barely Good Enough" thinking is being able to differentiate customer wants from needs. Robert Wysocki defines this as follows:

> "Wants and needs are closely linked to one another but are fundamentally different. Wants tend to be associated with a solution that the client envisions. Needs tend to be associated with the problem. If wants are derived from a clear understanding of needs, then it is safe to proceed based on what the client wants, but you cannot always know that this is the case. To be safe, I always ask the client why they want what they want. By continuing this practice of asking why, you will eventually get to the root of the problem and the needs become clear."[15]

---

[13] Ambler, Scott, *Agile Modeling Effective Practices for eXtreme Programming and the Unified Process*, Hoboken, NJ: John Wiley and Sons, 2002

[14] Ambler, Scott, "Agile Modeling," www.agilemodeling.com/essays/barelyGoodEnough.html

[15] Wysocki, Robert, *Effective Project Management—Traditional, Agile, Extreme*, Hoboken, NJ: Wiley, 2009, p. 52

The key idea here is that it is always a good idea to be sure that the problem is well understood before jumping too quickly into a solution. Charles Kettering, a famous inventor, once said "A problem well stated is a problem half solved."[16]

Agile methodologies do provide a mechanism for capturing a "vision statement" upfront, which would normally capture the business objectives and a succinct definition of the business problem to be solved prior to jumping too quickly into the design and development effort. However, there is a danger that, without a sufficient level of analysis, the effort will not get to the root problem the system needs to address.

Very often, it is necessary to drill down into the problem to find the root cause rather than simply react to what may be the symptoms of the problem. A very effective technique for doing that is called "the 5 why's method." It consists of starting with what appears to be the problem and repeatedly asking the question of "why" that problem occurred to get to the root cause. In many cases, the answer to the first "why" will prompt another "why," and the answer to the second "why" will prompt another and so on; hence the name the "5 Whys strategy." The following is an example of the 5 Whys analysis technique of analyzing a problem to get to the root cause:

> **1.** "Why is our client, Hinson Corp., unhappy? Because we did not deliver our services when we said we would.
> **2.** Why were we unable to meet the agreed-upon timeline or schedule for delivery? The job took much longer than we thought it would.
> **3.** Why did it take so much longer? Because we underestimated the complexity of the job.
> **4.** Why did we underestimate the complexity of the job? Because we made a quick estimate of the time needed to complete it, and did not list the individual stages needed to complete the project.
> **5.** Why didn't we do this? Because we were running behind on other projects. We clearly need to review our time estimation and specification procedures."[17]

Another commonly used prioritization technique in agile projects is called "MoSCoW." It consists of breaking up requirements into four categories:[18]

- **Must have**—Requirements labeled as *MUST* have to be included in the current delivery timebox in order for it to be a success. If even one *MUST* requirement is not included, the project delivery should be considered a failure.

---

[16] Kettering, Charles, Quote, www.quotationspage.com/quote/34282.html

[17] "5 Why's Problem Solving from MindTools.com," www.mindtools.com/pages/article/newTMC_5W.htm

[18] "MoSCoW Method," http://en.wikipedia.org/wiki/MoSCoW_Method

- **Should have**—*SHOULD* requirements are also critical to the success of the project but are not necessary for delivery in the current delivery timebox.
- **Could have**—Requirements labeled as *COULD* are less critical and often seen as *nice to have*.
- **Won't have**—*WON'T* requirements are either the least-critical, lowest-payback items, or not appropriate at that time.

The Role of Iterative Development

An iterative development approach can play an important role in prioritizing requirements. With traditional plan-drive projects, prioritization of requirements may have less impact because it's an all or nothing approach—either the requirements get included in the project or they don't, and there's a tendency for users to not want to give up anything, so everything gets rated as a high priority. With an iterative approach, users are not necessarily forced to make the choice to give up functionality; it's more of delaying the functionality to a later iteration or release, which is typically an easier decision to make. As a result, an iterative approach lends itself much more to prioritization of requirements.

Summary of Requirements Management Guidelines

1. The method for eliciting requirements is probably one of the most significant determinants of selecting a life-cycle model. The best method for eliciting requirements will depend on a number of factors including:
   - The nature and complexity of the product
   - The level of uncertainty and stability in the requirements and difficulty of accurately specifying requirements upfront
   - The importance of getting user input on some of the features and details
   - The availability and willingness of users to actively participate in the design
2. The interrelationship of the application and the business processes it is associated with should be considered before jumping too quickly into the design of the application.
3. The complexity of the requirements and the importance of validating the completeness, sufficiency, and consistency of the requirements is an important determinant of a requirements management strategy.
4. The testing strategy and product life-cycle support plan are also important considerations in determining a requirements management strategy.
5. Prioritization of requirements is very important to limit the complexity of the requirements to a reasonable level to avoid "gold-plating" an application.

RISK MANAGEMENT, UNCERTAINTY, AND PLANNING APPROACH

Risk Management Considerations

Risk management is also one of the fundamental principles of any project management methodology:

> "Risks and benefits always go hand in hand. The reason that a project is full of risk is that it leads you into uncharted waters. Projects with no real risks are losers. They are almost devoid of benefit; that's why they weren't done years ago."[19]

Planning can substantially reduce some of the risks in a project to a manageable level. Some people (particularly those that have never been burned by something going bad) tend to be naïve about risks and assume that "that will never happen to me" and don't even plan for risks. Effective risk management is a mark of maturity:

> "Taking explicit note of bad things that can happen (risks) and planning for them accordingly is a mark of maturity. But that's not the way we tend to use the word maturity in the IT industry. We software people tend to equate maturity with technical proficiency .... It is, rather, a quality of grown-up-ness, an indication that a person or organism has reached its adult state."[20]

The diagram below shows the general relationship of the level of risk to the level of planning in any project. In general, as the overall risk increases, more planning is needed to identify and mitigate the risks to reduce the overall level of risk in the project to an acceptable level as shown in Figure 7.2.

The level of risk is generally inversely proportional to the level of planning. Planning reduces the uncertainties in a project, and in general, the less the uncertainty, the less the risk. There are two stages of risk management:

1. Risk identification
   - There are two kinds of risks in a project: the ones you know about and the ones you don't know about. Planning reduces the uncertainty in a project and helps to identify risks that you might otherwise not have known about (risk identification).
   - Uncertainty is also related to complexity. In general, the higher the complexity, the higher the uncertainty because there are more things that could go wrong that are more difficult to predict and there is a

---

[19] DeMarco, Tom and Lister, Timothy, *Waltzing with Bears*, New York, NY: Dorset House, 2003

[20] DeMarco, Tom and Lister, Timothy, *Waltzing with Bears*, New York: Dorset House, 2003

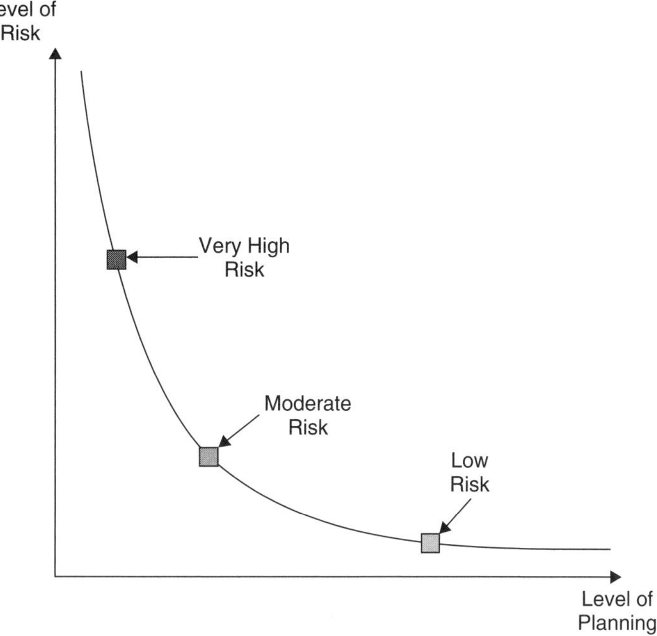

Figure 7.2 Risk versus Level of Planning curve

greater the need for planning to reduce the level of uncertainty and risk to an acceptable level.

- It's important to recognize that no project is without risk and that risk never goes to zero—you can only hope to reduce risk to a reasonable and manageable level.

2. Risk Mitigation

- Risk mitigation is the process of systematically reducing the impact of a risk and/or the likelihood of a risk occurring after a risk has been identified.
- Risk identification does not actually reduce the level of risk; it simply better defines what the actual level of risk is by removing some of the uncertainty. Planning only reduces the level of risk if it also includes contingency planning and risk mitigation.

It is important to note that planning does not all necessarily have to be done upfront as in the Waterfall approach; the planning can be spread throughout the project as in the "rolling wave" planning that is typically done in more agile methodologies. It would be naïve, in some cases, to believe that all risks can be detected and planned for at the beginning of a project. Risk planning and management should be continuous throughout the project; however, deferring the planning might mean that the risks are not identified until the project is in progress. In many cases, a more iterative approach may provide a better framework for managing risks, because it encourages a more continuous approach to risk management, and risks will generally be detected and resolved earlier in the project.

> "Planning doesn't eliminate project risks; constant gathering of information systematically reduces them over the life of the project. Gathering information costs money, so we want to constantly ask what information has the highest value. The strategies we employ to gather information should be guided in part by our risk analysis—It's an integral part of the product development process and a critical component of release planning."[21]

The company's tolerance for risk should be based on the potential business impact of the project.

- Some projects may have very low potential business impact, and it may be very acceptable to take a high-risk approach with a minimum level of planning. If a project has a very low level of complexity, as well as a low level of uncertainty and risk, it may not require very much planning at all. In that instance, doing excessive amounts of planning would probably be unwarranted and overkill.
- On the other hand, if a project is to redesign and replace a very mission-critical system that the company depends on for its operation, the business impact of something going wrong is much higher and the level of complexity and uncertainty is also probably much higher. For that reason, a much higher level of planning is probably needed to keep the risk at an acceptable level.

Summary of Risk Management Guidelines

1. The overall risk environment of the business that the project is associated with is a very important determinant in selecting an appropriate level of planning to mitigate the risks. It is also important to consider how planning is done in the life-cycle model (upfront or rolling wave) to determine if the level and nature of planning is appropriate and sufficient to mitigate the risks.
2. Even if most of the planning is done upfront, planning and risk management should always be ongoing activities throughout the project.
3. A project management methodology should be chosen that provides a level of planning and risk management that is appropriate for managing

---

[21] Highsmith, Jim, Agile *Project Management—Creating Innovative Products*, New Year: Addison-Wesley, 2010, p. 182

the risks, and that decision should be based on an assessment of the business impact, risks, and complexity associated with the project. Ideally, the business stakeholders should understand and buy into that decision.

Management of Uncertainty Considerations

Management of uncertainty is also a critical element in a project because uncertainty is directly related to risk—the higher the uncertainty, the higher the risk. Every project has something which is called "the fuzzy front end," as shown in Figure 7.3.

The "fuzzy front end" is the portion of the project where there is a very high level of uncertainty about many aspects of the project (requirements, design approach, risks, etc.). The goal of the upfront planning phase of the project should be to reduce that level of uncertainty to an *acceptable* level. (The level of uncertainty never goes to zero.)

The level of uncertainty is a combination of uncertainty associated with a number of project factors:

- Project requirements
- Scope, costs, and schedule associated with the project
- Design and architectural approach
- Risks and mitigation strategy
- Other factors

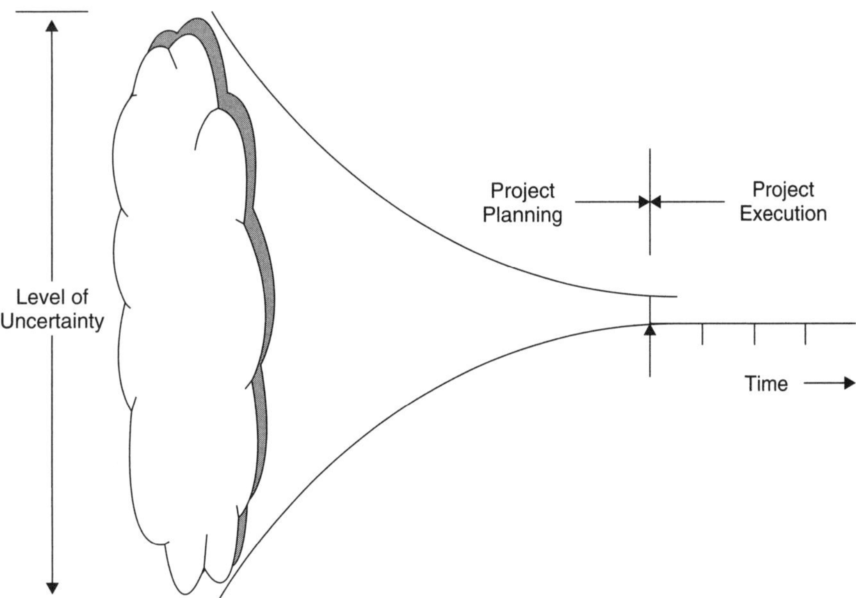

Figure 7.3 "Fuzzy front end" (conservative approach)

The Waterfall approach assumes that uncertainty can be reduced to a very low level of uncertainty prior to beginning the execution of the project, as shown in the preceding diagram. In some cases, however, it might take a long time to reduce the uncertainty to that level, and it may not even be practical to get it to that level early on in the project. A good example of that might be designing the user interface for a software application, sometimes it is much more efficient to start the project and work out the details as the project goes along.

Agile and iterative approaches encourage more of a just-in-time approach to planning and defer decision making based on planning until the "last responsible moment". The "last responsible moment" is the latest point that a decision must be made without impacting the project. The advantage of deferring planning decisions is that, in general, planning and decision making is easier when more information is known. Trying to do a lot of planning and decision making upfront in the project when less information is known generally requires a higher level of speculation, and there are two key problems associated with that. The first is that, because the planning and decision making are based on speculation, sometimes those decisions will be wrong. Second:

- A change of direction and potential rework of whatever portion of the project that was built around those assumptions will be needed later in the project, or
- Worse yet, those assumptions will be taken for granted and not revisited later in the project and the project will go off in the wrong direction

An example of that kind of approach is shown in the "More Aggressive Approach" in Figure 7.4. It acknowledges the fact that it is okay to start the execution of the project before all of the uncertainty is resolved through planning, and the remainder of the uncertainty will be resolved as the project progresses. There are naturally tradeoffs involved in doing that. The primary tradeoff is between the following pros and cons.

Pros:

- Getting started quicker with a higher level of uncertainty potentially has the benefit of reducing the overall development time.
- It may be more effective to defer planning till later in the project when more information is known. Attempting to do all the planning upfront many times results in unnecessary replanning and rework later.

Cons:

- The ability to accurately predict the costs and schedule of the project before starting the project execution is probably reduced because of the higher level of uncertainty.
- There may also may be more risk in starting the project with incomplete planning.

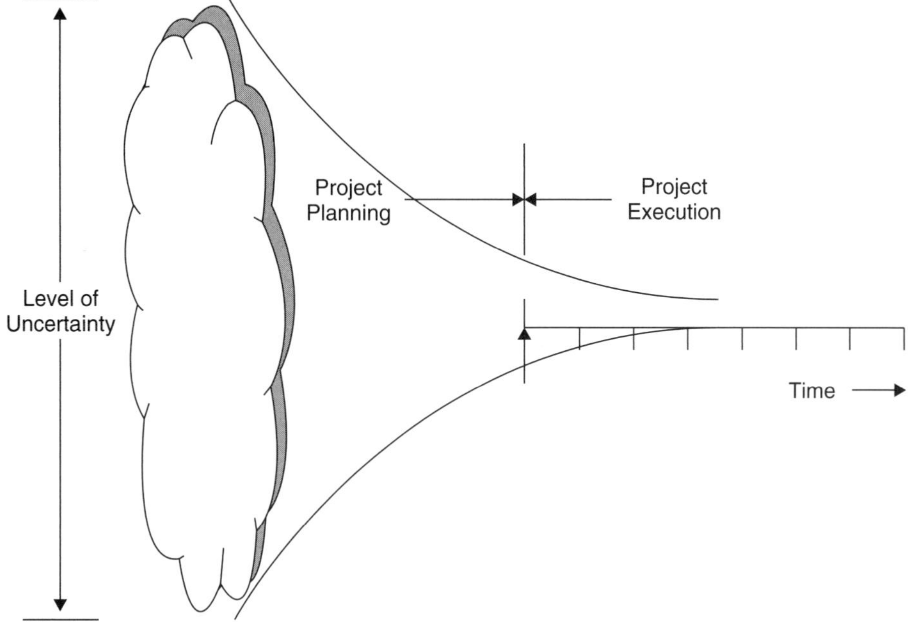

Figure 7.4 "Fuzzy front-end" (more aggressive approach)

Another approach would be to start the project with a very limited amount of upfront planning as shown in Figure 7.5. Naturally, the risks in this situation would probably be much higher, but it involves the same general tradeoffs.

It is perfectly acceptable for a project to begin with any of these levels of uncertainty, but it should be done knowingly with a full understanding of the risks involved and based on some analysis of the tradeoffs associated with alternative approaches. If a decision is made to start a project at a point of high uncertainty, it introduces more potential risk into the project and may call for some method of continuing to assess the level of uncertainty and risk as the project progresses.

Summary of Management of Uncertainty Guidelines

The following are a few good guidelines associated with management of uncertainty:

1. It is impossible to completely remove all uncertainty prior to the start of the project. In most situations, a project would never get started if it were necessary to completely resolve all uncertainties prior to the start of the project. An intelligent judgment should be made as to what is an *acceptable* level of uncertainty prior to starting a project.

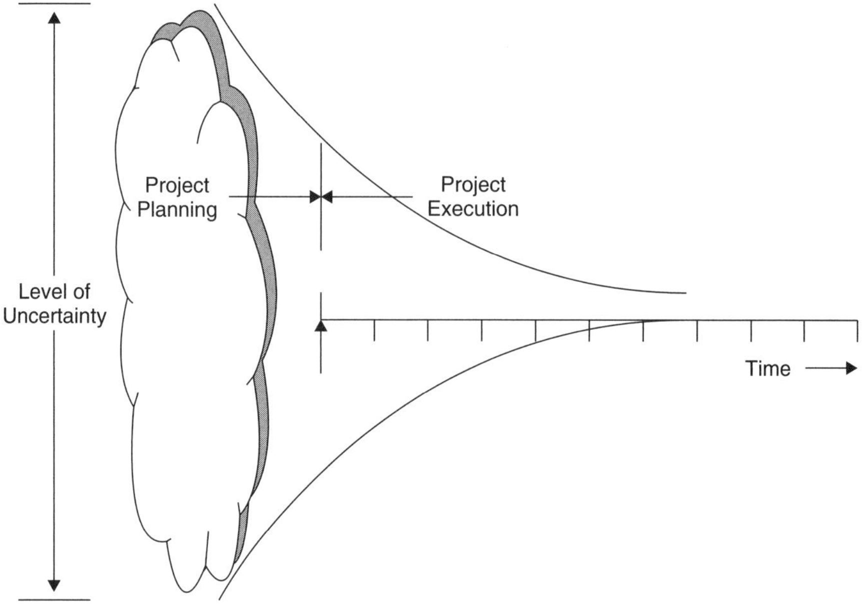

Figure 7.5 "Fuzzy front end" (very aggressive approach)

2. In most cases, a best practice is to resolve the major uncertainties associated with a project to a reasonable level and postpone many of the details if possible.
3. If an uncertainty cannot be completely resolved, a good practice is to make an assumption about how the uncertainty is *most likely* to be resolved, proceed on the basis of the assumption, and track the resolution of the assumption as a risk or issue until it is resolved. This is commonly known as a risk log.

The Role of Planning

Adopting the appropriate mindset about the role of planning is very important. Here are several quotations on the subject of planning[22]:

Quote	Source
"A plan is nothing; planning is everything."	Dwight D. Eisenhower
"Plans are of little importance, but planning is essential."	Winston S. Churchill
"No battle plan survives contact with the enemy."	Helmuth von Moltke the Elder
"A good plan, violently executed now, is better than a perfect plan next week."	George S. Patton

[22] "Plan" from Wikipedia the Free Encyclopedia, http://en.wikipedia.org/wiki/Plan

It's interesting that all of the above quotes come from the military environment, where the level of uncertainty is typically very high. In a military environment, you never know what the enemy or the terrorists are going to do next, and you have to react quickly and change plans rapidly as the situation evolves. This mode of thinking is very relevant to many product development initiatives.

The most common problems associated with project planning are:

1. Writing a plan and putting it on the shelf, where it gathers dust, and never revisiting it again. Planning should take place on an ongoing basis throughout any project—even if a very high level of planning was done prior to executing the project in a Waterfall model. No plan should be considered sacred; it is always wise to revisit some of the planning and assumptions behind that plan to see if they are still valid as the project progresses.
2. Taking planning to an extreme and never getting started on the project. A good project manager knows how to make an intelligent judgment about how much planning is essential to do before starting the project to manage the risk and how much planning can be deferred and done as the project progresses.

Agile projects take a different approach to planning and work well in environments that have a very high level of uncertainty that cannot easily be resolved prior to the start of the project:

> "The models are built on the assumption that the solution has to be discovered. Planning becomes less of a one-time task done at the outset and more of a just-in-time task done as late as possible. There is less and less reliance on a plan and more reliance on the tacit knowledge of the team. That doesn't reduce the complexity, but it does accommodate it."[23]

Developing an appropriate balance between planning and execution can be a challenge:

> "Every project has known's and unknown's, certainties and uncertainties, and therefore every project has to balance planning and adapting. Balancing is required because projects run the gamut from production-style ones in which uncertainty is low, to exploration-style ones in which uncertainty is high. Exploration-style projects... require a process that emphasizes envisioning and then exploring into that vision rather than detailed planning and relatively strict execution of tasks. It's not that one is right and the other is wrong, but that each style is more or less applicable to a particular project type.

[23] Wysocki, Robert, *Effective Project Management—Traditional, Agile, Extreme*, Hoboken, NJ: Wiley, 2009, p. 311

> Another factor that impacts project management style is the cost of an iteration; that is, the cost of experimenting. Even if the need for innovation is great, high iteration costs may dictate a process with greater anticipatory work. Low-cost iterations... enable an adaptive style of development in which plans, architectures, and designs evolve concurrently with the actual product."[24]

Summary of Planning Guidelines

The following are a few good guidelines associated with planning:

1. The overall nature and level of planning should be appropriate to the risk and should provide an effective overall framework for risk management (see the risk management section).
2. A key purpose of planning is to reduce the uncertainty in the project to a manageable level (see the management of uncertainty section).
3. The best approach to planning may be to do some reasonable amount of high-level, upfront planning and defer some of the more detailed planning until later in the project as it progresses. It may not make sense to try to resolve 100 percent of the uncertainties before the start of the project. In many cases, it is best to postpone a planning decision until more information is available to make that decision effectively if possible.
4. A plan should never be rigid, and planning should never stop:
   - Any plan should always leave open the possibility that the selected approach is not going to work as planned or that unforeseen events will occur that will invalidate or change the plan.
   - Lessons learned during the course of the project and new information gained should be fed back into the plan as the project progresses.

THE ROLE OF LEADERSHIP AND TRAINING

Leadership

Any project methodology requires leadership to execute it effectively. Too often, there's an assumption that a given methodology can be just executed by the book and people will just follow along. That kind of approach creates an environment where the process manages you instead of you managing the process and is one of the factors that sparked the agile movement to revolt and develop a more humanistic kind of approach.

Movement to an agile approach typically involves a softer form of leadership with more delegation of responsibility to empowered teams, but leadership does not necessarily mean abdicating the management role altogether.

---

[24] Highsmith, Jim, *Agile Project Management—Creating Innovative Products*, New York: Addison-Wesley, 2010, pp. 70–71

> "Leaders as opposed to managers, encourage change—by creating a vision of future possibilities (which may be short on details), by interacting with a large network of people to discover new information that will help turn the product vision into reality, and by creating a sense of purpose in the endeavor that will motivate people to work on something outside the norm.
>
> Leaders who steer rather than command are not abdicating decision making."[25]

People need to feel respected and have the freedom to use good judgment, creativity, and intelligence, but that doesn't require having an environment filled with chaos and anarchy. In fact, in many cases, if it is done properly, an agile environment has an even higher level of discipline, but it is a different kind of discipline. Instead of a traditional, hierarchical command-and-control environment, it is typically a flatter organizational environment with much higher levels of self-discipline.

The following are a few good quotes on the role of effective leadership:

Quote	Source
"Management is doing things right; leadership is doing the right things."	Peter F. Drucker
"Don't tell people how to do things, tell them what to do and let them surprise you with their results."	George S. Patton
"Leadership is the art of getting someone else to do something you want done because he wants to do it."	Dwight D. Eisenhower
"The best executive is the one who has sense enough to pick good men to do what he wants done, and self-restraint to keep from meddling with them while they do it."	Theodore Roosevelt

A key element of defining a project approach is finding the middle ground that has the right balance of control and agility, is consistent with the culture and business environment of the organization, and builds highly motivated, cohesive, collaborative, and cross-functional teams, and this requires strong and intelligent leadership.

Summary of Leadership Guidelines

The following are a few guidelines associated with leadership:

1. Any project methodology requires effective leadership and management to make it work, and the leadership and management style should be

---

[25] Highsmith, Jim, *Agile Project Management—Creating Innovative Products*, New York: Addison-Wesley, 2010, pp. 48–49

appropriate to the project and consistent with the culture and business environment of the organization.

2. Teamwork and respect for people is important whatever methodology you use.
3. Sapient has provided some excellent bullet points on leadership guidelines, which I think are very appropriate to consider in a more agile development approach:

> - Inspire a Shared Vision—Help people see, buy in, and commit to a compelling future state
> - Think Strategically—Keep people focused on the big picture, the real value, and the critical elements to success
> - Drive Accountability—Hold ourselves and others accountable for achieving clearly articulated business outcomes
> - Model the Way—Act the way you expect others to act; teach our values by example
> - Enable Others to Act—Set context and clear objectives, give ownership and support that empowers people to perform
> - Make the Hard Decisions—Face reality, communicate it clearly, and make the hard decisions you know are right
> - Challenge Assumptions—Understand the "why" behind things and drive change when the "why" no longer makes sense[26]

Training

Similarly, it is very difficult to get any project methodology to work without well-trained people. This becomes even more important when everyone on the project team is expected to play a very active role in participating in the team. Agile methodologies are particularly sensitive to the importance of having knowledgeable and well-trained people:

> "All of the agile methods put a premium on having premium people . . . both (plan-driven and agile) operate best with a mix of developer skills and understanding, but agile methods tend to need a richer mix of higher-skilled people . . . . The plan-driven methods, of course, do better with great people, but are generally more able to plan the project and architect the software so that less-capable people can contribute with low risk."[27]

---

[26] Gottesman, Erik, Sapient White Paper on Leadership

[27] Boehm, Barry and Turner, Richard, *Balancing Agility and Discipline—A Guide for the Perplexed*, New York: Addison-Wesley, 2003, pp. 46–47

With traditional methodologies, the primary emphasis is on training people on the project team in their functional discipline (development, testing, etc.), and they are not expected to need to know much about the project methodology, since that is the domain of the project manager. In an agile project:

- Everyone on the team is expected to much more actively engage in working as a team to jointly manage the project. As a result, they are expected to understand the methodology, as well as their own functional discipline.
- Since there is a heavy emphasis on cross-functional collaboration, there is also a need for each person on the team to be somewhat knowledgeable about other functional disciplines. For example, on an agile project, a developer should have a good understanding of QA and testing.

Training of an agile project team is typically more difficult than in a traditional environment, because the agile approach is less prescriptive and needs to be somewhat adaptive to the situation. For that reason, agile projects typically rely heavily on coaching and mentoring in addition to normal training. Naturally, all organizations may not have the level of people required to make an agile methodology work, and there is typically some turnover in people when companies move to an agile approach because some people will have difficulty in making the transition to an agile approach.

The role of training is many times overlooked:

> "When an organization has software development challenges, there is a tendency to impose a more disciplined process on the organization. The prevailing concept of a more disciplined software process is one with more rigorous sequential processing: requirements are documented more completely, all agreements with the customer are written, changes are controlled more carefully, and each requirement must be traced to code. This amounts to imposing additional deterministic controls on a dynamic environment, lengthening the feedback loop. Just as control theory predicts, this generally makes a bad situation worse."[28]

Imposing a more rigorous development process may be the wrong solution in many cases. In a more dynamic environment, training may be a more appropriate solution.

Summary of Training Guidelines

The following are a few good guidelines associated with training:

1. A project methodology cannot entirely substitute for highly qualified and well-trained people on the team; however, traditional plan-driven methodologies are probably less sensitive to the level of training of the team.

[28] Poppendiek, Tom and Mary, *Lean Software Development—An Agile Toolkit*, New York: Addison-Wesley, 2003, p. 26

2. The availability of trained and qualified people should be an important consideration in selecting a project methodology.

THE ROLE OF DOCUMENTATION

Some people become overly consumed with writing project documentation for the sake of documentation, and the people creating the documentation lose sight of what purpose the documentation was intended to serve. What is important is that:

- The information that will be contained in the document serves a useful purpose for better planning and/or managing the project.
- The approach taken to gather and analyze the information required was well-chosen based on the overall risks and complexity associated with the project.
- The analysis that went into developing that information was sufficiently complete for the purpose it was intended for.
- The consensus building that was used to reach agreement on the results of the analysis involved the appropriate people, and the level of consensus building was consistent with the importance of the information to the project.

A document is the result of the analysis used to develop the information that went into it. *It is the analysis that went into the information that's contained in the document that's generally what is important, not the document itself*; however, the document can serve a useful purpose of recording that event and communicating the information to others if necessary.

There is a tendency among some people in the agile community to think that documentation is a bad thing and should be avoided at all costs. It is always worthwhile to ensure that documentation provides value, but it shouldn't be assumed that all documentation is bad. Documentation can potentially serve several valuable purposes:

1. It is a record of decisions made and that can become important as the project progresses. Sometimes after months have passed on a project, people forget decisions that have been made early on in the project. In contractual situations where work is being performed under contract for a customer, that can be very critical.
2. It can be an effective tool for better planning and management of projects. For example, in large projects with distributed teams, it is essential to have some kind of documentation to keep everyone on the team informed of what's going on, but, of course, that doesn't mean that the project should rely exclusively on conventional paper-based

documentation. There are many web-based tools for documenting and sharing information that accomplish this task very effectively.

3. It can be an essential tool for understanding the interrelationship of complex requirements. For example, requirements management tools are often useful to analyze requirements and to perform traceability analysis of the requirements. Traceability provides a way of validating that:
   - The requirements are complete and consistent with the business objectives that they support
   - The different types of requirements are complete and consistent internally. For example business rules are defined as needed for all requirements.
   - The requirements are consistent with the business processes they're associated with.
   - Test cases that are associated with the requirements are complete, and there is a sufficient level of test coverage to adequately test the requirements at multiple levels of testing.

   It's impossible to do that kind of traceability analysis if the requirements are not documented and very well defined.
4. Documentation is also essential for configuration management of systems. Configuration management can be essential to effectively manage complex systems so that any changes in requirements that impact other related requirements, test cases, design objects, interfaces to other systems, and so forth are understood so that a change in one area of a system doesn't break another related area.

Summary of Documentation Guidelines

The following are a few good guidelines associated with documentation:

1. Documentation is only a tool, not an end in itself. Any document should fulfill some objective related to planning and management of the project and the level of documentation should be appropriate to the risks and complexities of the project.
2. It is always useful to question documentation to ensure that it provides value and serves a useful purpose; many times organizations either:
   - Go overboard in creating documentation that serves no useful purpose or outlives its useful purpose, or
   - Dismiss all documentation as unnecessary bureaucracy without considering downstream impact and unintended consequences that might result of eliminating documentation that serves a useful purpose

3. Documentation can be a good tool for developing an effective project management approach if it is used correctly to provide value. Potential areas of value include:
   - Recording and communicating information to everyone on the team; however, the strategy should always consider other means of communication such as shared portals that may accomplish that task more effectively
   - Consensus building among members of a team, but it is the consensus building that is important; the documentation is only a tool for achieving that consensus and should only be used to the extent needed to build consensus
4. The level and nature of documentation in a project should be determined by organizational culture as well as the scope and complexity of the project. Some large, complex projects might require a more documented approach because the people involved in the project are separated by time, organization, and process. An agile process typically relies heavily on more complex interactions and individual discipline rather than documentation—that approach works well for smaller projects; however, it is difficult to extend the heavy reliance on direct face-to-face communications to large distributed teams.

CHAPTER 8

SOFTWARE DEVELOPMENT LIFE CYCLES

Chapter 7 discussed some general principles that apply to all life-cycle models, which make sense to consider in selecting a life-cycle model for a project or tailoring it to fit a particular project. This chapter will discuss some general categories of life-cycle models that can provide a framework for those decisions.

The table that follows shows a summary of the major tradeoffs to be considered between two extreme life-cycle models (pure agile and extreme plan-driven Waterfall).

Pure Agile	Extreme Plan-Driven Waterfall
Potential Benefits	**Potential Benefits**
• Faster development times with higher levels of productivity and employee morale • Flexibility to adapt to uncertain and changing requirements • Faster learning curves to incorporate process improvements	• Higher levels of control and predictability over costs and schedules • Less dependent on highly skilled resources • Consistent with many typical company environments—doesn't require significant change • Higher levels of efficiency for products with low levels of uncertainty
Tradeoffs	**Tradeoffs**
• Can be difficult to implement and might require a large amount of retraining of the company's staff as well as a significantly increased level of participation from business resources. • Might require a significant change management initiative if the company's culture is not consistent with an agile strategy • May not be appropriate for all of the company's projects particularly if they are large and complex • Might not provide a sufficient level of risk management and control for high risk projects or regulated environments. • Might result in a lower level of control and predictability over product development costs and schedules.	• May have overly bureaucratic control and documentation requirements that: • Add unnecessary overhead, and • Raise product development costs and result in excessively long product development times • Emphasis on control may seriously impact the ability to react to emergent and changing business requirements if the environment the company operates in has a significant level of uncertainty in it • Inadequate emphasis on learning and continuous improvement

Because these tradeoffs can be so severe, the temptation may be to use no methodology at all, or some companies might just adopt the process on paper but not really follow it in practice. Developing a process that really fits the company's business environment, that is realistic to implement, and that people really believe in takes some skill. In many cases, the best solution is a hybrid approach in between these two extremes that provides a balance of control and agility to fit with the company's business and organizational environment.

TYPES OF SOFTWARE DEVELOPMENT LIFE CYCLES

There are many different variations on software development life cycles that are commonly used today. The purpose of this section is to break these life cycles up into logical high-level categories. These categories are intentionally somewhat general and conceptual to avoid getting too far down into the specific mechanics of any particular methodology. This is intended to provide an understanding of how these various life-cycle models provide a continuum of alternatives between an extreme traditional Waterfall model at one end and pure agile life-cycle models at the other end.

Bob Wysocki[1] has developed a model for characterizing life-cycle models by clarity of the goal and clarity of the solution. Projects where the goal is not clear are outside the scope of this book and are generally found only in a research and development environment. The following model expands the model originally developed by Bob Wysocki and provides more granular differentiation of the life-cycle models by clarity of the solution and the level of iteration needed to further define the solution, as shown in Figure 8.1.

The categories in the diagram are somewhat fuzzy, and they may have some level of overlap; however, the general framework is useful. To use a cooking analogy, these categories are like different kinds of sauces—chefs have five basic kinds of sauces that they generally work with for preparing a gourmet meal:

> "In the 19th century, the chef Antonin Carême classified sauces into four families, each of which was based on a mother sauce. Carême's four mother sauces were:
>
> - Allemande is based on stock with egg yolk & lemon juice
> - Béchamel is based on flour and milk
> - Espagnole is based on brown stock, beef etc.
> - Velouté is based on a light broth, fish, chicken or veal

[1] Wysocki, Robert, *Effective Project Management—Traditional, Agile, Extreme,* Hoboken, NJ: Wiley, 2009, p. 299

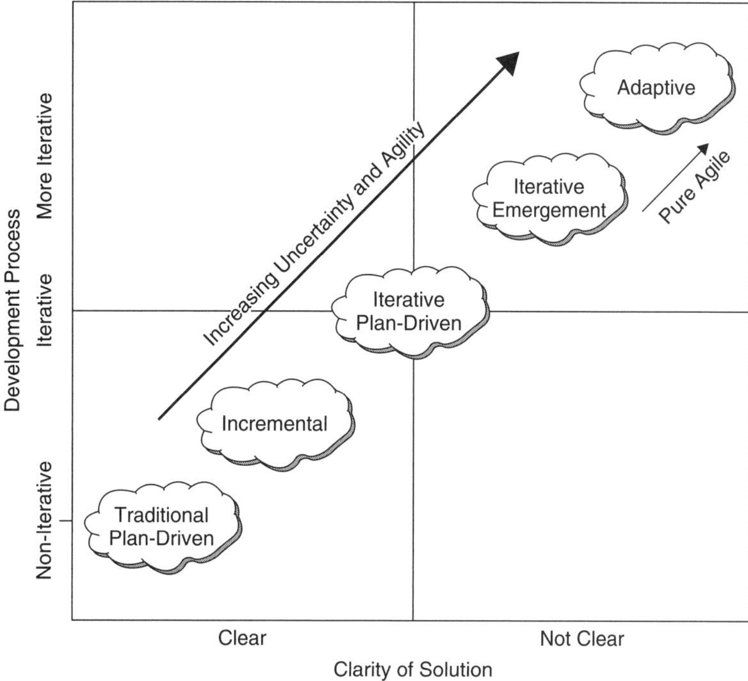

Figure 8.1 Categories of life-cycle models

> In the early 20th century, the chef Auguste Escoffier updated the classification, replacing sauce Allemande with egg-based emulsions (Hollandaise and mayonnaise), and adding tomato. Escoffier's schema is still taught to chefs today:
>
> - Béchamel
> - Espagnole
> - Hollandaise
> - Mayonnaise
> - Tomato sauce
> - Velouté
>
> Those sauces are called "mother sauces" because most other sauces can be derived from them. For example, Mornay sauce is a cheese sauce based on bechamel."[2]

The analogy to cooking sauces is a good one—these categories of lifecycle models can be thought of as different "sauces" or styles of cooking that can be

[2] "What are the 5 mother sauces and why are they called that?," http://answers.yahoo.com/question/index?qid=20061204192031AAuuq0x

used as a *base* for developing a number of different gourmet recipes (project methodologies) that are tuned to a particular "taste" for either a more agile or a more traditional approach.

The way life-cycle models deal with defining requirements is probably the most significant differentiator of these life-cycle models. Life-cycle models attempt to expand the breadth and depth of the definition of requirements in three ways:

1. By starting with a base of completely defined core requirements, defining those requirements in depth, and then incrementally expanding the definition of new features and capabilities (see Figure 8.2)
2. By starting with a high-level definition of all requirements and progressively adding more detail (see Figure 8.3)
3. By using a combination of both of these approaches (see Figure 8.4)

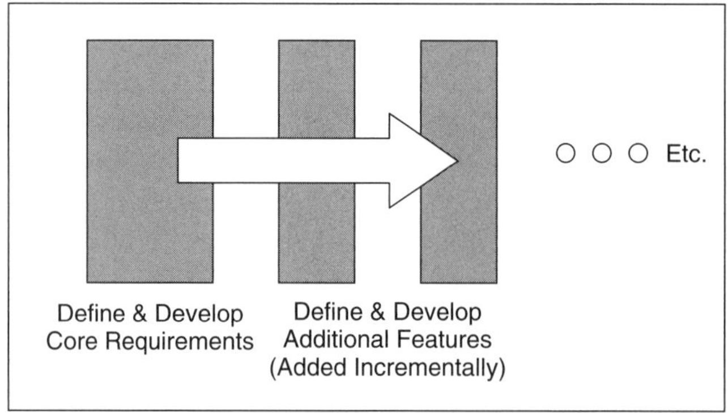

Figure 8.2 Incremental requirements definition approach

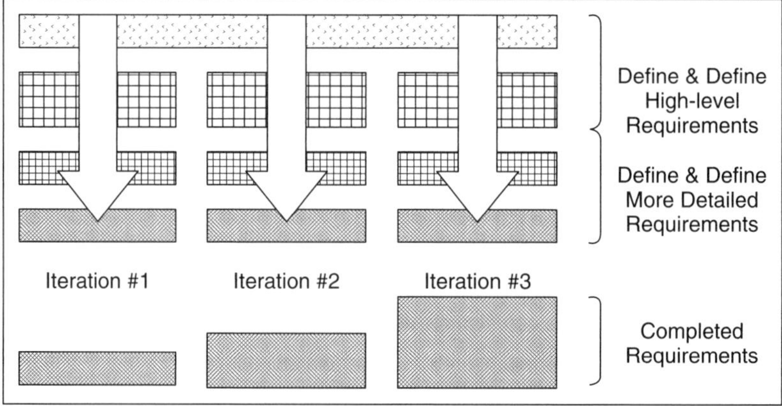

Figure 8.3 Progressive elaboration requirements definition approach

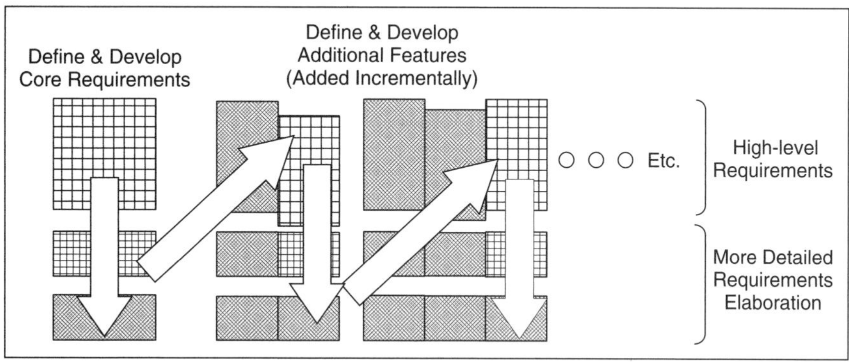

Figure 8.4 Combination requirements definition approach

The general characteristics of these categories are:

- Traditional plan-driven (Waterfall) approaches attempt to define both the breadth and depth of all the requirements upfront at the beginning of the project.
- Incremental approaches develop the product incrementally through a series of releases, and the life-cycle model for each release is essentially a mini-waterfall. Each release is intended to produce a releasable product, and it is assumed that the requirements for that release can be completely defined prior to the design of that release. The project planning can be truly incremental and does not require any planning beyond the current release. (See Figure 8.2.)
- Iterative plan-driven approaches are similar to the incremental approach in that requirements are completely defined prior to beginning the design effort for each iteration, and there should be little or no need for the user to further elaborate the requirements once the design has begun. The approach differs from the incremental model as follows:
  - There is typically a high-level plan that outlines the general high-level content of all iterations prior to the start of the project.
  - Iterations will typically be smaller units of functionality; they may not be completely independent of each other, and the result of each iteration may or may not be a releasable product.
- The iterative emergent approach is similar to the Iterative Plan-Driven approach with the following differences:
  - Only high-level requirements for each iteration are developed prior to the start of each iteration.
  - Detailed requirements for each iteration will be elaborated further as the design of the iteration progresses.

- Adaptive approaches are similar to the Iterative Emergent approach with the exception that the overall approach is expected to be much more adaptive and responsive to change and the solution is likely to evolve as each iteration is implemented.

There are a number of fundamental characteristics of these life-cycle models that are different. At one end of this spectrum, the life-cycle models are generally called "optimizing." The term "optimizing" is used to denote that the life cycle is designed to *optimize the efficiency of the process for getting to the solution* when the requirements for the solution are fairly certain and not likely to change. It does *not* necessarily optimize the solution, particularly if further adaptation is needed to define an optimum solution.

At the other end of the extreme, the life-cycle models are considered more "adaptive"—the solutions are less known and more likely to change and the life-cycle model is designed to adapt to those conditions.

> "An adaptive development process has a different character from an optimizing (Traditional) one. Optimizing reflects a basic prescriptive Plan-Design-Build lifecycle. Adapting reflects an organic, evolutionary Envision-Explore-Adapt lifecycle. An adaptive approach begins not with a single solution, but with multiple potential solutions (experiments). It explores and selects the best by applying a series of fitness tests (actual product features or simulations subjected to acceptance tests) and then adapting to feedback. When uncertainty is low, adaptive approaches run the risks of higher costs. When uncertainty is high, optimizing (traditional) approaches run the risk of settling too early on a particular solution and stifling innovation. The salient point is that these two fundamental approaches to development are very different, and they require different processes, different management approaches, and different measurements of success."[3]

An adaptive development process really is evolutionary, in that earlier work guides later work. It is particularly useful for subjective, highly user-focused development—user interfaces (UIs) are a prime example. It is also very good for ongoing enhancement of a product where real user/customer response drives where you go next. An adaptive approach is designed to *optimize the solution* when the requirements for the solution are not completely known in advance.

Traditional Plan-Driven Life-Cycle Model

Traditional plan-driven life-cycle models include the Waterfall and variations on the Waterfall model. These life-cycle models are appropriate when both

---

[3] Highsmith, Jim, *Agile Project Management—Creating Innovative Products*, New York: Addison-Wesley, 2010, p. 67

the goal of the project and the requirements for the project can be defined largely upfront prior to starting the project, and there is a low appetite for risk.

> "Traditional project management assumes that events affecting the project are predictable and that tools and activities are well understood. In addition, with traditional project management, once a phase is complete, it is assumed that it will not be revisited. The strengths of this approach are that it lays out the steps for development and stresses the importance of requirements. The limitations are that projects rarely follow the sequential flow, and clients usually find it difficult to completely state all requirements early in the project. This model is often viewed as a waterfall."[4]

A general conceptual model of a traditional plan-driven life-cycle model consists of some number of phases that happen sequentially (or mostly sequentially), as shown in Figure 8.5.

Traditional-plan driven models are used frequently when cost and schedules are important to manage, such as customer contractual commitments. In those environments, it may be essential to have a well-defined plan upfront with a clearly defined scope and change control to manage changes in scope in order to accurately predict and manage costs and schedules. In some of those instances, a traditional plan-driven model might be combined with a different kind of model for the startup phase of the project. For example, there might be an exploratory startup phase to define the requirements and scope of the project prior to committing to a fixed-price, plan-driven project.

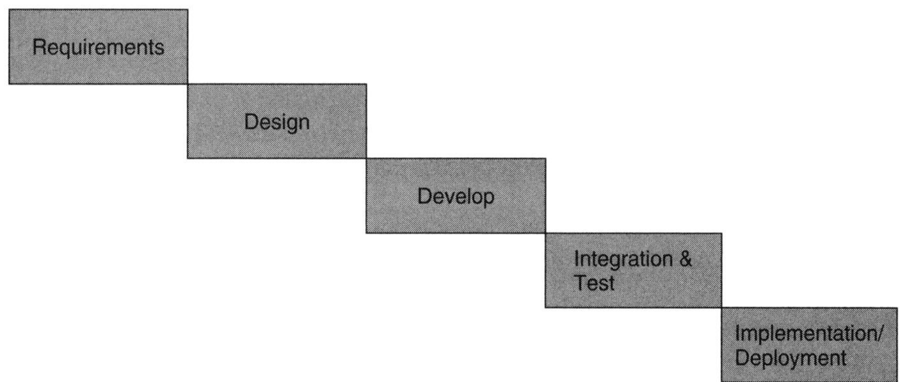

Figure 8.5 Traditional plan-driven conceptual life-cycle model

[4] Hass, Kathleen, "The Blending of Traditional and Agile Project Management," *PM World Today*, May 2007

Distinguishing Characteristics:

From the preceding, it should be clear that the stereotype of a very rigid and bureaucratic approach associated with a traditional plan-driven approach is not necessarily accurate. There are certainly some instances where that is the case, but it doesn't have to be that way. That kind of image results from companies that often attempt to implement a model without understanding the principles behind it and without tailoring the model to fit their business environment and the risks and complexity of their projects. The key things that are different about traditional plan-driven models are:

1. *Most* of the planning is done upfront—however, it is expected that some level of planning will continue throughout the project. Naturally, that tends to work best in environments with a low level of uncertainty and where only limited amounts of change are expected. It doesn't work well in environments with high levels of uncertainty and change. Many of the other aspects of the model can be tailored to provide higher levels of agility—there is no reason that it has to be rigidly implemented by the book.
2. *Most* of the requirements are defined prior to starting the design rather than concurrently with the design—however, it is also possible to allow some overlap to and allow the design to begin before the requirements definition is 100 percent complete.

Potential Variations:

There are a number of variations of the traditional plan-driven model including:

1. Number and Types of Phases
   There are many variations on the traditional plan-driven model have more or less phases and different definitions for the phases. The general characteristic that distinguishes a traditional plan-driven model is that the phases happen sequentially and most of the planning is done upfront. However, it should also be realized that there are many shades of gray in these distinctions, and planning should always continue to some extent throughout the whole project even in traditional plan-driven models.
2. Deliverables and Artifacts Required for Each Phase
   There is a common stereotype associated with traditional plan-driven models that they are loaded down with lots of unnecessary documentation. That is not necessarily the case—if a plan-driven model is done intelligently, there is no reason why the documentation and artifacts cannot be tailored as needed to fit the needs of the project.
3. Level of Formality to the Review Process between Phases
   Another stereotype is that traditional plan-driven approaches are loaded down with excessive bureaucratic controls that make it very cumbersome

to make progress. That is also not necessarily the case—there is no reason why the team cannot be empowered to make whatever decisions regarding approving phase transitions or whatever other approvals need to be made in the project. The level of control can and should be tailored to fit the risk, scope, and complexity of the project and the sponsoring organization's risk tolerance.

Phase "gates" in a traditional model fulfill a fundamental purpose to test that any prerequisites required for moving on to the next phase have been met and resources required for the next phase are committed. Agile methods involve similar decisions with less formality and on a shorter time scale.

4. Amount of Overlap Allowed between Phases
A pure Waterfall approach does not allow overlap between phases—but that also does not necessarily have to be the case. Instead of making the transition between phases highly controlled and rigid, it is perfectly acceptable to design a model that allows some overlap between the phases. The amount of overlap allowed should be based on evaluating the tradeoffs between increasing risks by allowing more overlap against the schedule, efficiency, and cost gains by accelerating progress on the project.

Strengths and Benefits:

- The costs, schedule, and resources required for the project are known from the start of the project and are more predictable *provided that the requirements can be accurately defined upfront*.
- It can be a more efficient process where there is little uncertainty about the project requirements, but that may not be realistic in many environments.
- The model is easily scalable to large complex projects and doesn't require the team to be co-located.
- The model isn't highly dependent on the culture of the organization and doesn't require much of a shift in thinking from established ways of doing things.
- The model is also adaptable to high-risk and regulated environments, where a higher level of project control may be required.

Risks and Limitations:

- Probably has more overhead for control purposes; however, that level of control may be needed in certain situations such as high risk or regulated environments
- The contractual style of relationship with the customer that this model is based on limits the ability to develop a true partnership with the customer to meet customer needs

- Typically requires documentation for the upfront portion of the effort; however, that investment may pay off in increased efficiency for types of projects where the solution can be easily defined up front with a very low level of uncertainty
- More resistant to change and limited adaptability and flexibility to adapt to uncertain and changing requirements
- Overall development schedule is probably longer because of the sequential nature of the process
- Can't take full advantage of lean and agile thinking
- Defers integration and acceptance testing till the end of the project, which can create significant risks because problems may not be discovered until the very end of the project

The use of traditional plan-driven life-cycle models for software projects has diminished significantly as companies migrate to more agile approaches that focus on increased levels of flexibility and adaptability to maximize business outcomes as opposed to focusing heavily on conformance to a plan with cost and schedule goals. Bob Wysocki describes traditional plan-driven life-cycle models as follows:

> "The limiting factor in these plan-driven approaches is that they are change-intolerant. They are focused on delivering according to time and budget constraints, and rely more on compliance to plan than on delivering business value. The plan is sacred, and conformance to it is the hallmark of the successful project team."[5]

Bob Wysocki is absolutely right—that is typically how many traditional plan-driven life-cycle models have been implemented; however:

- The focus on schedule and cost control is not necessarily a bad thing—in some environments, such as those involving customer contractual commitments, it is essential.
- On the other hand, it is important to recognize that the perception of high levels of predictability and control that plan-driven models provide is an illusion if requirements are uncertain.

In environments where the focus on schedules and costs is not as important, there is nothing that prevents allowing more flexibility and openness to change in a traditional plan-driven model, and the change management process does not have to be unnecessarily cumbersome. It is mostly a matter of changing the mindset of how it's implemented and relaxing some of the rigidity of the change control process associated with the model. However, this model clearly becomes

[5] Wysocki, Robert, *Effective Project Management—Traditional, Agile, Extreme*, Hoboken, NJ: Wiley, New York, 2009, p. 301

cumbersome and impractical when the level of changes becomes numerous and significant.

Incremental Life-Cycle Model

The incremental life-cycle model is a variation on the traditional plan-driven life-cycle model. An incremental life-cycle model is based on delivering the overall solution in releases that are spread out over a period of time. In this type of life-cycle model, there would be some overall level of planning at the solution level to break it up into releases, but that level of planning need not go too far beyond what's in release 1. Each release would then have an abbreviated life-cycle model associated with planning, designing, testing, and implementing the details of that release (see Figure 8.6). The detailed requirements for each release would be defined prior to starting development of that release.

Distinguishing Characteristics:

The key things that differentiate an incremental life-cycle model are similar to a traditional plan-driven life-cycle model with the exception that the overall life-cycle model is broken into individual releases and a release planning phase can be added on the front end to define what will be included in each release.

Potential Variations:

This model is a series of "mini" traditional plan-driven life-cycle models—the possible variations include:

1. Same variations as the traditional plan-driven model for each release life cycle:
   - Number and types of phases
   - Deliverables and artifacts required for each phase
   - Level of formality to the review process between phases
   - Amount of overlap allowed between phases

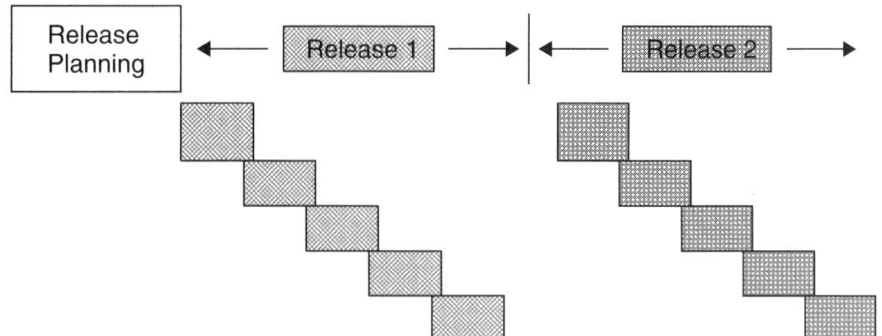

Figure 8.6 Incremental conceptual life-cycle model

2. The effort required for the incremental releases might be overlapped—for example, the requirements definition for release 2 might begin while release 1 is still being completed.

Strengths and Benefits:

Similar to the traditional plan-driven model, except that this model:

- Allows for earlier release of incremental functionality
- Defers detailed planning for future releases rather than trying to do it all upfront
- Provides some flexibility to adjust the contents of each release based on the previous release

Risks and Limitations:

Similar to traditional plan-driven life-cycle models. Except that this model allows a little more flexibility to adapt to changes between releases and defers the detailed planning for future releases:

- May have more overhead for control purposes; however, that level of control may be needed in certain situations such as high- risk or regulated environments
- The contractual style of relationship with the customer that this model is based on limits the ability to develop a true partnership with the customer to meet customer needs
- May require documentation for the upfront portion of the effort; however, that investment may pay off in increased efficiency for types of projects where the solution can be easily defined upfront with a very low level of uncertainty
- More resistant to change and limited adaptability and flexibility to adapt to uncertain and changing requirements
- Overall development schedule is probably longer because of the sequential nature of the process
- Can't take full advantage of lean and agile thinking
- Defers integration and acceptance testing till the end of the project, which can create significant risks

Iterative Plan-Driven Life-Cycle Model

An iterative plan-driven approach is similar to an incremental approach, except that the functionality in each increment (iteration) may not be releasable software, each iteration might be smaller increments of functionality. There would also typically be a higher-level of upfront planning at the solution level to define

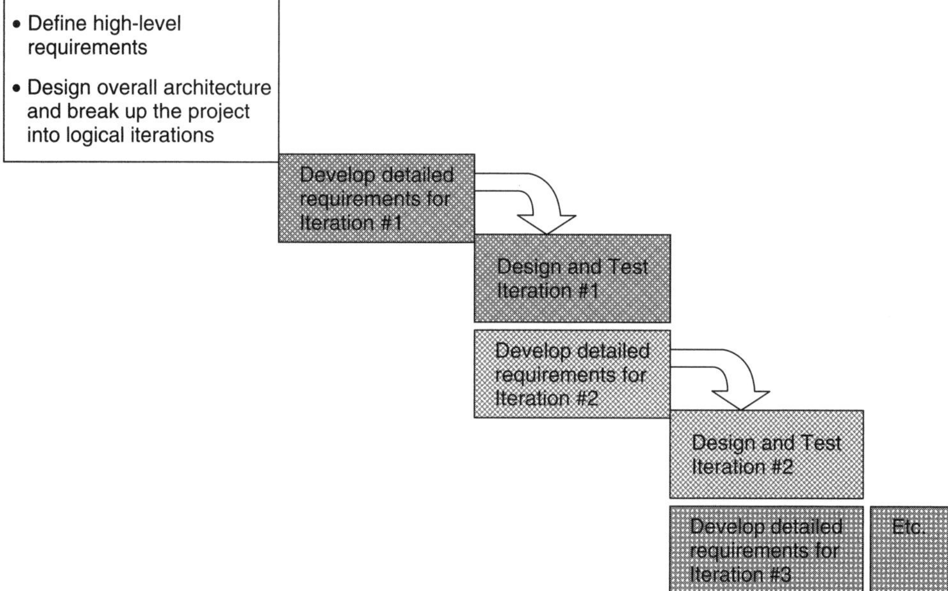

Figure 8.7 Iterative plan-driven conceptual life-cycle model

what is in each iteration. The detailed requirements for each iteration would be defined prior to starting development of that iteration; however, in many cases, the requirements for the next iteration can be developed in parallel with completing the development of the current iteration. After all iterations are complete, there would typically be a final system integration and test iteration for the completed system. An example of an iterative plan-driven life-cycle model is shown in Figure 8.7.

Distinguishing Characteristics:

The distinguishing characteristics associated with an iterative plan-driven life-cycle model are similar to those of an incremental life-cycle model with the exception that each iteration may not produce a releasable product and the process is more adaptive—each iteration is used to progressively build some level of functionality that gradually builds towards a releasable product.

Potential Variations:

1. Many of the basic variations in this model are similar to those of the incremental life-cycle model:
   - Number and types of phases for each iteration and for the overall solution
   - Deliverables and artifacts required for each iteration and for the overall solution

- Level of formality to the review process between iterations
- Amount of overlap allowed between iterations and between phases within an iteration

2. Another variation on this model is a "prototyping" approach, whereby the requirements for the functionality in a given iteration are not completely certain and a prototyping approach is used to progressively define the functionality required for each iteration. The iteration process is repeated as needed until the requirements for that iteration are well-defined.

Strengths and Benefits:

- It is similar to the incremental life-cycle model, except that this model is more iterative and more flexible for adapting to change because the solution is broken up into smaller increments of functionality.
- Detailed requirements for each iteration are deferred until required for that iteration, which should accelerate the startup of the project
- Iterations provide a mechanism for getting user feedback early and making "midcourse" corrections in the middle of the project if necessary.
- It provides a balance of control and agility for companies and projects that require a stronger emphasis on control.

Risks and Limitations:

- Doesn't provide the level of adaptability and flexibility provided by more adaptive agile methodologies—requirements are defined prior to the start of each iteration and do not generally change once the iteration has started.

Iterative Emergent Life-Cycle Model

An iterative emergent approach typically breaks up the solution into iterations; however, instead of defining all of the requirements prior to the beginning of each iteration, only the high-level requirements are defined prior to the start of the iteration and detailed requirements for each iteration are further defined during the iterations. The following is a list of some of the life-cycle models that would be included in this category:

Life-cycle Model	Reference
Rational Unified Process (RUP®)	www.ambysoft.com/unifiedprocess/rupIntroduction.html
Enterprise Unified Process	www.enterpriseunifiedprocess.com/
Agile Unified Process	www.ambysoft.com/unifiedprocess/agileUP.html

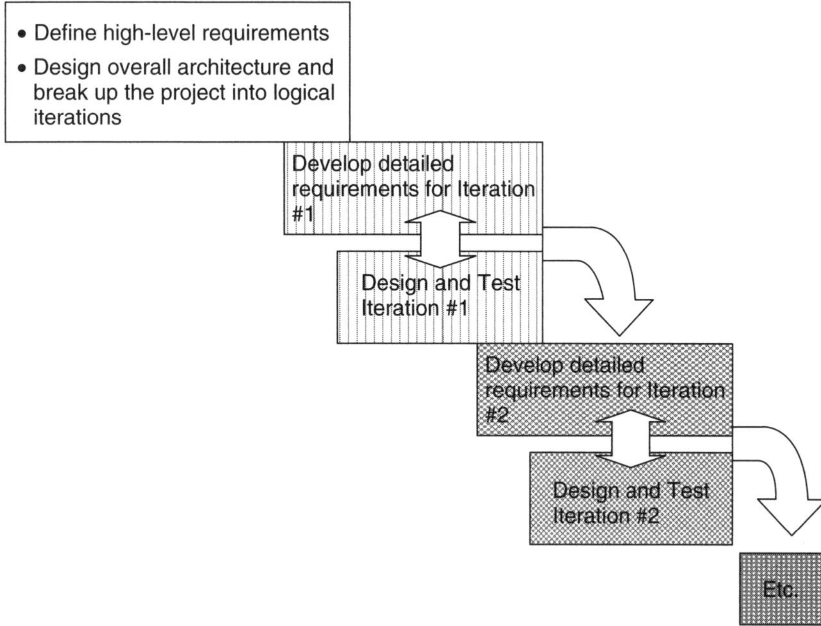

Figure 8.8 Iterative emergent conceptual life-cycle model

Figure 8.8 shows a general conceptual diagram of an iterative emergent approach that uses iterations for each increment of functionality. Instead of developing detailed requirements prior to the start of the iteration, a portion of the detailed requirements would be developed concurrently with the iteration. After all iterations are complete, there would typically be a final system integration and test iteration for the completed system.

Distinguishing Characteristics:

The distinguishing characteristics associated with an iterative emergent life-cycle model are similar to an iterative plan-driven life-cycle model with the exception that a portion of the detailed requirements for each iteration are developed concurrently with the design and development effort for that iteration rather than prior to the start of the iteration. Examples of life-cycle models that would be included in this category include the Unified Process, including the Rational Unified Process (RUP®) and other variations of the Unified Process.

Potential Variations:

1. The level of documentation and artifacts required for the process can vary significantly—for example, RUP® is noted for being fairly heavy on

documentation and artifacts, but those requirements can be customized and streamlined easily

2. The requirements process can be tailored to be more or less emergent:
   - Some of the requirements that might normally be defined upfront prior to the beginning of an iteration might be deferred to be completed during the design and development portion of the iteration.
   - Some of the detailed requirements that might normally be defined during the design and development portion of an iteration might be defined upfront prior to the iteration.
3. The length of iterations and the process for performing iterations can also vary widely.
4. Most of these processes do not rely on timeboxing of iterations; however, that is another option.

Strengths and Benefits:

- Deferring detailed requirements for each iteration allows the project to get started much more quickly.
- The user is more involved in the development, which should provide a higher level of assurance that the solution meets user requirements.
- The process is more flexible and adaptive for meeting user needs but still provides a good overall framework for control and planning.
- Iterations provide a mechanism for getting user feedback early and making "midcourse" corrections in the middle of the project if necessary.

Risks and Limitations:

- More difficult to predict and control overall project costs and schedules than a more traditional, plan-driven model
- Requires regression testing to ensure that changes introduced do not have an unintended impact on other functionality that has been implemented previously

Adaptive Life-Cycle Model

An adaptive life-cycle model is designed and optimized for environments with high levels of uncertainty. The amount of upfront planning is limited and a "rolling wave" planning approach is generally used concurrently with the development effort. The architecture and detailed requirements are also generally defined concurrently with the development effort. The following is a list of some of the life-cycle models that would be included in this category.

Approach	Reference
Extreme Programming (XP)	www.extremeprogramming.org
Scrum	www.scrumalliance.org

Figure 8.9 shows a general conceptual diagram of an adaptive approach that uses sprints for each increment of functionality. Instead of developing detailed requirements prior to the start of the sprint, the detailed requirements would be developed collaboratively with the development team during each sprint. After all sprints are complete, there would typically be a final system integration and test sprint for the completed system.

Distinguishing Characteristics:

The distinguishing characteristics associated with an adaptive life-cycle model are similar to those of an iterative emergent life-cycle model with the exception that because the solution is more uncertain:

- Upfront planning and definition of the solution is much more limited,
- The approach relies on a much higher level of collaborative engagement of the user in the design and development process.
- A higher level of change is anticipated and accommodated by the model.

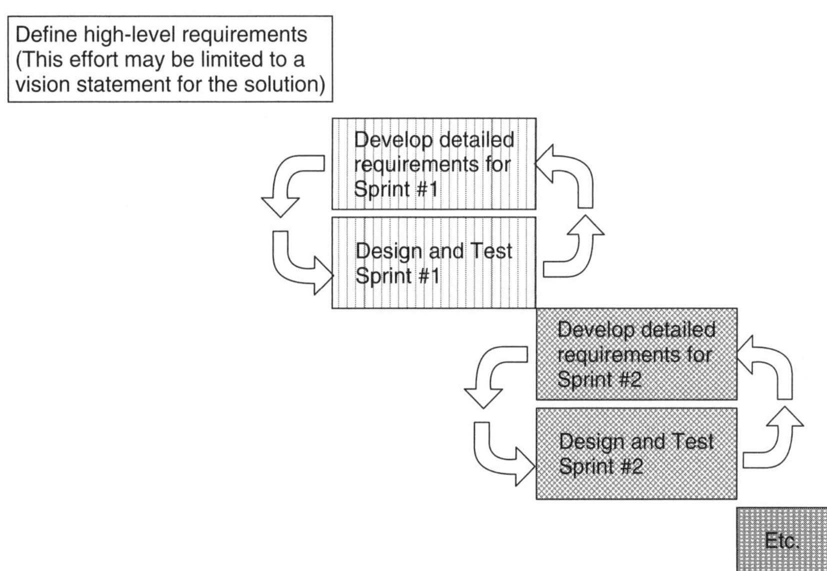

Figure 8.9 Adaptive conceptual life-cycle model

Potential Variations:

- The level of upfront planning and architecture development can vary significantly.
- The length of iterations and the process for performing iterations can also vary; however, iterations are generally timeboxed and constrained to fixed durations.

Strengths and Benefits:

Similar to the iterative emergent approach, except that:

- The user is much more closely coupled into the development, which should provide a higher-level of assurance that the solution meets user requirements.
- The process is more flexible and adaptive, and changes are expected.
- Sprints are very short, which should result in developing increments of functionality more rapidly and provide more immediate feedback.

Risks and Limitations:

- Requires a higher level of sophistication and training to implement this model.
- Requires a greater commitment of user resources to participate directly in the design and development process.
- Much more difficult to predict and control overall project costs and schedules.
- May need to be extended to scale to larger more complex projects.
- Because the solution evolves progressively, there is a risk that the overall architecture will not have a sound overall design and may require rework and cleanup.

SUMMARY OF SDLC GUIDELINES

In selecting a standard SDLC and/or customizing an SDLC to fit the needs of a project, it's important to keep in mind the potential purposes an SDLC can serve to make sure that the SDLC is providing the intended value without creating unnecessary overhead.

General Considerations

- **An SDLC provides a "road map."** This way all the members of the team understand their role and how it fits into accomplishing the goals of the project. It's like a play book for an athletic team—if all the players on an athletic team just ran around without a play book hoping to make a play, the team might not be very successful.

- **An SDLC helps use resources more efficiently**. Each resource on the team knows when and how he or she needs to engage in the project.
- **An SDLC that has been proven to work in the past on similar projects has a lot of value**. The chances of success in a project are much higher if there is a defined and reliable methodology that has been used successfully on similar projects in the past. Of course, for a methodology to be reusable, it has to be at least somewhat defined and documented.
- **An SDLC provides a basis for ongoing continuous improvement.** If an organization uses a defined methodology for executing projects, that methodology becomes a basis for incorporating lessons learned and it gets better over time. A key part of any SDLC should be a postmortem at the end of the project and at various points during the project to look back at what went right, what went wrong, and how the process could be done differently next time. Of course, if an SDLC isn't defined, there's no baseline process to incorporate those lessons learned into and no basis for ongoing improvement.

Requirements Management Considerations

Choose an SDLC based on the most appropriate requirements definition process (See "Requirements Management Principles"):

- If the requirements are relatively well-known or can be easily determined upfront, choose a more traditional plan-driven model.
- If the requirements are very uncertain and difficult to determine upfront, choose a more iterative or adaptive model to defer the requirements definition process.
- If the requirements are uncertain and the customer is not willing or able to provide the level of dedicated involvement required by an adaptive model, an adaptive model probably won't work and an iterative model may be best.
- If a commitment to date/cost is required upfront, a more plan-driven approach or a hybrid approach may be required to provide that level of control and predictability.

Risk Management Considerations

The overall level of risk management should be proportionate to the criticality of the project. On high-risk projects, it's essential to have some kind of process for managing the risks, and that should be built into the design of the SDLC. In general, a risk that is caught early in the project will have a lot less impact than if it is allowed to propagate further into the project and isn't discovered until later; however, it may not be possible to completely plan and identify all risks upfront. Detecting and mitigating risks may be much more difficult to do upfront in projects with a high level of uncertainty. (See the "Risk Management Section").

Project Scope and Complexity Considerations

Larger, more complex projects may either require a more plan-driven methodology or at least layering an additional level of planning and management on top of an agile foundation.

Other Considerations

There are a number of other considerations that might impact the choice of an SDLC:

1. The SDLC chosen must be consistent with the culture and capabilities of the organization. Factors include:
   - Need and desire for control—leadership and management style
   - Proficiency and level of training of employees
   - Tolerance for risk and project uncertainty
   - Customer commitment to participate in the process
   - Ability to collocate the team members and the separation of the team members across time zones and linguistic barriers
2. Contractual and business requirements may dictate the use of certain types of life-cycle models; for example:
   - Regulatory requirements may require a controlled process.
   - Contractual requirements may require a formalized change control approach and may require formal and documented approvals at different stages of progress.
   - Configuration management requirements may require a disciplined method for ensuring that all of the components of the entire system are consistent with each other.

SELECTING A SOFTWARE DEVELOPMENT LIFE CYCLE

Comparison of Approaches

The hybrid approaches can provide a compromise to balance the need for control and predictability against agility. The following is a summary of some of the general considerations that might play a role in selecting one of these approaches.

Factors Favoring Iterativeor Plan-Driven Approaches

	Traditional Plan-Driven	Iterative Plan-Driven	Iterative Emergent	Adaptive (PureAgile)
Limited capabilities for agile project teams				
Well-dened requirements with low levels of uncertainty				
Need to plan and estimate cost and schedule upfront				
Need to use geographically distributed teams				
Scalability for large projects				
Consistency with high risk and/or regulatory environments				
Minimize the impact on business sponsors				

Factors Favoring Iterativeor Plan-Driven Approaches

	Traditional Plan-Driven	Iterative Plan-Driven	Iterative Adaptive	Adaptive (PureAgile)
Uncertain requirements with signicant potential for change				
Aggressive timeframes to deliver functionality				
User involvement in development process				
Team empowerment and motivation				
Flexibility to adapt to changes				
Adaptability (ability to learn quickly as the project progresses)				
Minimum documentation requirements				

Life-Cycle Model Selection Examples

This section contains some examples of different actual scenarios where these life-cycle models have been used and provides some discussion on the rationale for choosing a particular life-cycle model in each situation.

Pure Waterfall Approach

Company Background:

A large insurance company planned to roll out a major new application to support a new insurance product.

Application Background:

- The company had recently rolled out another application that had not met user expectations.
- The company was also interested in better defining and reengineering some of their business processes concurrently with the introduction of the new insurance product.
- Accurate definition and implementation of the business rules associated with the implementation of the new insurance product were extremely critical to protect the company's business interests.
- Because this was such a critical effort and the previous insurance project had not met expectations, there was a very strong senior management commitment of user resources to define the requirements to make this effort successful.

Methodology:

A modified version of a traditional plan-driven life-cycle model was used:

- A team consisting of key business management stakeholders was assigned to define the business processes, business rules, and requirements for the system. The primary focus of that effort was defining the business processes, business rules, and use cases that the system had to support (not detailed design requirements). A very aggressive schedule was established for completing this portion of the effort—the team met in daily work sessions for approximately four hours a day, five days a week for almost three months to define and document the business processes, use cases, business rules, and requirements for the new system.
- A requirements management tool was used to track requirements and to perform requirements traceability to ensure that requirements were complete and consistent with the business objectives of the project.
- Further definition of detailed requirements, such as UI screen designs was deferred to a later phase of the project.

Rationale for This Methodology:

- A considerable amount of work was required to define the business processes and the business rules for how the application should work. Attempting to do that in parallel with the design effort would have made no sense. It would have tied up development resources unnecessarily and possibly resulted in a significant amount of rework as the definition of the business process and rules evolved.
- Ensuring the completeness, consistency, and accuracy of the business requirements and rules associated with the application was very critical for managing the risks associated with this application, and the use of requirements management tools was essential to performing that analysis.

Iterative Plan-Driven Approach—Example #1

Company Background:

A midsized IT consulting company that is in the business of recruiting and placing specialized contract consultants with clients used a home-grown CRM system to track and manage relationships with both consultants and clients. The same system is used to manage the placement process associated with placing consultants in client assignments.

Application Background:

- The CRM system needed to be replaced by a more modern architecture that would allow future expandability and improved maintainability; however, the company president wanted the ability to easily tailor the system to the company's own unique business processes. As a result, purchasing an off-the-shelf CRM system as a replacement was not considered to be a viable option.
- Selection of a design architecture for the new system that would allow for ease of maintainability and expandability in the future was considered very important.
- As part of the implementation of the replacement system, the company wanted to do some reengineering of their business processes at the same time, and those reengineered processes would be incorporated into the design of the new system.
- The company wanted to automate as much of their business processes as possible to maximize employee productivity. The business rules associated with those business processes were very critical to define and automate as much as possible in the new system.
- User involvement in the design process was critical because the usability of the system was an extremely important feature. The company hires

new employees with little or no prior experience as recruiters and account managers, and it is very important that they be able to learn their job functions easily with a minimum of training. The screen design and layout of the new system had to be designed to facilitate that.

- The company president wanted to see and approve a reasonably accurate cost and schedule for the project before the design team was hired to actually begin the project. A limited-scale prototyping effort to validate some of the design concepts with users prior to beginning the actual design was acceptable.

Methodology:

An iterative plan-driven life-cycle model approach was used for this project:

- A steering group was formed of the company's senior-level executives to reengineer the business processes and to establish the high-level business process, business rules, and system requirements at the same time.
- The high-level requirements were used to finalize the design approach for the overall system architecture, and because the architectural design approach was so important, it was also considered essential to define the architectural approach prior to the start of the detailed design phase.
- Because the user interface was so critical to the design of the system and had a big impact on the requirements as well as the cost and schedule, some limited prototyping of the UI was done to better define the requirements in that area as part of the requirements definition effort.

Rationale for This Methodology:

- Because the definition of the business processes and the business rules was considered so important, the requirements were completed to a sufficient level to include detailed business rules for how the system should work as part of the initial planning for the system. Attempting to reengineer the business processes and define the new business rules while the design of the new system was in process was not considered a viable option because it would have slowed down the design effort significantly and possibly resulted in significant rework.
- Because the company president wanted to approve a relatively accurate cost and schedule prior to committing to the start of the project, an iterative plan-driven life-cycle model was used to define the requirements to a sufficient level of detail to estimate the project schedule and cost as accurately as possible. However, detailed requirements were deferred till the design phase.
- Prototyping of the user interface (UI) upfront was done because that portion of the system was so important. That worked well in this case because

resources to do a completely detailed design weren't available until the project budget was approved. The simulated UI screens provided a low-cost way to get user feedback into the design requirements.

Iterative Plan-Driven Approach—Example #2

Company Background:

Rapidly growing financial services company with about 700 employees, needed to replace an aging legacy system that was used for performance analytics.

Application Background:

One particular software application used for performance analytics required a major redesign to improve maintainability and to build a more robust platform that was capable of adding new features required for new business requirements. This particular application performed many very complex and mission-critical tasks related to performance analytics that had to be very precise and accurate. The formulas and process that defined how those calculations were performed were buried in the code, and the code was a tangled mess that was almost impossible to maintain and also to unravel to discover the requirements and rules that were embedded in it.

Methodology:

The methodology chosen was to use an iterative plan-driven life-cycle model, where the goal of Iteration #1 was to simply replace the existing system functionality with a new architecture. Further iterations beyond Iteration #1 would build on that initial foundation and begin adding additional new functionality incrementally.

Rationale for This Methodology:

- An analysis of the existing system was performed to determine if the architecture could be broken up into components that could be replaced incrementally and that was determined not to be feasible. The existing software was so poorly designed that the effort required to refactor it in order to facilitate an incremental approach would be much too great.
- Since this system performed a very mission-critical application, the risks associated with replacing it were very high. Any replacement system had to duplicate the calculations that were performed by the existing system exactly and none of the existing system functionality could be left out of the replacement system when it was cutover to operational use. Therefore, the minimum goals for Iteration #1 had to be to replace the functionality in the existing system as accurately as possible.

- Keeping any new functionality out of Iteration #1 was essential for two key reasons: (1) to get Iteration #1 done as quickly as possible and (2) to minimize the risk

Adaptive Approach—Example

Company Background:

AOL Inc. has been in business for over 25 years (AOL was founded in 1983), and during that time their business has changed from primarily being a provider of e-mail services to dial-up subscribers to being a provider of news and information to their subscribers who also use e-mail services. The business of publishing news and information is a much more fast-paced business than the traditional dial-up e-mail services business, and AOL decided that a major change in their business processes and software development practices was essential to make it fast moving enough to keep pace with their new business direction. (The information in this example is based on a presentation by Jochen (Joe) Krebs to the Boston Agile Group)[6]

Application Background:

This case study was not limited to a particular application and was a total transformation of all of AOL's software development practices.

Methodology:

AOL implemented a major transformation of their entire business and software development processes across the whole company to a pure agile (Scrum) approach. The effort consisted of:

- 8,000 employees worldwide
- 1,000 AOL employees involved in software development:
  - Product
  - Technology
  - Editorial
  - Photo
  - User Experience
- Approximately:
  - 550 ScrumMasters within AOL
  - 25 Product Owners
  - 100 Acting ScrumMasters

---

[6] Krebs, Jochen (Joe), Presentation to the Agile Boston Group, February 2010

The effort affected the daily life of approximately 3,000 employees because it was a complete business process transformation (not just a development effort) and involved about 40–60 projects in parallel.

Rationale for This Methodology:

This change was considered an essential part of a strategic transformation of the AOL business that was led and driven from the top-down by their CEO. The CEO felt that a major transformation in AOL was needed from what used to be a provider of e-mail services to subscribers to focus on being a very aggressive online publisher of information. The implementation of agile methodologies in the development organization was a great catalyst to initiate that transformation, but the overall transformation impacted the whole company.

Summary of Results

Before:	A project was delivered after 2 years with fewer features, behind schedule (after competitor) with frustrated employees.
After:	Similar project was launched in 6 months with more features, ahead of schedule with high morale employees.

Before:	One product manager worked on one product.
After:	One product manager served as product owner for three products.

CHAPTER 9

PART II SUMMARY AND ACTION PLAN

SUMMARY OF IMPACT ON PROJECT MANAGERS AND PMI®

Moving to a more agile approach has some significant implications for project managers and also for the Project Management Institute (PMI®):

1. **Balancing Flexibility and Adaptability with Control**
   In many situations, there is a need for a shift in thinking in project management to put more focus on successfully achieving business results. Traditionally, project managers may have focused very heavily on managing costs and schedules and on controlling the scope of a project. That focus is still very appropriate in some situations; however, it typically results in a very planned and controlled management style that may be successful in meeting costs and schedules but doesn't have sufficient flexibility and adaptability in environments where there is a high level of uncertainty to successfully provide successful business results.

   For both project managers and PMI®, there is a general need to rethink how we apply many of the traditional project management practices and principles. In an agile environment, many of the practices and principles are still very sound, but they need to be applied in an entirely different context with the right balance between control and agility. A major effort is probably needed to merge the process-oriented thinking behind the *A Guide to the Product Management Body of Knowledge*—Fourth Edition (*PMBOK® Guide*—Fourth Edition) with the value-oriented thinking behind agile.
2. **Becoming a Project Management "Chef"**
   As I mentioned, we need to develop more high-level project managers into "chefs" rather than "cooks." To help their companies become more agile might mean that the role of the project manager needs to shift from just implementing a standard methodology to playing a broader role of helping to design and/or choose an appropriate customized methodology as well as making recommendations to tailor it as needed to fit a given project. That requires a higher level of skill—it requires understanding a broader range of methodologies (agile as well as non-agile) at a deeper

level to know how to create the right set of "recipes" that have the right blend of "ingredients" to provide a balance of control and agility for a given business environment.

3. Going All the Way to Agile
   In many cases in the past, a lot of the actual project work may have been done primarily in functional departments and the primary role of the project manager may have been a planner, coordinator, and administrator. The movement to more agile methodologies may require project managers to take a much more active role in leading cross-functional teams engaged in agile projects. That probably requires a much broader range of skills to take a major leadership role in leading that kind of effort; for example:
   - More technical skills may be needed because the boundary between management of the development team and overall project management will begin to blur.
   - More business analysis skills may be needed because the requirements definition effort may also become much more of an integral part of the development effort.
   - More people management and leadership skills may be needed because the functional managers in different departments may play less of a role in management of cross-functional teams
   - More quality management and process knowledge may be needed because much of the QA function may also become more of an integral part of the development effort.

   In the extreme case, the role of a project manager within a project might change to becoming a ScrumMaster, which is a very different role than a traditional project management role. Becoming a ScrumMaster would probably require developing some new skills for many project managers.
   - The ScrumMaster is much more of a facilitator of the process than a controller of the process.
   - The ScrumMaster will be very directly involved in the actual development effort and needs to have an understanding of the technical details of the product design as well as the process for managing it.
4. Developing and Leading Organizational Transformations
   Moving to a more agile approach may require a major organizational transformation. In that situation, there is probably also a need and an opportunity for project managers to play a higher-level role in helping to lead and implement that organizational transformation to move to a more agile environment. This role might include:
   - Working with senior-level managers to help them understand the trade-offs involved in adopting a business processes and development processes with an appropriate level of agility and control.

- Helping to facilitate organizational change management initiatives that might be needed to move towards a more agile approach.
- Facilitating the cross-functional teamwork that is needed among senior managers to implement the approach.

DEVELOPING AN ACTION PLAN FOR PROJECT MANAGERS

For project managers who work inside companies making a transition to agile, their own personal direction will need to become consistent with their company's direction. For all project managers, there are some general career-planning questions that are similar to the questions posed for businesses:

- What is the impact of agile on project management, and are you satisfied that your current approach to project management will be consistent with more agile project management in the future?
- How agile do you want to be and when do you want to get there? It is not necessary for all project managers to move to the most extreme forms of agile project manager, but even implementing hybrid approaches may require some shifts in thinking about project management.
- How do you get from where you are to where you want to be?

The level of change required for project managers is also similar to companies and organizations, but it's more of a personal change than an organizational change. It may either be a major and radical shift in your project management approach and the way you think about project management or only be a minor shift in direction, depending on where you are today and where you want to get to.

There still will be a need for traditional project managers who are used to doing traditional plan-driven project methodologies, but over time, the need for the plan-driven approach is likely to decline, and it is clear that there is a growing need for more agile forms of project management.

The approach for developing new project management skills might also follow three similar paths:

Incremental Improvements

Even project managers who operate in traditional environments can benefit from a shift in thinking towards a more agile approach if it is consistent with their company's business environment and direction:

- Tailor the life-cycle methodology for projects to better fit the business environment and project goals based on an understanding of the principles behind it.
- Recognize the importance of successfully meeting business outcomes in addition to managing cost and schedule goals, and develop an approach

that provides the right balance of control and agility to do achieve both of those objectives.

- Shift to a management and leadership style that is based on teamwork, collective ownership, and empowerment and respect for people.
- Develop a flexible and value-based approach to streamline process documentation and artifacts associated with projects.

All of these things can be done, to some extent, even in a traditional plan-driven project environment. In most cases, the key thing that is needed is just a shift in thinking—that will be easy for some and not so easy for others. Project managers who have been deeply engrained in the kind of "command and control" thinking that has been prevalent in project management for so long may have the most difficulty in making that shift.

Designing and Implementing Hybrid Approaches

There is a huge need for project managers who can operate successfully in the "middle ground" between extreme Waterfall approaches and pure agile approaches. Many companies will choose to operate in this space either because a pure agile approach isn't feasible for them or as part of an incremental migration to get to a pure agile approach over time.

Operating in this space also requires some new skills—it isn't just a matter of taking a standard iterative approach like RUP® and implementing it by the book. In many cases, it will mean designing and implementing customized approaches that blend the right levels of control and agility and have the right level of lean thinking built into them to streamline documents and artifacts as needed.

There is also a significant need for project managers who have knowledge of a number of different methodologies and can help companies pick and choose an appropriate methodology for a project or blend elements of multiple methodologies together if necessary. In many environments, one methodology doesn't fit all projects. Many project managers are schooled primarily in one methodology (whatever it might be, agile or non-agile) and might try to force-fit projects to that methodology because that's what they're most familiar with. The right approach is to tailor the methodology (or combination of methodologies) to fit the project rather than attempting to force-fit a project to any given methodology (agile or non-agile). It takes much more skill and a broader and deeper understanding of a number of different methodologies to do that.

Implementing Pure Agile Project Management Approaches

Some project managers may choose to move to a pure agile form of project management. That might mean becoming a ScrumMaster (and developing those skills is certainly worthwhile); but in an agile approach, a ScrumMaster operates primarily at the iteration management level. Depending on the scope and complexity of the project, there is still a need for a project management role above the iteration management level in many agile projects. That role might be performed by the ScrumMaster, or the project might be large enough to justify a separate project manager to fill that role.

In either case, the project manager certainly needs to deeply understand agile principles and methodologies to operate in that environment and needs to develop a project management approach that is consistent with operating in that environment.

Helping Companies Move in the Right Direction

There is also a need for project managers who can operate at a very high level and help companies define and implement a migration strategy that is well aligned with their business goals and direction. This kind of effort might include developing the initial business strategy and plan, defining and implementing a change management initiative if required, and coaching and mentoring others in the organization to help implement that plan.

PART III

APPENDICES

APPENDIX A

Overview of Agile Development Practices

A number of technical practices are commonly used at the development level in agile projects. This appendix provides an overview of some of the most commonly used technical practices.

EXTREME PROGRAMMING

Extreme programming (XP) is a development approach that advocates frequent releases of software in short development cycles (timeboxing).

> "Extreme Programming improves a software project in five essential ways; communication, simplicity, feedback, respect, and courage. Extreme Programmers constantly communicate with their customers and fellow programmers. They keep their design simple and clean. They get feedback by testing their software starting on day one. They deliver the system to the customers as early as possible and implement changes as suggested. Every small success deepens their respect for the unique contributions of each and every team member. With this foundation Extreme Programmers are able to courageously respond to changing requirements and technology."[1]

XP does not attempt to define all of the requirements upfront as is commonly done in the Waterfall approach. Instead, it relies on close collaboration between the business users and developers to define and refine the requirements as the design progresses. XP advocates frequent releases of software in short development cycles (timeboxing).

The following is a brief description of the XP planning process.

1. User Stories
   The XP process begins with the development of "user stories." The purpose of a user story is not to provide all the details of any particular scenario, but rather to be able to describe the requirement at a high level sufficient to estimate how complex a part of the system will be, and how long it may take to implement it. The details of the story will be clarified

[1] "Extreme Programming," www.extremeprogramming.org

with the customer just prior to and during the implementation of the user story. The following is an example of a user story:

"As a customer representative, I can search for my customers by their first and last name."

2. Release Planning

   The Release Planning Process consists of estimating the difficulty of each user story and assigning them to releases for the life of the project. The release plan is based on rough estimates that will be further refined as the project progresses. The prioritization of assigning user stories to each release is based generally on developing the features that have highest value to the customer as early as possible, but that prioritization may include other factors and needs to be balanced with developing other architectural needs that the customer may not be aware of at all. For example, if you're building a house, the roof, bedrooms, and kitchen probably provide the most value to the home buyer; however, you really need to start with the foundation and some basic services like plumbing and electricity before adding some of those features.

3. Iteration Planning

   Each release is broken up into iterations, and the iterations are designed to produce working code as quickly as possible. At the beginning of each iteration, an iteration planning meeting is held to produce that iteration's plan of programming tasks. Each iteration is 1 to 3 weeks long—the duration of an iteration is called a "timebox." The length of the timebox is based on the velocity of the team (the rate of implementing user stories). User stories are chosen for this iteration by the customer from the release plan in order of the most valuable to the customer first.

4. Test-Driven Development

   XP uses a Test-Driven Development approach, whereby a unit test is developed for each user story prior to coding that user test. (See the "Test-Driven Development" section.)

5. Collective Ownership of Code

   Any developer can change any line of code to add functionality, fix bugs, improve the design or refactor. No one person becomes a bottleneck for changes.

6. Pair Programming

   All code to be sent into production is created by two people working together at a single computer. Pair programming increases software quality without impacting time to deliver. (See the "Pair Programming" section.)

7. Continuous Integration

   Developers should be integrating and committing code into the code repository whenever possible. Continuous integration often avoids diverging or fragmented development efforts, in which developers are not communicating with each other about what can be reused or what could be shared. (See the "Continuous Integration" section.)

8. Process Improvement
XP is designed to making improving the development process a normal part of the development. At the end of each iteration, there is a retrospective to critique the process (what went well, what didn't go well) and to make adjustments in the process if necessary for the next iteration. Because each iteration is short, learning happens quickly as the development progresses.

The following are some of the key principles associated with Extreme Programming:

1. Rapid Software Development
The software is broken up into small iterations to deliver working functionality as quickly as possible.

2. Communications
XP emphasizes very close communications among everyone on the team:

- The development team is normally co-located in close proximity to each other.
- The customer is expected to work closely with the development team throughout the development effort to define detailed requirements as the development progresses, provide regular feedback, and approve acceptance test results as development items are completed.

3. Simplicity
XP emphasizes keeping the solution as simple as possible, which includes:

- Limiting the design to known current requirements only (future requirements are not included in the development effort)
- Using refactoring to simplify the design whenever possible so that the code is easily understood by everyone on the development team

Strengths and Benefits:

- Close collaboration between developers and users throughout the development process will likely result in code that is more consistent with user requirements and maximizing business value.
- The flexibility to adapt to changes makes it easier to adapt to changing business requirements.
- XP efforts typically keep developers and business users focused on current design requirements and do not generally attempt to anticipate future

requirements. That implies an iterative approach that can make incremental business value available to the user much faster.

Risks and Limitations:

- Without detailed requirements to begin with, it is very difficult to accurately estimate the costs and schedule for the overall project upfront.
- Without a clear overall understanding of the requirements before starting the design, it may be difficult to define an optimum architecture for meeting those requirements until a substantial part of the code is already developed.
- It is difficult to use an XP approach for deep and complex functionality (and even more so for nonfunctional requirements such as regulatory compliance). For example, it may be difficult to express all the details of complex business rules on an index card.
- Changing requirements, an architecture that evolves as the design progresses, and failure to anticipate future requirements may require a substantial amount of rework to the code.
- Team distribution is also a challenge due to XP's emphasis on close collaboration, just-in-time story design, pair programming, continuous integration, and limited documentation. This limitation can be addressed, but not entirely overcome, through collaborative, enabling technologies such as portals for sharing information.

FEATURE-DRIVEN DEVELOPMENT

Feature-Driven Development (FDD) is a model-driven approach that puts more emphasis on defining an overall model of the system and a list of features to be included in the system prior to starting the design effort.

> "As the name implies, features are an important aspect of FDD. A feature is a small, client-valued function expressed in the form <action><result><object>. For example,
>
> - Calculate the total of a sale
> - Validate the password of a user, and
> - Authorize the sales transaction of a customer".
>
> Features are to FDD as use cases are to the Rational Unified Process (RUP®) and user stories are to XP—they're a primary source of requirements and the primary input into your planning efforts."[2]

[2] "Feature Driven Development (FDD) and Agile Modeling," www.agilemodeling.com/essays/fdd.htm

The key difference between XP and FDD is the amount of upfront design activity prior to beginning the design effort. Typically, agile and Scrum projects have what is called an "Iteration 0," which is used to resolve any significant uncertainties that need to be resolved prior to starting the design effort; however, that effort is always optional and it's completely up to the development team to decide:

- If it is needed
- What should be included
- How the analysis should be performed

FDD defines a more specific modeling approach, which is equivalent to what might be done in "Iteration 0" of an XP project. The level of depth of the FDD analysis can be scaled based on the scope and complexity of the project; however, doing the analysis is not optional. Feature-Driven Development may be a more appropriate design approach than Extreme Programming for large and complex agile projects.

The FDD development process comprises five basic activities:

1. Develop Overall Model
   The first step in FDD is to develop an overall object model. This is an important step to get both the domain (subject matter) experts and the development team to come to a shared understanding of the problem domain. The object model at this point is a high-level model and further depth and detail will be added as the project progresses.

   > "... In FDD ... the building of an object model is not a long, drawn-out, activity performed by an elite few using expensive CASE tools. The modelers do not format the resulting model into a large document and throw it over the wall for developers to implement.
   >
   > Instead, building an initial object model in FDD is an intense, highly iterative, collaborative and generally enjoyable activity involving domain and development members under the guidance of an experienced object modeler in the role of Chief Architect."[3]

2. Build Feature List
   The next step in the FDD process is to define the feature list hierarchy that will define the set of features that will be included in the solution. The feature list is typically hierarchical: it starts with high-level features, and then each high-level feature is further broken down into activities that are associated with that high-level feature.

   > "Unlike Scrum and Xtreme Programming that use a flat list of backlog items or user stories, FDD organizes its features into a three level

[3] "An Introduction to Feature-Driven Development," http://agile.dzone.com/articles/introduction-feature-driven

> hierarchy that it unimaginatively calls the feature list. Larger projects/teams need this extra organization. It helps them manage the larger numbers of items that are typically found on an FDD features list than on a Scrum-style backlog."[4]

3. Plan by Feature
   The "Plan by Feature" portion of FDD involves developing an initial development schedule and assigning initial development responsibilities. FDD differs from other agile methodologies in that it chooses not to adopt collective ownership of software source code. Instead, individual developers are assigned to be responsible for particular classes.

   > "The planning team initially sequence the feature sets representing activities by relative business value. Feature sets are also assigned to a Chief Programmer who will be responsible for their development. At the end of this process, each Chief Programmer effectively has a subset of the features list assigned to them. For a Chief Programmer this is their backlog or 'virtual inbox' of features to implement."[5]

4. Design by Feature
   At that point in the FDD process, the design is developed for each feature.

   > "A chief programmer selects a small group of features that are to be developed within two weeks. Together with the corresponding class owners, the chief programmer works out detailed sequence diagrams for each feature and refines the overall model. Next, the class and method prologues are written and finally a design inspection is held."[6]

5. Build by Feature
   Once the design is completed, the class owners develop the actual code for the classes that they are responsible for.

   > "After a successful design inspection a per feature activity to produce a completed client-valued function (feature) is being produced. The class owners develop the actual code for their classes. After a unit test and a successful code inspection, the completed feature is promoted to the main build."[7]

---

[4] "An Introduction to Feature-Driven Development," http://agile.dzone.com/articles/introduction-feature-driven

[5] "An Introduction to Feature-Driven Development," http://agile.dzone.com/articles/introduction-feature-driven

[6] "Feature-Driven Development," http://en.wikipedia.org/wiki/Feature_Driven_Development

[7] "Feature-Driven Development," http://en.wikipedia.org/wiki/Feature_Driven_Development

Strengths and Benefits:

- FDD is a much more planned approach, which can significantly reduce the risk in large complex projects. Finding the true problem (and taking the time to do so) is an upfront investment that can produce better results and also reduce the time required for the remainder of the project.
- Breaking up the design into discrete features encourages an iterative development approach and modularity of functionality so that individual features can be tested and validated as the design progresses.
- FDD generally involves developing a more complete understanding of the problem domain and breaking it up into features before beginning the actual design of each feature. This approach should provide a much better understanding of the scope and complexity of the overall problem and can provide a better foundation for developing a sound object-oriented architectural design approach with more accurate cost and schedule estimates than Extreme Programming. It also will probably result in less major rework of the code as the design progresses.
- The FDD approach is much more scalable and extensible to large, complex problems than the Extreme Programming approach.

Risks and Limitations:

- Because FDD requires developing an understanding of all the features that make up the problem domain prior to starting the design, it is likely to take longer to get started than an Extreme Programming approach, but that is certainly an acceptable tradeoff in many cases.
- The FDD approach is less agile than an Extreme Programming approach and is more difficult to adapt to changing requirements.
- The FDD approach generally requires more documentation than Extreme Programming to define the features that will be included in the design.

TEST-DRIVEN DEVELOPMENT

Test-Driven Development (TDD) is commonly used in agile methodologies to integrate testing directly into the software development effort:

> “Instead of writing functional code first and then your testing code as an afterthought, if you write it at all, you instead write your test code before your functional code. Furthermore, you do so in very small steps—one test and a small bit of corresponding functional code at a time. A programmer taking a TDD approach refuses to write a new function until there is first a test that fails because that function isn’t present. In fact, they refuse to add even a single line of code until a test exists for it.

> Once the test is in place they then do the work required to ensure that the test suite now passes."[8]

However, Test-Driven Development is not unique to agile development methodologies and is more of a best practice for code development that can be used with any development methodology, but in practice it is highly reliant on continuous integration.

> "Agile teams almost always develop test plans at the same time they define requirements; if a requirement isn't testable, then the requirement is not yet fully developed. This is a best practice that can be used in traditional development to ensure requirements are complete, accurate and testable."[9]

Test-Driven Development may include different levels of testing. At a minimum, it normally includes unit testing that is built into the software so that each module of the code can be tested as it is developed, but it is good practice to include functional testing and acceptance testing as well so that a functional regression test can also be performed as the code is developed a limited acceptance test can be performed on the results of each iteration as the work in each iteration is completed.

Strengths and Benefits:

Test-Driven Development works particularly well with agile methodologies because:

- It encourages the development of small incremental modules of code that can be easily tested and integrated with a Continuous Integration process.
- It is well suited to testing of the design as it progresses and provides immediate feedback to the developers on how well the design meets the requirements. If it is extended to include functional testing and some limited user acceptance testing, it is also a way to validate that the software meets user needs early on in the project.
- It also encourages developers to write only the minimal amount of code necessary to pass a given test.

Risks and Limitations:

- Some implementations of Test-Driven Development primarily address only unit testing of code modules, and much more testing may be needed at

---

[8] "Introduction to Test-Driven Design," www.agiledata.org/essays/tdd.html

[9] Hass, Kathleen, "The Blending of Traditional and Agile Project Management," *PM World Today*, May 2007

different levels of the application. For example, functional testing may be needed to test the complete system at a higher level to include user interface testing and other aspects of system testing that are not tested at the unit test level. User acceptance testing will probably also be needed of the complete system.

- Test-Driven Development puts the emphasis on rapidly implementing software to provide a minimum level of required functionality and relies on later refactoring the code to clean it up to meet acceptable design standards. There is a risk that the refactoring won't be done and the code might provide the desired functionality but may not be reliable and supportable.

PAIR PROGRAMMING

Pair programming is an agile software development technique in which two programmers work together at one work station. This kind of approach has been used successfully for many years in aviation—in commercial airliners; there are always two people in the cockpit—the captain and a copilot—to provide a higher level of safety. In an aircraft, the two people alternate roles—one might be flying the aircraft while the other observes. The observer is stepping back and looking at the big picture while the pilot who is flying the aircraft might be immersed in watching the instruments. This system has become essential for air safety in commercial aviation.

A similar approach is used for agile methodologies—one developer plays the role of an observer while the other developer in the pair writes the code. "While reviewing, the observer also considers the strategic direction of the work, coming up with ideas for improvements and likely future problems to address. This frees the driver to focus all of his or her attention on the 'tactical' aspects of completing the current task, using the observer as a safety net and guide."[10]

Pair programming is most commonly used with Extreme Programming and is less commonly used with Feature-Driven Development. Feature-Driven development encourages the idea that there should be one primary owner for a given feature.

Strengths and Benefits:

1. Design Quality
   One developer observing the other person's work should result in better quality software with better designs and fewer bugs. Any defects should also be caught much earlier in the development process as the code is being developed. The cost of the second developer who is required may or may not be at least partially offset by productivity gains.

---

[10] "Pair Programming," http://en.wikipedia.org/wiki/Pair_programming

2. Learning and Training
   Sharing knowledge about the system as the development progresses increases learning.
3. Overcoming Difficult Problems
   Pairs are able to more easily resolve difficult problems.

Risks and Limitations:

1. Work Preference
   Some developers prefer to work alone and a less experienced or less confident developer may feel intimidated when pairing with a more experienced developer and participate less as a result.
2. Costs
   Experienced developers may find it tedious to tutor a less experienced developer, and the productivity gains may not offset the additional costs of adding a second developer.

CODE REFACTORING

Code refactoring involves removing redundancy, eliminating unused functionality, and rejuvenating obsolete designs and improving the design of existing software in order to improve reliability and maintainability of the software. Refactoring throughout the entire project life cycle saves time and increases quality of the software. Code Refactoring is more commonly used with Extreme Programming—it is less commonly used with Feature-Driven Development.

Traditional plan-driven software development methods in the past have emphasized a very well-planned and structured design approach to create code that is well designed to begin with to avoid unnecessary and expensive rework of code. A potential problem with that approach is that it can put a higher level of emphasis on the structure and design of the code over the functionality of the code. Developers might produce very well-architected and well-structured code but lose sight of the functionality the code is intended to provide.

Agile approaches tend to emphasize quickly creating code to meet functional requirements *first*, for example, by using a Test-Driven Development approach, and then refactoring the code as necessary *later* to clean it up to reduce the complexity of the code and improve the maintainability. Modern design tools have made it easier to do refactoring of code and have enabled this to be a much more viable practice.

Strengths and Benefits:

- Encourages developers to put the primary focus on the functionality provided by the code first and clean it up later to make the code more structured and maintainable.

- Reduces the time required to produce functional code that can be available for prototyping and user validation

Risks and Limitations:

- In a project that relies heavily on refactoring, the amount of rework of the code required might be significant and, in most cases, it's much better to do it right the first time if possible and avoid the need to do refactoring altogether.
- If the architecture of the software is allowed to evolve through code refactoring rather than from a planned development approach, the structure of the code may not be optimized around the most desirable architectural approach.
- Time pressures to complete the iteration may short-circuit the code-refactoring effort and allow poorly organized code to be released.

CONTINUOUS INTEGRATION

Continuous integration is the practice of frequently integrating new or changed software with the code repository. It provides for early detection of problems that may occur when individual software developers are working on code changes that may potentially conflict with each other. In many typical software development environments, integration may not be performed until the application is ready for final release.

In one extreme case, I was involved in a very large hardware/software development effort in the early 1990s where a major electronics company spent over $150 million on the development of a complex communications switching system. We had already signed up beta test customers to test the product, and I was a program manager responsible for managing one of the beta test customers. During final system integration testing of the product, the development team was unable to resolve some very complex integration issues that had developed, and the product had to be withdrawn from the market. These problems arose as a result of different groups working on different components of the design without clearly defined interface specifications, and they were not discovered until the very last minute before the product was scheduled to be released. The results were significant:

- The company had to withdraw the product from the market and approximately $150 million in investment was lost.
- The beta test customers who had waited for the arrival of the product had to be told it was no longer going to be available and they would have to find an alternative solution from a competitor.

Discovering and resolving this kind of integration problem is not an easy thing to do sometimes if it is delayed until the last minute and if the potential integration issues are allowed to compound themselves. It's like unraveling a giant ball of twine that is full of tangles and knots: if you can catch the tangles and knots early enough and do it incrementally, it's relatively easy to untangle, but if they become too numerous, it becomes much more difficult. In a fast-paced agile development environment, these problems can compound themselves rapidly if they are not discovered early and that is the major purpose of Continuous Integration.

Continuous Integration is very consistent with the principle of "fail fast, fail early, and fail often." It brings problems to the surface early in the project rather than allowing them to be discovered later.[11]

Strengths and Benefits:

Other benefits of Continuous Integration include:[12]

- Developers detect and fix integration problems continuously, avoiding last-minute chaos at release dates, (when everyone tries to check in their slightly incompatible versions).
- Early warning of broken/incompatible code and of conflicting changes
- Constant availability of a "current" build for testing, demo, or release purposes
- There is immediate feedback to developers on the quality, functionality, or systemwide impact of code they are writing.
- Frequent code check-in pushes developers to create modular, less complex code.
- Metrics generated from automated testing and Continuous Integration (such as metrics for code coverage, code complexity, and features complete) focus developers on developing functional, high-quality code, and help develop momentum in a team.

Risks and Limitations:

- The primary limitation of Continuous Integration is that it may be difficult to implement on larger code development projects, where the integration effort may be too complex to do as frequently. It also requires a level of sophistication and close teamwork on the part of the team to make it work especially on large, complex projects.
- Resources and tools to automate the continuous integration, building, and testing process are also essential in many cases.

---

[11] Gottesman, Erik, comments on book review

[12] "Continuous Integration," http://en.wikipedia.org/wiki/Continuous_integration

APPENDIX B

Overview of Agile Project Delivery Frameworks

This section discusses several agile "project delivery frameworks" that have been commonly used. The word "framework" is important—it should be understood that these "delivery frameworks" are not as explicitly defined as some traditional development processes. That is by design—as a "framework," they are intended to provide a basic foundational approach, and they may need to be customized, tailored, and expanded for a given project, depending on the risks and complexity of the project.

SCRUM

Scrum is heavily focused on the iteration management level of agile and has become the most dominant model for agile software development management. It does address some basic project management considerations, such as how the overall product backlog is established and release planning, but the roots of Scrum are heavily in the iteration management level and that's the level that is most mature at this time. Scrum doesn't specifically address some of the higher-level project management considerations that may be important such as risk management and planning and management of large, complex efforts that may require multiple teams. For that reason, in some cases, there is a need to wrap an additional layer of project management around Scrum. (See the discussion on agile project management.)

Scrum has become the most widely accepted agile methodology, to the extent that the word "agile" has almost become synonymous with Scrum. Scrum is typically based on an Extreme Programming development model and defines a "process framework" which contains sets of practices and predefined roles to extend the development model to more of a project model. The main roles in Scrum are:[1]

1. The "**ScrumMaster**" maintains the processes (typically in lieu of a project manager). The ScrumMaster's responsibilities include:[2]
   - Facilitating the work of the team, developing teamwork among everyone on the project team, and creating an environment based on empowerment and respect for people

[1] "Scrum (Development)," http://en.wikipedia.org/wiki/Scrum_ (development)

[2] "Scrum Alliance—Scrum Roles," www.scrumalliance.org/pages/scrum_roles

- Shielding the team from external interference and removing any impediments that hinder progress by the team
- Building consensus among all team members and acting as a facilitator to resolve any conflicts
- Serving as a focal point for communication for the team to ensure everyone on the team and any external stakeholders are kept informed
- Supporting the Product Owner as required
- Ensuring that the process is followed and tracking progress against assigned tasks
- Raising awareness of dependencies among tasks to ensure that they are prioritized and tracked
- Managing the process and tools used by the team to maximize the efficiency of the team and facilitating Scrum Reviews and Scrum Retrospectives for ongoing process improvement

2. The "**Product Owner**" represents the stakeholders and the business. The responsibilities of the Product Owner include:[3]
   - Defining the features of the product
   - Deciding on the product release date and content (based on discussion with the team)
   - Being responsible for the profitability of the product (ROI)
   - Prioritizing features according to market value, risk, and other factors
   - Adjusting features and priority at the end of each iteration, as needed
   - Accepting or rejecting work results
3. The "**Team**" is a cross-functional group of about seven people who do the actual analysis, design, implementation, testing, and so on. The responsibilities of the team include:[4]
   - Selecting the sprint goals and specifying work results and task requirements
   - Completing all required work within the boundaries of the project guidelines to reach the sprint goal, including testing of the work to confirm that it is complete and meets all required tests
   - Organizing itself and its work
   - Demoing work results to the product owner and any other interested parties

Although Scrum heavily emphasizes the development approach, Scrum is more than just a development methodology and provides a framework for a

---

[3] "Scrum Alliance—Product Owner Roles and Responsibilities," www.scrumalliance.org/resources/617

[4] "Scrum Alliance—Scrum Roles," www.scrumalliance.org/pages/scrum_roles

project-level methodology based on an iterative approach to breaking up a development effort into releases and iterations called sprints. Scrum borrows its name from Rugby, where a sprint is the process of stopping play, then vigorously playing until the sprint ends and a new one begins.

A "sprint" in Scrum is typically a two to four week period and during each "sprint," the team creates a potentially shippable product increment (for example, working and tested software). The set of features that go into a sprint come from the product backlog, which is a prioritized set of high-level requirements of work to be done. The backlog items that go into the sprint are determined during the sprint planning meeting prior to the beginning of the sprint.

During the Sprint Planning meeting, the Product Owner informs the team of the items in the product backlog that he or she wants completed. The team then determines how much of this they can commit to complete during the next sprint. During a sprint, no one is allowed to change the sprint backlog, which means that the requirements are frozen for that sprint. After a sprint is completed, the team demonstrates the use of the software. Figure B.1 shows the organization of a typical Scrum project.

1. The process starts with the Product Owner defining the Product Backlog. The Product Backlog is a list of backlog items which are broad descriptions of all required features, wish-list items, and so forth prioritized by business value that describe what will be built.
   - Each item in the Product Backlog is typically described by a brief user story. The Product Backlog also typically contains a rough work estimate for each item in the backlog. These estimates will be refined as the detailed requirements for each item are further defined during the course of the development effort.
   - The Product Backlog is typically broken down further into releases and each release is typically broken down further into iterations (sprints).
   - The Product Backlog is updated frequently over each iteration of the Scrum project. During each sprint, items in the Product Backlog are refined and elaborated as they are being implemented by the team. Scrum does not specify a development approach but typically uses an Extreme Programming approach for development and relies heavily on direct customer interaction with the development team to further define detailed requirements as the development progresses.
   - New features/functionality that is identified during a sprint will be captured in the Product Backlog. "These may be portions of features that were not completed in the Sprint, or new ideas surfaced by reaction to the work produced. It may include team process improvements revealed by the Sprint Retrospective. All this is crucial feedback that needs to be incorporated into the planning process, and so must be captured in

the Product Backlog and prioritized before the next Sprint Planning Meeting."[5]

2. Prior to the start of each release, a Release Planning Meeting is typically held, where the team defines a high-level plan for the iterations and sprints that will be included in that release.
3. Prior to the start of each sprint, there is a Sprint Kickoff Meeting, where the team defines the "sprint backlog" for that sprint. The Sprint Backlog is extracted from the Product Backlog and is the set of features from the product backlog that will be addressed in that sprint.
   - During each sprint, the detailed requirements for each feature are developed collaboratively between the Product Owner and the Development Team as the design progresses.
   - A "burn down" chart is typically used to track the progress of completing the Sprint Backlog items required to be completed during that sprint.
4. During each sprint, the team has daily meetings called Daily Scrum Meetings. The Daily Scrum Meetings are typically limited to 15 minutes and are usually standup meetings so that the time and discussion will be

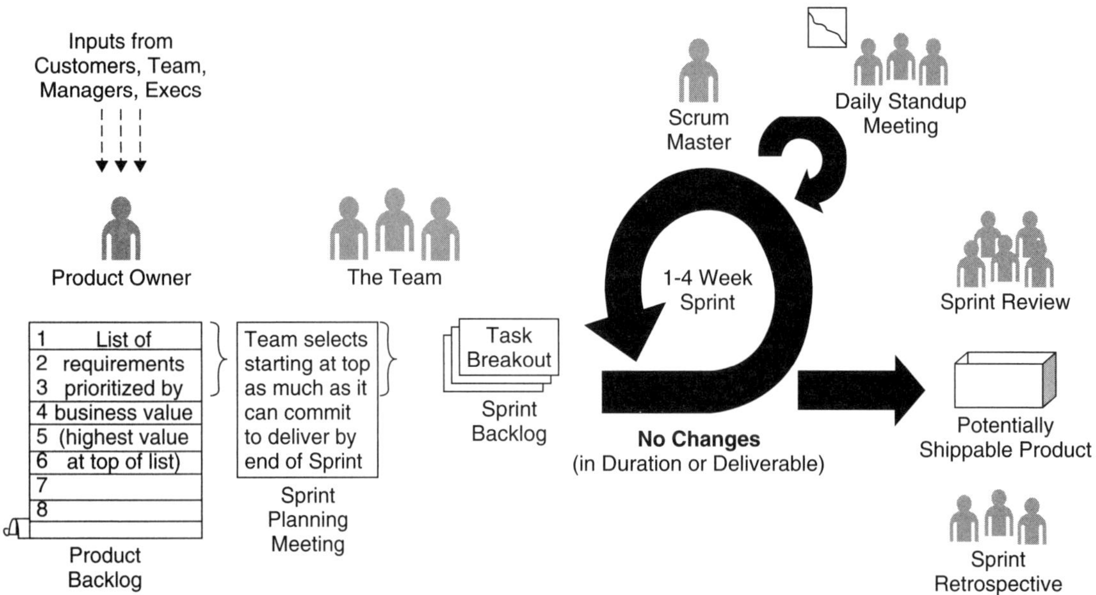

Figure B.1 Detailed Scrum process flow[6]

---

[5] "Scrum Alliance—How Scrum Works," www.scrumalliance.org/articles/47-how-scrum-works

[6] Copyright 2002–2010, Rally Software Development Corp. All Rights Reserved

limited. During the Daily Scrum Meeting each member of the team is asked three questions:

- What have you accomplished since the last Daily Scrum Meeting?
- What will you do before the next Daily Scrum Meeting?
- Is there anything that is impeding your progress (and remedies are discussed)?

5. Scrum enables the creation of self-organizing teams by encouraging co-location of all team members, and relies primarily on direct verbal communication across all team members and disciplines that are involved in the project.
6. The goal of each sprint is to produce working software, although it may not be releasable software, and the software should be tested against unit tests by the development team and acceptance tests by the product owner to determine if it is done.
7. At the end of each sprint, there is a Sprint Review, where the team demos what they've built during the sprint. There is also a Sprint Retrospective, where the team gets together to discuss what's working and not working in the process and makes adjustments as necessary to the process for the next sprint.

Figures B.1 and B.2 show two different views of the Scrum process flow.

DYNAMIC SYSTEMS DEVELOPMENT MODEL (DSDM)

Dynamic Systems Development Method (DSDM) is a framework based originally around Rapid Application Development (RAD), supported by continuous user involvement in an iterative development and incremental approach, which is responsive to changing requirements, in order to develop a system that meets the business needs on time and on budget. DSDM was developed in the United Kingdom in the 1990s by a consortium of vendors and experts in the field of information system (IS) development, the DSDM Consortium, combining their best-practice experiences.[7] It is most frequently used outside of the United States. The word "dynamic" in DSDM is a keyword:

> "... It is the relationship between the development activity and the business goals that is 'dynamic.' The critical challenge for teams that develop products and systems is that business goals present a relentlessly moving target, and the technology is also constantly evolving.
>
> DSDM is a business-driven and multi-disciplinary approach to developing products and systems that delivers more and better feedback earlier. Prototypes and user contact ensure that, instead of working

[7] "What is DSDM?," www.selectbs.com/adt/process-maturity/what-is-dsdm

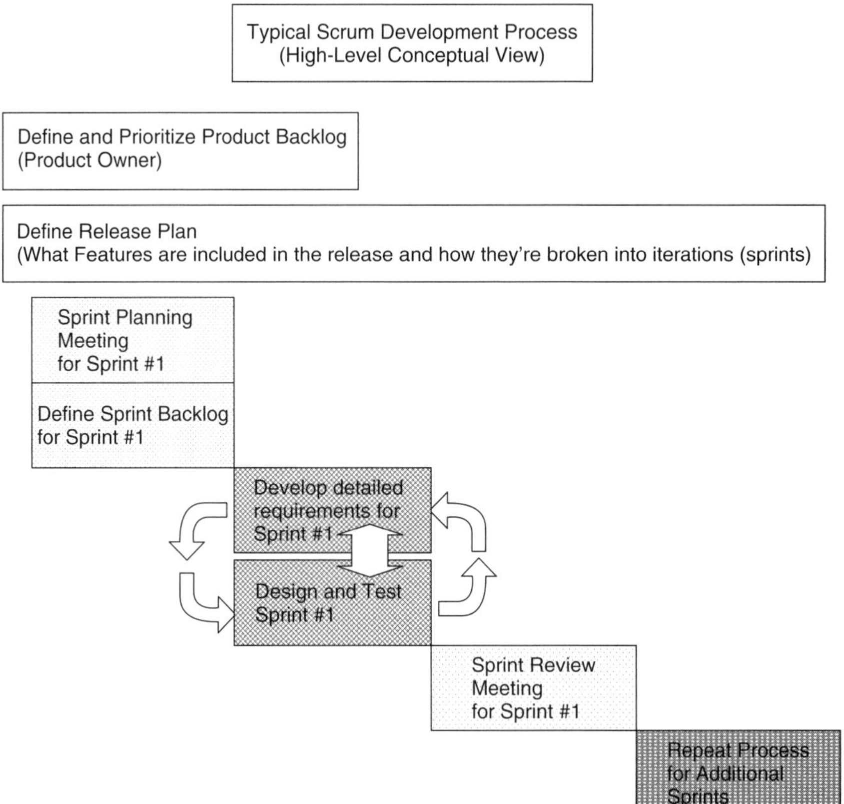

Figure B.2 Conceptual life-cycle model of a Scrum project

> towards a frozen and detailed specification, the team is continuously focusing on delivering the most important objectives that add real value to the business."[8]

Many of the major characteristics of DSDM are similar to other agile approaches:

> - "DSDM concentrates on managing output and results, rather than inputs and activities. It facilitates a partnering spirit, thanks to which the parties genuinely cooperate to continuously prioritize and to deliver what matters to the business.
> - DSDM offers a high degree of adherence to business goals, because it concentrates on high-level shared and integrated objectives, instead

[8] "What is DSDM?, The Business Case for integrating DSDM practices into a Design and Product Development Processes," www.cis.gsu.edu

> of getting stuck in the technical details that concern each individual discipline.
>
> - DSDM is value-driven, rather than cost-driven. It is a design-to-cost and design-to-time approach that builds in customer contact via modeling and prototyping so that all parties gain a better understanding both of the possibilities and the practicalities.
> - DSDM encourages agility, because it recognizes that change is a reality and that, in order to reduce costs and to increase value, change tolerance must be built into the architecture and managed into the organization.
> - DSDM is realistic by accepting that clients and suppliers must both understand the problem together and work on the solution together, instead of strictly and artificially dividing the responsibility for understanding the problem from the responsibility for developing solutions."[9]

DSDM is a framework similar to Scrum—the principles underlying DSDM are very similar to other agile methodologies such as Scrum; however, it is a much more structured approach than Scrum. There are nine underlying principles of DSDM consisting of four foundations and five starting points for the structure of the method. These nine principles form the cornerstones of development using DSDM:[10]

DSDM Principles
1. Active user involvement is imperative
2. DSDM teams must be empowered to make decisions
3. The focus is on frequent delivery of products
4. Fitness for business purpose is the essential criterion for acceptance of deliverables
5. Iterative and incremental development is necessary to converge on an accurate business solution
6. All changes during development are reversible
7. Requirements are baselined at a high level
8. Testing is integrated throughout the life cycle
9. A collaborative and cooperative approach among all stakeholders is essential

There are two major prerequisites for using DSDM that are also similar to other agile frameworks:[11]

- DSDM relies on interactivity between the project team, future end users and higher management.

[9] What is DSDM?, The Business Case for integrating DSDM practices into a Design and Product Development Processes," www.cis.gsu.edu

[10] DSDM Public Version 4.2, www.dsdm.org/version4/2/public/Principles.asp

[11] "What is DSDM?," www.selectbs.com/adt/process-maturity/what-is-dsdm

- It also relies on the ability to decompose a project into smaller parts to enable an iterative approach.

DSDM is based on the 80/20 rule: 80 percent of the benefits can be delivered in 20 percent of the time. Through prioritizing and timeboxing, the most important goals are satisfied on time and measurable results are delivered in short timescales, typically of 3 to 6 months.[12]

The DSDM framework consists of three sequential phases:[13]

- **Pre-Project Phase**—"In the pre-project phase, candidate projects are identified, project funding is realized and project commitment is ensured. Handling these issues at an early stage avoids problems at later stages of the project."
- **Project Life-Cycle Phase**—The project life-cycle phase of DSDM consists of the five stages a project will have to go through to fulfill the project requirements. (Each of the phases is repeated iteratively as many times as necessary to refine the approach and solution before proceeding to the next phase):
  - Feasibility Study
  - Business Study
  - Functional Model Iteration
  - Design and Build Iteration
  - Implementation
- **Post-Project Phase**—The post-project phase ensures that the system is operating effectively and efficiently and includes maintenance, enhancements, and any necessary fixes.

Figure B.3 shows a high-level view of the DSDM project life-cycle phase.

DSDM includes some commonly used agile practices, such as:

- Timeboxing
- Emphasis on testing as the design progresses
- Iterative approach and prototyping

However, the DSDM process is considerably more rigorous than other agile frameworks in a number of respects and considers factors that are not explicitly included in other agile frameworks, such as:

- Stronger emphasis on upfront planning to include a feasibility study and business study
- Decomposition of a functional model similar to FDD

---

[12] "What is DSDM?, The Business Case for integrating DSDM practices into a Design and Product Development Processes," www.cis.gsu.edu

[13] "What is DSDM?," www.selectbs.com/adt/process-maturity/what-is-dsdm

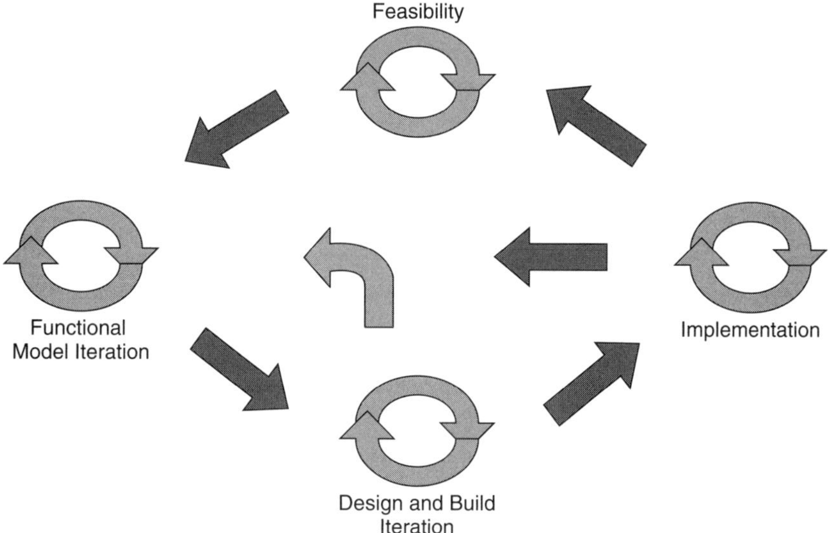

Figure B.3 DSDM life-cycle phases—high-level conceptual view

- Use of UML modeling tools to define the system architecture
- Configuration management

DSDM is sometimes layered on top of an Extreme Programming (XP) development approach.

AGILE MODELING

Agile Modeling (AM) is a methodology developed by Scott Ambler that is a collection of values, principles, and practices for modeling software that can be applied on a software development project in an effective and lightweight manner.[14] The core principles of Agile Modeling are very similar to those of other agile methodologies, with a greater emphasis on modeling of the solution:

> "The values of AM, adopting and extending those of Extreme Programming, are communication, simplicity, feedback, courage, and humility. The keys to modeling success are to have effective communication between all project stakeholders, to strive to develop the simplest solution possible that meets all of your needs, to obtain feedback regarding your efforts often and early, to have the courage to make and stick to your decisions, and to have the humility to admit that you may not know everything, that others have value to add to your project efforts."[15]

[14] "Agile Modeling," www.agilemodeling.com

[15] "An Introduction to Agile Modeling," www.agilemodeling.com/essays/introductionToAM.htm

Agile Modeling advocates:

- Architecture Envisioning at the beginning of the project to define the high-level architecture
- Model-Storming during the development effort to work out further details of the architecture
- The principle of "Modeling with a Purpose," which is based on using models of the system effectively to serve a particular purpose for a particular audience:

> "... With respect to modeling, perhaps you need to understand an aspect of your software better, perhaps you need to communicate your approach to senior management to justify your project, or perhaps you need to create documentation that describes your system to the people who will be operating and/or maintaining/evolving it over time.
>
> If you cannot identify why and for whom you are creating a model then why are you bothering to work on it all? Your first step is to identify a valid purpose for creating a model and the audience for that model, then based on that purpose and audience develop it to the point where it is both sufficiently accurate and sufficiently detailed....
>
> An important implication of this principle is that you need to know your audience, even when that audience is yourself."[16]

The Agile Modeling Methodology includes the following agile practices:

- Test-Driven Development
- Prioritized requirements
- Active stakeholder participation

It is many times used with an Extreme Programming (XP) development approach.

The principles and practices of Agile Modeling can be combined with other software processes, as shown in Figure B.4.[17] Figure B.5 shows the general structure of an Agile Modeling project.

Principles and Practices of Agile Modeling (AM)	Other Techniques (e.g., Scrum)
A Base Software Process (e.g. XP, RUP, AUP)	

Figure B.4 Combining Agile Modeling with other methodologies

[16] "Agile Modeling," www.agilemodeling.com/principles.htm#ModelWithAPurpose

[17] "An Introduction to Agile Modeling," www.agilemodeling.com/essays/introductionToAM.htm

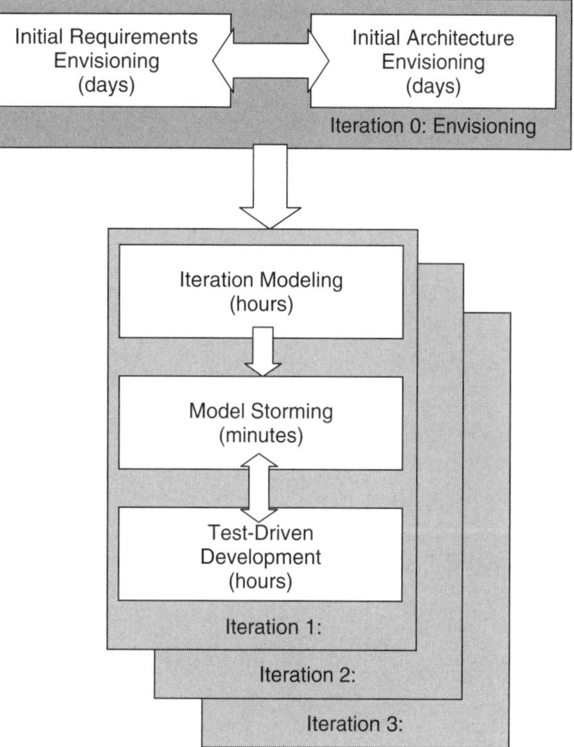

• Identity the high-level scope
• Identity initial "requirements stack"
• Identity an architectural vision
Initial Requirements Envisioning (days)
Initial Architecture Envisioning (days)
Iteration 0: Envisioning
• Modeling is part of the iteration planning effort
• Need to model enough to give good estimates
• Need to plan the work for the iteration
Iteration Modeling (hours)
• Work through specific issues on a JIT manner
• Stakeholders actively participate
• Requirements evolve throughout the project
• Model just enough for now, you can always come back later
Model Storming (minutes)
• Develop working software via a test-first approach
• Details captured in the form of executable specifications
Test-Driven Development (hours)
Iteration 1:
Iteration 2:
Iteration 3:

Figure B.5 General structure of an Agile Modeling project

Figure B.5 shows the general structure of an Agile Modeling project:[18]

AGILE UNIFIED PROCESS

The Agile Unified Process (Agile UP) is a simplified version of the Rational Unified Process (RUP) developed by Scott Ambler. It describes a simple, easy-to-understand approach to developing business application software using agile techniques and concepts yet still remaining true to the Rational Unified Process (RUP).[19]

The Agile Unified Process is based on the following principles[20]:

1. Your staff knows what they're doing. People aren't going to read detailed process documentation, but they will want some high-level

[18] "An Introduction to Agile Modeling," www.agilemodeling.com/essays/introductionToAM.htm

[19] "Agile Unified Process," www.ambysoft.com/unifiedprocess/agileUP.html

[20] The Agile Unified Process (AUP) Home Page, www.ambysoft.com/unifiedprocess/agileUP.html#Serial

guidance and/or training from time to time. The AUP product provides links to many of the details, if you're interested, but doesn't force them upon you.

2. Simplicity. Everything is described concisely using a handful of pages, not thousands of them.
3. Agility. The Agile UP conforms to the values and principles of the Agile Alliance.
4. Focus on high-value activities. The focus is on the activities which actually count, not every possible thing that could happen to you on a project.
5. Tool independence. You can use any toolset that you want with the Agile UP. My suggestion is that you use the tools which are best suited for the job, which are often simple tools or even open source tools.
6. You'll want to tailor this product to meet your own needs. The AUP product is easily tailor-able via any common HTML editing tool. You don't need to purchase a special tool, or take a course, to tailor the AUP.

It follows the same general phases as RUP and other variations of the unified process:[21]

1. Inception Phase –
   "During the inception phase, you establish the business case for the system and delimit the project scope. To accomplish this you must identify all external entities with which the system will interact (actors) and define the nature of this interaction at a high level. This involves identifying all use cases and describing a few significant ones. The business case includes success criteria, risk assessment, and estimate of the resources needed, and a phase plan showing dates of major milestones."
2. Elaboration Phase –
   "The purpose of the elaboration phase is to analyze the problem domain, establish a sound architectural foundation, develop the project plan, and eliminate the highest risk elements of the project. To accomplish these objectives, you must have the "mile wide and inch deep" view of the system. Architectural decisions have to be made with an

[21] "Rational Unified Process—Best Practices for Software Development Teams," www.ibm.com/developerworks/rational/library/content/03July/1000/1251/1251_bestpractices_TP026B.pdf

understanding of the whole system: its scope, major functionality and nonfunctional requirements such as performance requirements."

3. Construction Phase –
"During the construction phase, all remaining components and application features are developed and integrated into the product, and all features are thoroughly tested. The construction phase is, in one sense, a manufacturing process where emphasis is placed on managing resources and controlling operations to optimize costs, schedules, and quality. In this sense, the management mindset undergoes a transition from the development of intellectual property during inception and elaboration, to the development of deployable products during construction and transition."
4. Transition Phase –
"The purpose of the transition phase is to transition the software product to the user community. Once the product has been given to the end user, issues usually arise that require you to develop new releases, correct some problems, or finish the features that were postponed."

The phases of the Agile Unified Process are shown in Figure B.6.[22]

Instead of the "big bang" approach, where you deliver software all at once, you instead release it into production in portions (e.g., version 1, then version 2, and so on). AUP teams typically deliver development releases at the end of each iteration into pre-production staging area(s). A development release of an application is something that could potentially be released into production if it were to be put through your pre-production quality assurance (QA), testing, and deployment processes.

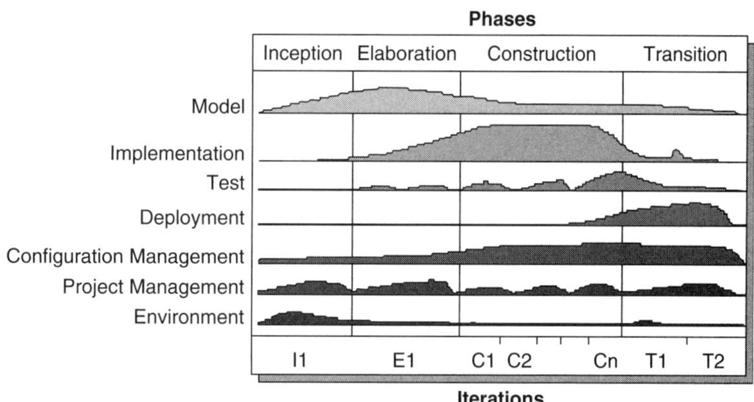

Figure B.6 Agile Unified Process phases (Source: Copyright 2005 Scott W. Ambler.)

[22] "Agile Unified Process," www.ambysoft.com/unifiedprocess/agileUP.html

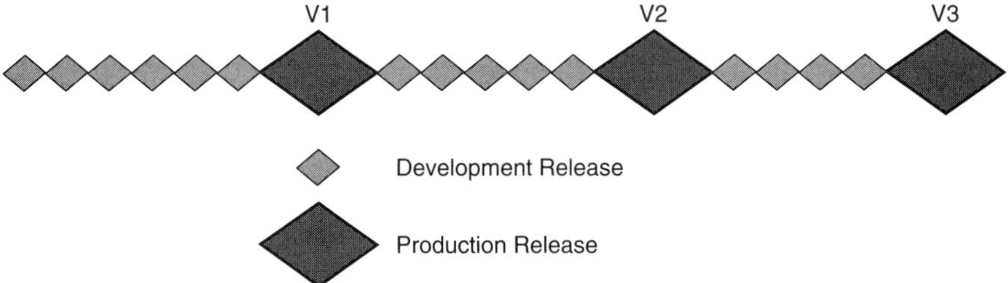

Figure B.7 AUP incremental release approach

Figure B.7 shows how this process would work over a period of time.

The Rational Unified Process (RUP) has often been criticized for being very heavy on tools and artifacts, but the underlying iterative methodology is very sound. The Agile Unified Process demonstrates how to apply the underlying iterative methodology behind RUP in a more agile context without the heavy emphasis on tools and artifacts that is normally found in RUP.

Lean Software Development

Lean Software Development is an iterative methodology originally developed by Mary and Tom Poppendiek. It is much more of a set of principles that can be applied to other methodologies than it is a well-defined methodology in itself:

> "Lean Software Development owes much of its principles and practices to the Lean Enterprise movement, and the practices of companies like Toyota. Lean Software Development focuses the team on delivering Value to the customer, and on the efficiency of the "Value Stream," the mechanisms that deliver that Value. The main principles of Lean include:
>
> 1. Eliminating Waste
> 2. Amplifying Learning
> 3. Deciding as Late as Possible
> 4. Delivering as Fast as Possible
> 5. Empowering the Team
> 6. Building Integrity In
> 7. Seeing the Whole
>
> Lean eliminates waste through such practices as:
>
> - Selecting only the truly valuable features for a system,
> - Prioritizing those selected, and
> - Delivering them in small batches"[23]

[23] "Agile Methodologies," www.versionone.com/Agile101/Methodologies.asp?c-aws=i&gr-isdsdm&gclid=CMCdk9zUkKICFR_E3Aod_SrBcg

Each of these principles is discussed in more detail in the material that follows:

1. Eliminate Waste
   "Waste is anything that does not add value to a product, value as perceived by the customer. In lean thinking, the concept of waste is a high hurdle. If a component is sitting on a shelf gathering dust, that is waste. If a development cycle has collected requirements in a book gathering dust that is waste. If a manufacturing plant makes more stuff than is immediately needed, that is waste. If developers code more features than are immediately needed, that is waste."[24]
2. Amplify Learning
   "Development is an exercise in discovery, while production is an exercise in reducing variation, and for this reason, a lean approach to development results in practices that are quite different than lean production practices. Development is like creating a recipe, while production is like making the dish. Recipes are designed by experienced chefs who have developed an instinct for what works and the capability to adapt available ingredients to suit the occasion. Yet even great chefs produce several variations of a new dish as they iterate toward a recipe that will taste great and be easy to reproduce. Chefs are not expected to get a recipe perfect on the first attempt; they are expected to produce several variations on a theme as part of the learning process."[25]
3. Decide as Late as Possible
   "Development processes that provide for late decision-making [sic] are effective in domains that involve uncertainty, because they can provide an options-based approach. In the face of uncertainty, most economic markets develop options to provide a way for the investor to avoid locking in decisions until the future is closer and easier to predict. Delaying decisions is valuable because better decisions can be made when they are based on fact."[26]
4. Deliver as Fast as Possible
   "Until recently, rapid software development has not been valued; taking a careful, don't-make-any-mistakes approach has seemed to be more important.... Rapid development has many advantages. Without speed, you cannot delay decisions. Without speed, you do not

[24] Poppendiek, Tom and Mary, *Lean Software Development—An Agile Toolkit*, New York: Addison-Wesley, 2003, p. xxv

[25] Poppendiek, Tom and Mary, *Lean Software Development—An Agile Toolkit*, New York: Addison-Wesley, 2003, p. xxvi

[26] Poppendiek, Tom and Mary, *Lean Software Development—An Agile Toolkit*, New York: Addison-Wesley, 2003, p. xxvi

have reliable feedback. In development, the discovery cycle is critical for learning: design, implement, feedback, improve. The shorter these cycles are, the more can be learned."[27]

5. Empower the Team
"Top-notch execution lies in getting the details right, and no one understands the details better than the people who actually do the work. Involving developers in the details of technical decisions is fundamental to achieving excellence. The people on the front lines combine the knowledge of the minute details with the power of many minds. When equipped with necessary expertise and guided by a leader, they will make better technical decisions and better process decisions than anyone can make for them. Because decisions are made late and execution is fast, it is not possible for a central authority to orchestrate activities of workers."[28]

6. Build Integrity In
"A system is perceived to have integrity when a user thinks, "Yes! That is exactly what I want. Somebody got inside my mind!" Market share is a rough measure of perceived integrity for products, because it measures customer perception over time. Conceptual integrity means that the system's central concepts work together as a smooth, cohesive whole and it is a critical factor in creating perceived integrity."[29]

Mary Poppendiek defines conceptual integrity and perceived integrity as follows:

"Perceived integrity means that the totality of the product achieves a balance of function, usability, reliability, and economy that delights customers."[30]

"Software with integrity has a coherent architecture, scores high on usability and fitness for purpose, and is maintainable, adaptable, and extensible. Research has shown that integrity comes from wise leadership, relevant expertise, effective communication, and healthy discipline; processes, procedures and measurements are not adequate substitutes."[31]

[27] Poppendiek, Tom and Mary, *Lean Software Development—An Agile Toolkit*, New York: Addison-Wesley, 2003, p. xxvi

[28] Poppendiek, Tom and Mary, *Lean Software Development—An Agile Toolkit*, New York: Addison-Wesley, 2003, p. xxvii

[29] Poppendiek, Tom and Mary, *Lean Software Development—An Agile Toolkit*, New York: Addison-Wesley, 2003, p. xxvii

[30] Poppendiek, Tom and Mary, *Lean Software Development—An Agile Toolkit*, New York: Addison-Wesley, 2003, p. 125

[31] Poppendiek, Tom and Mary, "*Lean Software Development—An Agile Toolkit*," New York: Addison-Wesley, 2003, p. xxvii

7. See the Whole

"Integrity in complex systems requires a deep expertise in many diverse areas. One of the most intractable problems with product development is that experts in any area (e.g., database or GUI) have a tendency to maximize the performance of the part of the product representing their own specialty rather than focusing on overall system performance. Quite often, the common good suffers if people attend first to their own specialized interests."[32]

Lean Software Development is similar to other agile methodologies in that it emphasizes the speed and efficiency of development workflow and relies on rapid and reliable feedback between developers and customers.

"Lean uses the idea of work product being "pulled" via customer request. It focuses decision-making authority and ability on individuals and small teams, since research shows this to be faster and more efficient than hierarchical flow of control. Lean also concentrates on the efficiency of the use of team resources, trying to ensure that everyone is productive as much of the time as possible. It concentrates on concurrent work and the fewest possible intra-team workflow dependencies. Lean also strongly recommends that automated unit tests be written at the same time the code is written."[33]

Lean Software Development also uses an agile practice of deferring planning and detailed requirements decisions as long as possible until better information is available to support those decisions:

"Programming is a lot like die-cutting. The stakes are often high, and mistakes can be costly, so sequential development, that is, establishing requirements before development begins, is commonly thought of as a way to protect against serious errors. The problem with sequential development is that it forces designers to take a depth-first rather than a breadth-first approach to design. Depth-first forces making low-level dependent decisions before experiencing the consequences of the high-level decisions. The most costly mistakes are made by forgetting to consider something important at the beginning. The easiest way to make such a big mistake is to drill down to detail to fast. Once you set down the detailed path, you can't back up and are unlikely to realize that you should. When big mistakes may be made, it is best to survey the landscape and delay the detailed decisions."[34]

---

[32] Poppendiek, Tom and Mary, *Lean Software Development—An Agile Toolkit*, New York: Addison-Wesley, 2003, p. xxvii

[33] "Agile Methodologies," www.versionone.com/Agile101/Methodologies.asp?c-aws=i&gr-is dsdm&gclid=CMCdk9zUkKICFR_E3Aod_SrBcg

[34] Poppendiek, Tom and Mary, *Lean Software Development—An Agile Toolkit*, New York: Addison-Wesley, 2003, p. 48–49

> Delaying irreversible decisions until uncertainty is reduced has economic value. It leads to better decisions, it limits risk, it helps manage complexity, it reduces waste, and it makes customers happy."[35]

ADDITIONAL READING

There are a number of good books on the subject of agile and agile project management that I highly recommend for additional reading on agile development and agile project management.

Title	Author	Publisher, Date
Agile Project Management	Jim Highsmith	Addison-Wesley, 2010
Effective Project Management Traditional, Agile, Extreme	Robert Wysocki	Wiley, 2009
Succeeding with Agile Software Development Using Scrum	Mike Cohn	Addison-Wesley, 2010
The Software Manager's Bridge to Agility	Michele Sliger and Stacia Broderick	Addison-Wesley, 2008
Balancing Agility and Discipline—A Guide for the Perplexed	Barry Boehm and Richard Turner	Addison-Wesley, 2003
Agile & Iterative Development—A Manager's Guide	Craig Larman	Addison-Wesley, 2003
Agile Project Management with Scrum	Ken Schwaber	Microsoft Press, 2003
The Enterprise and Scrum	Ken Schwaber	Microsoft Press, 2003
Agile Estimating and Planning	Mike Cohn	Prentice Hall, 2006
Lean Software Development—An Agile Toolkit	Mary and Tom Poppendiek	Addison-Wesley, 2003
Implementing Lean Software Development—From Concept to Cash	Mary and Tom Poppendiek	Addison-Wesley, 2007
Leading Lean Software Development	Mary and Tom Poppendiek	Addison-Wesley, 2010

GLOSSARY OF TERMS

Term	Definition
Agile Modeling	Agile Modeling is a methodology developed by Scott Ambler that is a collection of values, principles, and practices for modeling software that can be applied on a software development project in an effective and lightweight manner.[36]

[35] Poppendiek, Tom and Mary, *Lean Software Development—An Agile Toolkit*, New York: Addison-Wesley, 2003, p. 54

[36] "Agile Modeling," www.agilemodeling.com

Term	Definition
Agile Unified Process	The Agile Unified Process is a simplified version of the Rational Unified Process (RUP) developed by Scott Ambler. It describes a simple, easy to understand approach to developing business application software using agile techniques and concepts yet still remaining true to the RUP.[37]
AUP	See Agile Unified Process
Code Refactoring	Code refactoring involves removing redundancy, eliminating unused functionality, and rejuvenating obsolete designs and improving the design of existing software in order to improve reliability and maintainability of the software. Refactoring throughout the entire project life cycle saves time and increases quality of the software. Code refactoring is more commonly used with Extreme Programming; it is less commonly used with Feature-Driven Development.
Continuous Integration	Continuous integration is the practice of frequently integrating new or changed software with the code repository. It is a way of early detection of problems that may occur when individual software developers are working on code changes that may potentially conflict with each other. In many typical software development environments, integration may not be performed until the application is ready for final release.
DSDM	See Dynamic Systems Development Model
Dynamic Systems Development Model (DSDM)	Dynamic Systems Development Method (DSDM) is a framework based originally around Rapid Application Development (RAD), supported by continuous user involvement in an iterative development and incremental approach that is responsive to changing requirements, in order to develop a system that meets the business needs on time and on budget. DSDM was developed in the United Kingdom in the 1990s by a consortium of vendors and experts in the field of Information System (IS) development, the DSDM Consortium, combining their best-practice experiences.[38] It is most frequently used outside of the United States.
Epic	An "epic" is a large user story that needs to be broken down into smaller user stories prior to the start of an agile iteration.
Extreme Programming (XP)	"Extreme Programming is a discipline of software development based on values of simplicity, communication, feedback, and courage. It works by bringing the whole team together in the presence of simple practices, with enough feedback to enable the team to see where they are and to tune the practices to their unique situation. In Extreme Programming, every contributor to the project is an integral part of the "Whole Team." The team forms around a business representative called "the Customer," who sits with the team and works with them daily.

[37] "Agile Unified Process," www.ambysoft.com/unifiedprocess/agileUP.html

[38] "What is DSDM?," www.selectbs.com/adt/process-maturity/what-is-dsdm

Term	Definition
	Extreme Programming teams use a simple form of planning and tracking to decide what should be done next and to predict when the project will be done. Focused on business value, the team produces the software in a series of small fully-integrated releases that pass all the tests the Customer has defined."[39] (See the "Extreme Programming section in Appendix A for more detail.)
Feature-Driven Development	Feature-Driven Development (FDD) is a model-driven approach that puts more emphasis on defining an overall model of the system and a list of features to be included in the system prior to starting the design effort.
Lean Manufacturing	"Lean manufacturing is a comprehensive term referring to manufacturing methodologies based on maximizing value and minimizing waste in the manufacturing process. Lean manufacturing has evolved in North America from its beginnings in the Toyota Production System (TPS) in Japan. Many of the most recognizable phrases, including *kaizen* and *kanban*, are Japanese terms that have become standard terms in lean manufacturing. At the heart of lean is the determination of value. Value is defined as an item or feature for which a customer is willing to pay. All other aspects of the manufacturing process are deemed waste. Lean manufacturing is used as a tool to focus resources and energies on producing the value-added features while identifying and eliminating non value added [sic] activities."[40]
Lean Software Development	Lean Software Development is a translation of lean manufacturing and Lean IT principles and practices to the software development domain. It is heavily based on the work of Tom and Mary Poppendiek.
Pair Programming	Pair programming is an agile software development technique in which two programmers work together at one work station—one developer plays the role of an observer while the other developer in the pair writes the code.
Product Backlog	The product backlog is a high-level document list of all required features, wish-list items, etc. prioritized by business value in an agile project. It is the "What" that will be built. It is owned by the product owner and continuously prioritized and reprioritized as the project progresses, work is completed, and detailed requirements are better understood.
Prototype Model	A prototype model is a type of software development life cycle model that is used to progressively define the requirements for a product or application. It involves developing the requirements as much as possible from user input, then a prototype model is built based on the known requirements. User feedback is then used to progressively refine the model as necessary until it satisfies the user. Prototyping can also be an effective method to demonstrate the feasibility of a certain approach.

[39] "What is Extreme Programming?", http://xprogramming.com/book/whatisxp/

[40] "Lean Manufacturing Learning Center," www.vorne.com/learning-center/lean-manufacturing .htm

Term	Definition
	The basic reason for limited use of prototyping is the cost involved in this build-it-twice approach. However, with modern software development tools, prototyping need not be very costly and can actually reduce the overall development cost.[41]
Rational Unified Process	The Rational Unified Process (RUP) is a software development process from Rational, a division of IBM. It divides the development process into four distinct phases that each involve business modeling, analysis and design, implementation, testing, and deployment. The four phases are: **Inception**—The idea for the project is stated. The development team determines if the project is worth pursuing and what resources will be needed. **Elaboration**—The project's architecture and required resources are further evaluated. Developers consider possible applications of the software and costs associated with the development. **Construction**—The project is developed and completed. The software is designed, written, and tested. **Transition**—The software is released to the public. Final adjustments or updates are made based on feedback from end users.[42]
RUP	See Rational Unified Process
Scrum	Scrum is an agile software development model based on multiple small teams working in an intensive and interdependent manner. The term is named for the scrum (or scrummage) formation in rugby, which is used to restart the game after an event that causes play to stop, such as an infringement. Scrum employs real-time decision-making processes based on actual events and information. This requires well-trained and specialized teams capable of self-management, communication, and decision making. The teams in the organization work together while constantly focusing on their common interests.[43] (See the Scrum section in Appendix B for more detail)
SDLC	See Software Development Life Cycle
Software Development Life Cycle	A software development life cycle (SDLC) is a process or framework that describes the activities performed at each stage of the software development process and provides an overall roadmap for the project. It provides a template for executing a project that can be tailored to fit a particular project. An example of an SDLC is the Waterfall model; however, as used in this book, an SDLC would include any project framework such as Scrum.

[41] "Prototyping Software Lifecycle Model," www.freetutes.com/systemanalysis/sa2-prototyping-model.html

[42] "RUP (Rational Unified Process Definition)," www.techterms.com/definition/rup

[43] "What is Scrum?," http://searchsoftwarequality.techtarget.com/sDefinition/0,,sid92_gci1230820,00.html

Term	Definition
Spike	"A spike is an experiment that allows developers to learn just enough about the unknown elements in a user story, e.g., a new technology, to be able to estimate that user story. Often, a spike is a quick and dirty implementation or a prototype which will be thrown away. When a user story on the product backlog contains unknown elements that seriously hamper a usable estimation, the item should be split into a spike to investigate these elements plus a user story to develop the functionality."[44]
Story Points	"Story Points" are a method of estimating the level of effort associated with implementing a user story. The typical form of story points is a Fibonacci series such as 1, 2, 3, 5, 8, 13, with 1 being a minimal level of effort and 13 being a maximum level of effort for a user story in an iteration.
TDD	See Test Driven Development
Test-Driven Development	Test-Driven Development (TDD) is commonly used in agile methodologies to integrate testing directly into the software development effort: "Instead of writing functional code first and then your testing code as an afterthought, if you write it at all, you instead write your test code before your functional code. Furthermore, you do so in very small steps—one test and a small bit of corresponding functional code at a time. A programmer taking a TDD approach refuses to write a new function until there is first a test that fails because that function isn't present. In fact, they refuse to add even a single line of code until a test exists for it. Once the test is in place they then do the work required to ensure that the test suite now passes."[45] (See the Test-Driven Development section in Appendix A)
User Persona	A "User Persona" is a description of a specific type of user that impacts the requirements. For instance, a "Banking Customer" would be an example of a User Persona. User Personas are useful ways of characterizing the users of the system and keeping the development effort focused on satisfying their needs.
User Stories	"User stories are one of the primary development artifacts for Scrum and Extreme Programming (XP) project teams. A user story is a very high-level definition of a requirement, containing just enough information so that the developers can produce a reasonable estimate of the effort to implement it." "User stories are small, much smaller than other usage requirement artifacts such as use cases or usage scenarios. Each of the following statements represents a single user story: Students can purchase monthly parking passes online. Parking passes can be paid via credit cards. Parking passes can be paid via PayPal™. Professors can input student marks.

[44] "Phillipus, Erik, Architecture Spikes," www.agile-architecting.com/Architecture%20Spikes.pdf

[45] "Introduction to Test-Driven Design," www.agiledata.org/essays/tdd.html

Term	Definition
	Students can obtain their current seminar schedule. Students can order official transcripts. Students can only enroll in seminars for which they have prerequisites. Transcripts will be available online via a standard browser."[46] User stories provide a way of breaking up the project into individual work items that can provide a way of estimating and tracking work to be done. Each user story may be further refined as necessary as the design progresses.
Waterfall Model	The waterfall model is a software development life cycle model that describes a linear and sequential development method. Waterfall development has distinct goals for each phase of development and once a phase of development is completed, the development typically proceeds to the next phase and there is no turning back. The advantage of waterfall development is that it allows for departmentalization and managerial control. A schedule can be set with deadlines for each stage of development and a product can proceed through the development process sequentially. Development moves through the phases of the model such as concept, design, implementation, and testing, and ends up at deployment and operation and maintenance. Each phase of development normally proceeds in a prescribed order, without any overlapping or iterative steps; however, tailoring is often done to make the process more efficient. The disadvantages of waterfall development are that: It does not allow for much reflection or revision—once an application is in the testing stage, it is very difficult to go back and change something that was not well thought out in the concept stage. It assumes that all requirements can be defined upfront prior to any design work, and that is not a realistic assumption in many situations, and it doesn't provide an approach that is flexible and adaptive to customer needs. It may require an excessive amount of documentation artifacts.[47]
XP	See Extreme Programming

46 "Introduction to User Stories," www.agilemodeling.com/artifacts/userStory.htm

47 "What is Waterfall Model," http://searchsoftwarequality.techtarget.com/sDefinition/0,,sid92_gci519580,00.html

Index